The Global Leadership Challenge
Second edition

The economy is global, businesses are increasingly global, management has gone global, and there is an increasing demand (and reward) for truly skilled global leaders, managers, and executives. Black and Morrison address this change by asking why and when globalization truly began and explain how businesses can adapt themselves to remain competitive in increasingly global markets.

Written by authoritative experts and based on extensive, up-to-date research and interviews with leading global leaders, *The Global Leadership Challenge* provides practical tools to develop global leadership skills, laying down the capabilities that must be developed and the plans that must be made to meet the globalization challenge.

This will be truly vital reading for middle managers who have ambition for more senior positions, senior managers who are already bumping up against the challenges of global leadership, and top executives who are in the midst of the challenges of global leadership.

J. Stewart Black is Professor of Global Leadership and Strategy at IMD, Switzerland.

Allen J. Morrison is Professor of Global Management and the holder of the Kristian Gerhard Jebsen Chair for Responsible Leadership at IMD, Switzerland.

The Global Leadership Challenge is a stimulating, practical guide to managing effectively in an ever-globalizing business world. It's an excellent read with real-life examples for how to deliver value for your company and improve yourself as a global leader. I highly recommend the book to anyone interested in enhancing their global leadership skills.

Doug Tough, *Chairman and CEO, International Flavors and Fragrances, Inc.*

In a world of possibly too many publications on leadership, Black and Morrison's book stands out, offering great insights, tools, and techniques that are critical for successful global leaders.

Steven Holliday, *CEO, National Grid plc.*

Global leaders were made 20 years ago; their children were born global, and will now compete with you for the best jobs. It's time to up your game, and this book is the best global passport you can hope for.

Michel Demaré, *Chairman of the Board, Syngenta*

The first edition *Global Explorers* was my instructional guide for my first international assignment. In this second edition, Black and Morrison lay out a research-based but practical framework that is a must-read for any leader facing the challenge of globalization!

William Chisholm, *CEO, Samuel Son & Co.*

This lucidly written book provides guidance for acquiring and nurturing leadership qualities for confidently facing a rapidly globalizing world undergoing increasing uncertainty, complexity and pace of change.

Ravi Kant, *Vice Chairman of Tata Motors*

The Global Leadership Challenge

Second edition

**J. Stewart Black and
Allen J. Morrison**

Routledge
Taylor & Francis Group

LONDON AND NEW YORK

First published 1999
Second edition 2014
by Routledge
2 Park Square, Milton Park, Abingdon, Oxon OX14 4RN

and by Routledge
711 Third Avenue, New York, NY 10017

Routledge is an imprint of the Taylor & Francis Group, an informa business

British Library Cataloguing in Publication Data
A catalogue record for this book is available from the British Library

Library of Congress Cataloging in Publication Data
Black, J. Stewart, 1959–
[Global explorers]
   The global leadership challenge / J. Stewart Black and Allen J.
   Morrison.—Second edition.
      pages cm
   Revised and updated edition of : Global explorers : the next generation
   of leaders / J. Stewart Black, Allen J. Morrison, Hal B. Gregersen.
   Includes bibliographical references and index.
   ISBN 978-0-415-70339-0 (hardback)—ISBN 978-0-415-70340-6
   (pbk.)—ISBN 978-0-203-79463-0 (ebook)   1. Leadership.
   2. Executive ability.   3. International business enterprises—
   Management.   I. Morrison, Allen J.   II. Title.
   HD57.7.B538 2014
   658.4'092–dc23   2013041612

ISBN: 978-0-415-70339-0 (hbk)
ISBN: 978-0-415-70340-6 (pbk)
ISBN: 978-0-203-79463-0 (ebk)

Typeset in Times New Roman
by RefineCatch Limited, Bungay, Suffolk

Printed and bound in the United States of America by
Edwards Brothers Malloy

Contents

Illustrations

Figures

Tables

Boxes

Foreword

We were fortunate enough in our first edition to have had our good friend and former professor Stephen Covey contribute the foreword. Sadly, he passed away in July 2012 before the second phase of our work was completed. We miss his wisdom and support but are grateful for his past encouragement. In this foreword we reiterate and quote from some of his original points.

In addition, we had the great fortune of co-authoring the first edition with a good friend and brilliant colleague Hal Gregersen. In fact, Hal was the catalyst for the global explorer focus of our earlier work. He has always had an exceptionally creative mind and artistic eye and recently decided to devote time in class and in the field to perfecting these gifts and talents. As a consequence, we conducted this second phase of research and writing on our own without the benefit of Hal's great insights. As a consequence, any shortcomings in this edition are ours alone to bear.

We extend to Professor Covey's family our sincere sympathies and prayers for their comfort and to Hal we offer our best wishes and appreciation.

This phase of our research is an important extension of our earlier work. There are a number of new insights but many of the original ideas were supported in the new data we gathered. As a consequence, one of the key points that Professor Covey made in his foreword to the first edition applies to what we put forward in this second edition. As a consequence, we quote here an incident from Professor Covey's original foreword:

> A few years ago, my mother attended one of my presentations. Arriving early, she sat near the front, and, like a mother, proudly awaited the introduction of her son. Right after I began, I caught a glimpse of her beaming face—nodding and encouraging at every phrase. You can just imagine it.
>
> But all that changed. Before long, two people talking in the front row distracted her. It's not that they exchanged just a comment or two. They had the brazenness to carry on an extended conversation during *her* son's speech! With each minute that passed, she became more and more irritated. By the end she was absolutely fuming, tempted to give them a piece of her mind.

Instead, she went up to the person who had introduced me and said, "Could you believe how those two people in the front talked on and on through Stephen's whole presentation?" He replied, "Oh yes, that woman is from Korea and the person sitting next to her is an interpreter."

My mother's heart sank. Though ashamed at how severely she had judged them, she graciously approached the woman, greeted her, and wished her well. The new, unexpected information my mother received created within her mind and heart what I call a paradigm shift—a new perspective, a new way of seeing things. And the new information transformed her whole experience. So instead of giving the Korean woman a piece of her mind, my mother constructed a new mind.

I am convinced that most significant paradigm shifts are preceded by the shock of new light, awareness, and understanding.

We agreed with Professor Covey then, and believe his point is even more relevant today. Doing business in a global context is different from doing business at home. As a consequence, most leaders need a paradigm shift. However, like Professor Covey's mother, our interviews with senior executives found that for most people this shift requires a bit of an unexpected shock. In our more than 200 interviews, one of the most common and powerful shocks occurred when people had the opportunity to live and work in a foreign country. The daily reality that people really are quite different around the world came home to these business leaders, not just in an intellectual way, but in a visceral and experiential way that literally opened their minds and hearts to the depth and breadth of the challenge of global leadership.

In *The Global Leadership Challenge*, we highlight the accelerating and growing scope of global business and the difference it creates in what it takes to be an effective leader. In his original foreword, Professor Covey said, "I personally believe that there are still relatively few who fully comprehend the significance of the global shift that has been set in motion and that continues to gather force and momentum in the world." Our interviews suggest that this is still true, though the pace with which leaders are being thrust into needing to understand the global shift and what it means for effective leadership is such that soon most leaders will be confronted by and will not be able to sidestep the challenges of global leadership.

It has been our enduring goal for more than 20 years to (1) understand the nature of global business, (2) crystalize what it means for effective leadership, and (3) outline how talented and motivated individuals can develop the required global leadership capabilities. We hope that culmination of our driving goal and two decades of effort would be worthy of Professor Covey's support and praise again. But, most importantly, we hope that this book is helpful to you and your company in navigating the challenge of global leadership.

J. Stewart Black, Ph.D.
Allen J. Morrison, Ph.D.

Preface

Today you can hardly pick up a newspaper or business magazine without reading about global business. However, as we show in the very first chapter of this book, globalization is a relatively new phenomenon of only about the last 15 years for most leaders. For evidence of its recency, we need only look at three key statistics. First, if we look at exports as a percentage of gross domestic product (GDP), in the last 15 years, it has soared from around 15 percent to 30 percent. Second, if we look at the percentage of revenues coming from outside a firm's home country (i.e., foreign sales), it has tripled for S&P 500 companies from around 15 percent to 45 percent in the same time frame. Finally, if we look at foreign direct investment (FDI) where leaders have to put real money into setting up offices, factories, warehouses, distribution networks, research facilities, etc. in foreign lands, we have seen a tripling of FDI from about 10 percent to 30 percent of world GDP. It is amazing how globalization has accelerated. Thus, while global business and global leadership have been the concern and purview of a few leaders for decades, within the last 15 years they have become the concern of most leaders. As a consequence, what it takes to be an effective global leader has moved from a topic of interest of a few to a central focus of most current and future leaders. Consequently, this book comes at an opportune time. Our focus on the characteristics of effective global leaders and on how to develop these characteristics should be of great interest to aspiring leaders and their companies around the world.

Developing a global leadership model

Our basic premise is this: Corporations today need to look at their markets, competitors, and technologies on a global basis and develop products and strategies that work across borders. Today's corporate leaders need to develop business and leadership capabilities that are effective not only at home but also outside of their own national boundaries.

The research

In examining global leadership we addressed two major questions: (1) What capabilities do leaders who are charged with directing operations that span the entire world of diverse cultures, capabilities, and customers need to acquire? (2) Given the growing need for global leaders, how can managers most effectively develop these capabilities?

We tackled these questions in a two-part research project. The first phase of this research was carried out in the late 1990s and was published in our earlier edition, *Global Explorers: The Next Generation of Leaders*. The second phase was completed 15 years later. In both phases of research, our approach was simple. We interviewed over 200 senior line and human-resource executives, including nearly 50 CEOs, in over 100 companies throughout Europe, North America, Latin America, the Middle East, and Asia. We asked these individuals to describe the capabilities of effective global leaders and how those characteristics are best developed. We also asked these managers to identify "archetypal" global leaders, or executives in their companies who were recognized as global role models. We took the opportunity to interview these individuals as well. In all of these interviews, we asked the same pair of questions: "What are the capabilities of effective global leaders?" and "What have been the most powerful experiences in your life in developing these attributes?" These interviews, along with the results of several different surveys we have conducted, serve as the foundation for this book.

In some ways the world has changed a great deal since the late 1990s. Yet, through all these changes, the need for more and better global leaders has only grown. Twenty years of researching global leadership has deepened our under- standing of this complex topic. We have been able to reconsider, test, and update our earlier work. The result is the *The Global Leadership Challenge*, which is filled with countless new examples of successful global leaders and company practices.

Relevance to you

Regardless of your current management position and responsibilities, if you want to lead organizations in the future, this book is required reading. Maybe you are a young manager and have little previous experience with international busi- ness issues. You might be on an international assignment right now. Perhaps you are serving on a task force or team grappling with an international challenge or opportunity for your firm. You might head a unit with global responsibility for products, services, or business functions. Whatever your current responsibilities are, and no matter how secure you feel today, you will be unable to avoid the effects of the growing tidal wave of globalization. Sooner or later *you* will need to master the key capabilities of global leadership.

Keep in mind, however, that we do not define leaders only as those in the upper echelons of corporations. Leadership is not a function of position as much as it is a function of action. Some of the most senior executives we have met fell far short of being world-class leaders. While they barked out orders and were greeted with compliance, they failed to inspire anyone. Leadership is about determining direction, and then inspiring and coordinating action.

Leadership is not about coercion; it is about affecting people, what they do and what they believe. You do not need the vantage point of the pinnacle of the organization to see this. In our explorations, we have often found inspiring leaders deep within even the lowest parts of organizations.

Structuring the model

Our research objective was to identify a set of global leadership capabilities that was comprehensive and broad without being unwieldy. We were mindful that a number of companies have generated competency models that often provide little meaning for employees. One company we worked with, for example, tracked almost 250 different competencies. The complexity of models like this often led to confusion, indifference, and, in some cases, even contempt from employees. Finding the right balance between identifying too many and too few competencies is always a challenge.

In our research, we found that overall global leadership success is a function of capabilities driven by both general global dynamics and business-specific dynamics. About two-thirds of the capabilities for success are driven by global dynamics that apply to businesses everywhere, while the remaining one-third are driven by business-specific dynamics.

Global capabilities

Our research and experience found that *every global leader must have a core set of global capabilities.* These capabilities are essential for global leaders regardless of their countries of origin, the industries they work in, the companies they work for, or their functional orientations. In essence, these characteristics are driven by the global dynamics of business. Effective global leaders are different from average managers because they master these global aspects of leadership. Given our research and experience, we have concluded that you cannot become an effective global leader without developing these core characteristics.

We found that global leaders are consistently competent in four important areas:

- inquisitiveness
- perspective
- character
- savvy.

Business specific characteristics

While the focus of this book is on those capabilities of global leadership that are driven by global dynamics, there are capabilities critical to overall success that are driven by a leader's specific situation. Roughly one-third of what makes a global leader successful arises from these specific dynamics. These dynamics can be grouped into three major categories: industry, country, company.

The first dynamic is *industry*. Different industries have different product cycle times, roles for technology, and so on. Consequently, specific skills to deal with these dynamics vary from industry to industry. The second important dynamic is *country affiliation*. Without doubt, certain leadership characteristics are vital in India, while others are essential in the United States, France, or Korea. The third dynamic is *company affiliation*. Each company has a unique culture, set of values, and management philosophy. The skills and know-how associated with effective leadership at Toyota are in some ways unique and can be quite different from those required at Hitachi.

Each of these three dynamics plays an important, but supporting, role in determining the complete portfolio of competencies required for effective global leadership. We must be clear about this at the outset: *Every global leader requires a certain set of unique skills and abilities that arise from industry, country affiliation, and company dynamics.* Every leader's personal situation differs and requires a number of unique skills that fit his or her specific context. Furthermore, whenever a manager changes contexts, an entirely new set of specific competencies may be required. While there are an almost limitless number of combinations of specific capabilities, these capabilities account for only one-third of what global leaders need to be successful. Therefore, though it is a natural temptation, it would be a mistake for any manager to focus myopically on the capabilities driven by specific dynamics versus the capabilities driven by global dynamics. Both are essential.

Becoming a global leader

After investigating the competencies needed for global leadership, we wanted to find out what it took to develop global leaders. We asked the question: "Are global leaders *born or made?*" We concluded that global leaders are born and then made. This means that the future of a global leader is a function of being *competent* at and being *interested* in global business. Exemplar global leaders are both highly competent and interested. They are constantly pushing the frontiers of their own knowledge and understanding; they thrive in a chaotic, ambiguous environment; they love people; they have uncompromising ethical standards; they love global business; they are organizationally savvy. In reality, precious few fully competent global leaders exist. Many managers, however, have the potential to become global leaders.

This potential for leadership is innate: High-potential managers are born with a certain degree of inquisitiveness and ability much like the potential musician or athlete. You need some level of interest to even start off on the development journey. In addition, to be a good musician or athlete, you need some basic talent. Once a certain threshold of raw talent is met, experience plays an essential role in "making" global leaders. Key experiences beget international curiosity and interest, which in turn foster the development of critical global competencies.

But which experiences are the most effective in accelerating your development as a global leader? In our research, we asked global leaders about their career and personal experiences. We wanted to know what experiences helped most in their development into capable global leaders.

The executives described four primary development options: Transfers, Training, Teams, and Travel (what we call the 4Ts). While each kind of experience can provide valuable lessons, international transfers were judged to be by far the most powerful global leader development tool. Approximately 80 percent of participants in our research identified *living and working in a foreign country as the single most influential developmental experience in their lives.* However, taking advantage of all four types of experiences over the course of their careers was found to be the most effective way to acquire the complete set of global leadership competencies for the arduous journey through the uncharted waters of today's business world: the New World of global commerce.

A broader approach to global leadership

This guidebook for the global leadership journey is organized into two main sections. Part I sets the stage. In Chapter 1, we review the recent rise of globalization and the forces behind the globalization tsunami and the reason why there is such a shortage of quality global leaders. In Chapter 2, we describe why this matters to more leaders. In Chapter 3, we describe the two fundamental global dynamics that drive the critical global leadership characteristics and we briefly introduce the overall global leadership model. Part II includes detailed discussions of each of the global leadership characteristics. In Chapter 4, we describe the glue that holds it all together—unbridled inquisitiveness. In Chapter 5, we discuss the importance of proper perspective as a global leader. How will you manage the huge degree of uncertainty in the global business environment? How will you balance constant tensions between the demands for global integration and local responsiveness? In Chapter 6, we talk about the character and interpersonal abilities of global leaders by looking at the importance of connecting emotionally with people across the world. We also explore how you can tackle serious ethical conflicts and maintain your integrity. Chapter 7 shows what you need to know in order to demonstrate global business and organizational savvy.

In Part III, we show you how to become a better global leader. We discuss strategies you can pursue to master each global leadership competency. In Chapter 8, we consider whether global leaders are born or made, and whether to buy or build them. In Chapter 9, we show you how to use transfers, training, teams, and travel and to develop greater global leader capabilities. In Chapter 10, we explain how you should vary the application of different development experiences, depending on your career stage, and finally, in Chapter 11, we discuss the conclusions we have arrived at and offer some final advice on how to reach your global leadership potential.

We have written this book to help individuals as well as companies achieve their global leadership aspirations. One of our consistent observations of the best global leaders is that they are driven by an innate sense of opportunity and yearning for challenge. They are not satisfied to stroll around in known and famil-iar territory. Instead, they push the envelope to discover new possibilities. Just like the Old World explorers, they are excited by the opportunity and challenges of the uncharted waters of global business. In this fantastic journey, we wish you the very best. Bon Voyage!

Acknowledgments

The development of a comprehensive study of a complex topic like global leadership is time-consuming and arduous. While conducting seemingly countless interviews was vital to our research, it necessitated an enormous amount of travel and time away from family. The encouragement and support of family members were essential. We gratefully acknowledge their patience and support.

We are also indebted to our colleague Hal Gregersen for his contributions to our first edition, *Global Explorers: The Next Generation of Leaders*. As a co-author, Hal's insights, wisdom, and experience were essential in creating the first edition. Many of his contributions have been carried forward in *The Global Leadership Challenge*. We have worked together so long and shared so many experiences that it becomes difficult at times to identify the source of ideas. Suffice it to say, even though other commitments prevented Hal from participating in this round of research and writing, his presence has been deeply felt and his contributions remain. His friendship and support were critical in inspiring us to proceed with this book. We will be forever indebted to him.

We also acknowledge the support and encouragement of countless executive participants of leadership programs which we have directed or in which we have taught. These participants have challenged our thinking and pushed us to ask deeper questions and look for more complex explanations. Without their encouragement, and without their insatiable curiosity, we never would have proceeded with this volume.

We are thankful to a host of research assistants who, through the years, have added to our understanding of this complex topic. In particular, we recognize the efforts of Celia Chui, Heidi Streibel, and Tom Gleave for their contributions in this regard.

Finally, we acknowledge the support of the Jebsen Chair and CEO Global Center and IMD for financial support that covered travel and research assistants.

Part I

The context of global leadership

1 The rise of globalization

Recently, one of the authors (Stewart Black) was giving a presentation on global leadership, and during the Q&A session, someone from the audience asked, "When did all this globalization start?"

Feeling a bit feisty, Stewart responded with a question of his own, "Do you want an approximate point in time or do you want the day, month, and year?"

Not to be outdone, the participant emphatically replied, "Day, month, and year, please."

How would you answer this question? When did globalization start? Ten years ago? Twenty years ago? Fifty years ago? Is there a single event and date to which you would point as the beginning of globalization?

Without hesitation, Stewart replied, "Globalization began on the sixth day of September, 1522."

"September 6, 1522? Where did you come up with that date?" queried the persistent participant.

"That was the date on which the surviving 18 men of the original 237-member crew of Ferdinand Magellan's expedition arrived back in Spain, after circumnavigating the globe for the first time in the history of mankind," Stewart concluded. Or so he thought.

After the session was over, a different participant came up and offered an alternative start date of globalization. He argued that, while it was true that Magellan was the first to circumnavigate the world, Niccolò and Maffeo Polo, the father and uncle of Marco Polo, opened the world up to systemic international trade in 1260 with their travels to and trade with Asia over 250 years before Magellan. "Marco Polo then subsequently built upon the pioneering trade routes of his father and uncle but he got most of the credit and fame," the participant concluded.

Whether one points to the first circumnavigation of the globe by Magellan or the major international trade expeditions by the Polos, the key issue is that globalization has been going on for some time—arguably for centuries. Given that globalization is, in principle at least, *not* new, several questions spring to mind:

- If globalization in principle is not new, is there anything new and different under the globalization sun today? Or are the pontificating globalization gurus just trying to put old wine in new bottles?

- Assuming that there are in fact some things that are new and different about globalization today versus the past, *why* should we care about them?
- Assuming that there are compelling reasons to care about the new aspects of globalization, what does it take to be an effective global leader today and tomorrow?
- Assuming that there are certain capabilities that can indeed make one more or less effective at global leadership, how can we systematically develop those capabilities in ourselves and others?

For us, these are not just idle questions. Rather they have been the driving force of our research and consulting for nearly two decades. As a consequence, they are the core questions that we will address in this book—but not all in this first chapter. In this first chapter we take on the first question: What's new about globalization today versus the past? In Chapter 2 we address the second question: Why should we care? In Chapters 3–7, we address the question: What does it take to be an effective global leader? In Chapters 8–10, we examine the question: How can we systematically develop ourselves and others to be effective global leaders? As we will explain in more detail in Chapter 3, the answers to these questions across all the chapters of this book are based on years of systematic field research which we have conducted, and on a combined experience base of over 50 years working as consultants with companies and their senior leaders trying to understand and meet the challenges of globalization and global leadership. On the basis of this significant base of research and practice, we hope that you will find the answers to these key questions both rigorous and relevant; we believe you will.

Common globalization path

In addressing the question of what's new under the globalization sun, we have developed a simple but robust framework that helps put globalization in context. While on a micro level the details of every company's globalization journey are unique, at a more macro level our research shows that there is a general development path that many, if not most, companies follow. The simplicity and power of the framework and the commonality of the path stem from the fact that there are two fundamental mechanisms by which all companies can grow outside their home market.

First, companies can move things (e.g., components, products, knowledge, people, etc.) from one place to another to create and capture value. For convenience, we label this movement "trade." For example, you can make a product in one country and sell it in another. Or, as another example, you can take a leader from France and move her to Singapore where she can apply her skills and capabilities in the new location and create and capture value for you there.

Second, companies can make financial investments directly in a foreign locale to build up capabilities there. For convenience, we label this activity "investment" or "foreign direct investment (FDI)." For example, you can invest in building a factory or a service center in a given country. As another example, you can invest time and money identifying and building up leadership capabilities in a given locale.

Each of these two mechanisms (i.e., trade and investment) constitutes an axis in a two-dimensional model. The two dimensions are conceptually independent and do not need to move in unison or in opposition. Therefore, companies could emphasize or deemphasize each dimension to any degree and in any sequence they wanted. Despite this independence and a myriad of possible paths and sequences, it is interesting that the majority of companies follow a common path through this two-dimensional space. As we examined the common pattern across companies, we discovered that it did not happen by accident but was the outcome of common economic and psychological drivers that were strong enough to largely trump industry, country, or even company differences. The outcome is a 5-stage path to globalization depicted in Figure 1.1. In the subsequent sub-sections, we describe the nature of each stage and the drivers that tend to move companies from one stage to the next.

Stage 1: domestic birth and focus

Until recently, it was virtually impossible for a firm to be born global. Instead firms were born or started in a given country and usually spent much of their life, and certainly their early life, in their "birth country." To appreciate this, you only need to look at today's largest firms. Most were born 30, 40, and some over 100 years ago. For example, if you take the Fortune Global 500, which is a list of the largest 500 companies in the world by revenue, virtually every one of them started in a particular country and started there many decades ago. For example, General Electric (GE) was born in the United States in 1892. Michelin was started

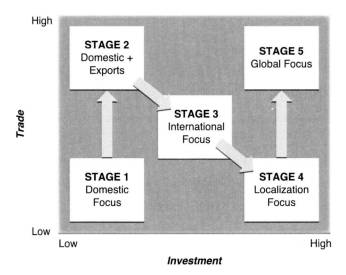

Figure 1.1 Five stages on the path of globalization

in France in 1888. Toyota was founded in Japan in 1937. Siemens was established in Germany in 1847. Nokia was born in Finland in 1865. Even 50 years after each company was started, every one had more than 80 percent of their assets and employees based in their home market.

In their early days, these and most companies focus on competing and growing at home. After all, if you don't focus on competing where you are born, you are unlikely to survive long enough to compete, let alone thrive and grow, somewhere else. However, as companies focus on their home market and are successful there, they can start to run into growth limits. For example, if you are a top executive at Gillette and after 50 years of growth since the company's founding in 1901 you have 70 percent of your home razor market and you still want to grow, it is natural for you to think about expanding internationally and therefore consider moving out of Stage 1. In fact, the faster company executives want to grow the firm and the smaller the home market, the greater and the earlier the catalyst to leave Stage 1. However, even if the company resides in a country with a large domestic market, eventually, as the home market matures and saturates, growth rates decline. Granted, to reach this point of diminishing growth can take decades. For example, GE spent its first 80 years primarily focused on its domestic market with more than 90 percent of its sales coming from the United States. If company executives are content with and accept declining growth rates, the company could stay in Stage 1 indefinitely. However, most company executives, especially those of public companies, are not willing to accept these declining growth rates, and so they start to think about leaving Stage 1.

Stage 2: export focus

If it is accepted that growth rates at some point are likely to stall out and then decline if a company just stays in Stage 1, why do most companies typically move from a domestic focus to exports? Why don't they jump straight into making big investments in foreign markets? In our research, we found that there are two principle forces that move most companies from Stage 1 (domestic focus) to Stage 2 (exports). One force is mostly grounded in economics and the second primarily in psychology.

Economic drivers

The economic driver of movement from Stage 1 to 2 is fairly straightforward. For manufactured goods with any degree of economies of scale, it just makes economic sense to get full utilization out of existing capacity, capture the economies of scale, lower per-unit costs, increase margins, and make more money by exporting. However, we need to stress that for most firms, the increased profits do not primarily come from the exports themselves. Yes, exports bring greater revenue and with that hopefully increased profits. However, the greatest capture of the increased margins due to the greater capacity utilization and economies of scale that exports provide is in domestic sales. For example, when Toyota started to move into exports in the early 1960s, domestic sales were five times greater than exports. Therefore, the increased capacity utilization and enhanced margins that exports provided to all the cars Toyota produced had their greatest benefits for cars produced for domestic sales, which as we mentioned were five times those of cars produced for exports.

Conversely, if Toyota had gone straight to building a factory abroad, say in the United States, for example, the economies of scale, capacity utilization, margin benefits, etc. could not have been applied to or captured in Toyota's domestic sales in Japan; they would have been limited to the production and sales out of their new factory in the United States. This is partly why Toyota didn't invest in building a car factory outside of Japan for more than 25 years after it started exporting cars. As we already pointed out, early in the process of moving out of Stage 1, domestic sales are always larger and usually much, much larger than international sales. Therefore, moving from Stage 1 directly into Stage 3 or Stage 4 by investing directly in foreign markets typically doesn't make as much economic sense as going for exports (i.e., moving into Stage 2). In addition, unless your products have a terrible weight-to-value ratio, such as bricks or cement, the savings captured through economies of scale typically are much larger than the shipping and other transaction costs associated with exporting. As a consequence, exports not only allow you to win the big prize of capturing the economy of scale benefits on domestic sales but also enable you to make money on the exports themselves.

In addition to the economic incentive to capture returns via the economies of scale on tangible assets like plant and equipment, there are also economic incentives to capture returns on economies of scale related to intangible assets. For example, after years of working and succeeding at home, a company typically builds up intangible assets, such as knowledge of and relationships with existing suppliers, employees, regulators, and the like. Exports in Stage 2 allow you to leverage those intangible assets and thereby enhance your return on investment (ROI) relative to the investments you have put into building up those intangible assets. To put it more simply, exports increase your ROI on intangible domestic assets because exports give you increased revenues without having to make much new investment in your intangible assets.

If we return to our example of Toyota, in addition to already having the plant and equipment to make cars at home in Japan for export to the United States and elsewhere, it already knows and has relationships with its workforce. Those workers know the Toyota way of manufacturing. Toyota already has relationships with suppliers and its suppliers know how to work within the "Toyota Way." To make more cars for export, Toyota doesn't really need to make any new investments in these intangible but very valuable assets. The numerator (i.e., revenues) goes up without much increase in the denominator (i.e., investments in intangible assets), and therefore the return improves. It is simple math that any executive can understand and is naturally incentivized to pursue.

In contrast, if Toyota moved out of Stage 1 by building production capacity in the United States, it would have to make significant investments not just in tangible assets like plant and equipment but in intangible assets as well. For example, it would have to invest time and money into figuring out how to effectively work with U.S. autoworkers and their unions. Given that the structure and orientation of U.S. autoworker unions are quite different from Japan's, Toyota would have to invest significant time and money into building up the intangible asset of understanding and working effectively with U.S. autoworker unions. This increased investment actually delivers a double negative effect. First, it causes Toyota to lose out on the ROI benefits of leveraging existing investments into its intangible asset of good working relations with Japanese unions that exports would have provided. Second, the greater this increased investment into understanding and working with U.S. unions, the lower the near-term ROI relative to its expansion in the United States and, all other things being equal, the longer it would take Toyota before it passed the breakeven point on those investments.

Thus, leaving one's home turf (Stage 1) via exports (Stage 2) for Toyota and many, many firms provides a much better ROI (especially early on) than leaving via the other alternatives (i.e., Stage 3, 4, or 5). *Bottom line*: exports can cut per-unit costs and grow revenues and profits all at the same time by leveraging both existing tangible *and* intangible assets. Therefore, moving from a domestic focus next to exports makes logical and financial sense for most companies and is followed by a majority of firms.

However, there are exceptions. For example, if you are in the hotel business and want to expand outside your home market, you will have a difficult time simply exporting your services. You typically have to have a hotel in the foreign market in order to capture revenues in that market. In this case, a hotel company is almost forced to go from Stage 1 (domestic focus) to Stage 3 (international focus). This can be true of other service firms as well, but not all. For example, there are a variety of legal, software, and accounting firms that do the work at "home" and then export the product (e.g., legal advice, programming code, accounting ledger entry) to "offshore" customers.

Psychological drivers

In addition to the economic incentives to move from Stage 1 to 2 that we just covered, there are psychological drivers, which our research suggests are nearly as important. As we mentioned, not only are most companies born in a single country, but they also spend their early years primarily in their birth country. As an example, young children are influenced by the language, culture, customs, and practices that surround them in their birth country. In business, the equivalent of influential parents, friends, and neighbors are domestic customers, competitors, employees, suppliers, regulators, and shareholders. So just as these societal differences lead to behavioral differences at the individual level country to country, so too do the business environment differences lead to strategy, structure, leadership style, and other differences at the firm level country to country.

The key point here is that during Stage 1, companies and their executives are focused on domestic competition and pursue winning at home in a way that makes sense in that home market. Because home country markets are different, Michelin's formula for success in France will be different from Bridgestone's in Japan. Siemen's recipe for success in Germany will not be the same as GE's in the United States, and so on. While the way each company succeeds at home could be (and in most cases is) different from country to country, the levels of success at home can be quite similar. In other words, Michelin could be as successful in France as Bridgestone is in Japan, even if the respective "ways" were quite different. Siemen's could be as successful in Germany as GE in the United States, even if their strategies, structures, and leadership styles were quite different. The key outcome of the differences across the home markets and different firms succeeding at home is that over time companies in the same industry often build up unique and different "ways" of achieving success at home.

Despite the differences in the "ways," the underlying key factors and dynamics are similar. First, the more difficult the home market and the more successful the way of the company, the more committed the company becomes to its way. Second, the longer the history of the company's success and the greater the magnitude of that success, the more committed the company becomes to its way. Given enough challenge, success, and time, the company's way typically evolves from "a way" into "*The* Way." At this point, top executives often feel that it is not only unwise or not smart to deviate from The Way but it is disloyal too.

This creates a psychological catalyst that complements the economic forces for moving from Stage 1 to Stage 2 rather than jumping straight to Stage 3 or 4 or 5. Moving to Stage 2 and emphasizing export allows you to stick with success— what you have done and the way you have done it. For example, when Toyota was building up its success in Japan from the 1930s through the 1940s, it competed with over a dozen different Japanese auto manufacturers. The "Toyota Way" helped it rise through this crowd of competition. After World War II, the number of domestic competitors decreased, but again it was the "Toyota Way" that helped the company rise to become the largest auto manufacturer in Japan. If the Toyota Way had helped the company succeed at home, and home was a very tough market, it was natural for executives to want to stick to The Way. When Toyota executives were looking at expanding outside of Japan, exports (Stage 2) enabled them to stick to the Toyota Way better than any other option.

This underlying psychological driver applies not just to Toyota's early growth and globalization actions but to most companies'. As we mentioned, the three ingredients that cause any company and its executives to view their way as "The Way" are tough competitive conditions at home, success, and time. This then creates a natural force to leave Stage 1 via Stage 2, because exports give you the greatest opportunity to stick with The Way. We will discuss in the next section how this natural progression can actually create challenges when a company tries to move from Stage 2 to 3, but we don't want to get ahead of ourselves.

In summary of this point, we want to emphasize four key issues:

1. After some period of focusing on the domestic market, executives typically face domestic growth limits (especially if the birth country is small).

2. This pushes them to think about leaving Stage 1.
3. The economic incentives for most firms stack up in favor of moving from Stage 1 to Stage 2 rather than to Stage 3, 4, or 5.
4. In addition, the psychological commitment that develops over time for "The Way" that led to success at home also causes executives to leave Stage 1 via Stage 2 rather than the other options.

This raises the question: "If there are so many benefits to Stage 2, why do firms ever leave it and why to most then move via Stage 3?"

Stage 3: international focus

Just as domestic growth limits lead executives to leave Stage 1, export growth limits cause executives to think about leaving Stage 2. These export growth limits stem from two inconvenient truths:

1. Customers are different around the world. They want different things; they have different price sensitivities; they prefer different packaging; they react differently to advertising messages; and they purchase what they want through different distribution channels.
2. The segment of customers willing to accept standardized exports is typically a much smaller one than the segment that wants something better positioned, tailored, or priced to meet its particular needs, wants, and preferences.

Like an iceberg, company executives can more easily see the above-water "export acceptor" customers, and, for all the reasons we already discussed, they are naturally inclined and motivated to focus on them. However, over time they come to realize that there is much more to the foreign customer iceberg that lies below rather than above the waterline, as Figure 1.2 illustrates.

As a consequence, once company executives start bumping into the growth ceiling for their exports, they start thinking about what it would take to penetrate into the larger segment of foreign customers who want products and services tailored to their needs. To reach them, companies typically have to change not only aspects of their products and services, but also the way they distribute, market, sell, and provide after-sales service. This typically requires companies to increase their direct investments in foreign markets and on a relative basis deemphasize exports. Thus, within the framework presented in Figure 1.1, companies move right on the "Investment" axis as they increase their foreign direct investments and move down on the "Trade" axis as they put less relative emphasis on exports.

As companies make greater local investment in one country and then another, over time they build up presence across multiple countries. Early on these might be combined under an international division or department. At some point, when the company has a presence across many countries and multiple regions, they typically cluster certain countries together, forming regional structures and strategies. In fact, given enough time and investment, companies could have a

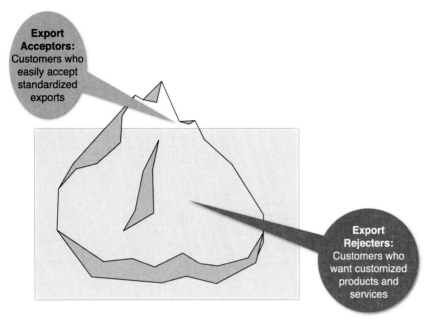

Figure 1.2 Segments of foreign customers

presence in most countries around the world and virtually every region in the world. While this might constitute global presence, as you will see from our later description of Stage 5, it is not what we would label a global company. Rather it is an international company with global presence.

Interestingly, many companies basically stop their globalization journey at Stage 3. To be clear, this is not necessarily bad. In fact, a company could stop at Stage 3 and continue to grow for years, even decades. After all, the world is a very big place and it can take a very long time to gain a presence in most countries and in all the regions on the planet.

Those companies that stay in Stage 3 typically create not only regional structures but strategies as well. Research has demonstrated that if companies stay at Stage 3, forming regional strategies and structure is generally a smart and effective move.[1] In fact, in Stage 3, the more countries in which a company is present, the more a regional approach makes sense. To appreciate why this is the case, just imagine a corporation with subsidiaries in 100 or more countries where each one reported directly back into headquarters. Such an approach would be just too unwieldy. In addition, a regional approach makes sense because scale economies are generally higher at regional—not local country—production levels. As a result, regional strategies have the potential to be relatively effective, particularly in Stage 3.[2]

However, there are some companies that have such attractive economies of scale and whose exports are so successful that they are very reluctant to move out of Stage 2 and into Stage 3. In some cases, it may even seem that the segment of customers who want the company's products tailored to their needs is *not* larger than those who are willing to purchase the standardized exported product. For example, even in 2013, Toyota produced more cars in Japan for export abroad than it built outside of Japan. However, even where this is the case, it is often difficult for these firms to avoid moving to the right along the investment axis. Often these companies find that they have to invest in local markets to manage distribution problems, warranty and repair work, provide after-sales service and support, and the like. Our point here is that while a move from Stage 2 to Stage 3 is not inevitable, the forces to do so are strong and prevalent. As a consequence, most company executives who have strong growth objectives will likely over time (though that time could be many years) find themselves moving their firm to one degree or another from Stage 2 to Stage 3.

One of the common challenges when companies initially move into Stage 3 is that they often try to operate and do things in the same way as proved successful for them in Stages 1 and 2. As we previously discussed at length, given some time and success in Stage 1, companies develop "their way." Given enough time and success, their way becomes "The Way." Stage 2 typically allows companies to continue with The Way. The greater and the longer The Way is successful in Stage 2, the more likely a firm is to try to implement The Way as it moves into Stage 3. This highlights a natural paradox. On the one hand, firms move out of Stage 2 and into Stage 3 because they start to see the limits of export growth and the need to modify products and services to tap into the larger segment of customers who want products and services more tailored to their specific needs. At the same time, the longer and more successful The Way has been up to that point, the more executives try to leverage The Way even as they move into Stage 3.

Some companies and their executives learn very quickly that in order to tap into the larger segment of "Export Rejecters" in foreign markets, they have to modify, and often significantly, not just their products and services but The Way as well. Other companies and their executives learn only slowly, largely through the school of hard knocks, that they must make adjustments. In a separate book entitled, *The Failure to Launch Globally*, we document this process in greater detail, but for our purposes here it is sufficient simply to point out that success in Stages 1 and 2 can actually get in the way of success in Stage 3.

Stage 4: localization focus

But assuming companies and their executives see the need to modify or even abandon parts of The Way in order to be successful at Stage 3, then success can breed success. By that we mean that as firms move deeper into Stage 3 and are successful customizing, adapting, and even creating new products and services that meet and appeal to local needs, this localization process becomes ever more attractive as it leads to deeper market penetration and higher sales. Consequently, there is a natural progression from Stage 3 to Stage 4 in which firms increase their investment in foreign markets and adapt to the local requirements in each market. As companies make this transition, they make ever-larger investments in building up local capabilities. This localization can involve not just products and services but support functions and processes as well. For example, information technology (IT) systems get designed and created that fit the local environment. Financial monitoring and reporting systems are adjusted to fit the local laws and regulations. Hiring, performance management, compensation, and training policies, processes, and practices are localized so that they can be more effective. In fact, the list and description of what can and often does get localized can become very long.

Not surprisingly, some companies make a virtue out of their ability to localize their services in and their understanding of the local environment. For example, HSBC has the tagline "The World's Local Bank." They utilize advertisements wherein the same item is seen differently through the eyes of different countries and cultures. For example, they show a picture of the same rug three times with three different captions: décor, souvenir, and place of prayer. Their point is that just as a rug is not the same thing to everyone everywhere, so too is banking not the same to everyone everywhere and HSBC makes the adjustments needed for their banking to be what you need wherever you are.

As companies adapt both products and business practices to meet the differences around the world, the success of this effort is evidenced and rewarded by increased sales. However, moving deeper into Stage 4 is not without its costs. Customizing the packaging, the design, the quality, or the functionality of different products and creating different IT platforms, finance systems, job-grading procedures, or hiring processes are not free.

However, early in Stage 4 these costs are often not nearly as visible as the increased revenues that come from localization. This is because both on an individual country basis and even on a larger aggregate basis the individual localization efforts and associated costs are not made at one time across all countries. To some extent it is simply math. Just as companies do not enter 100 different countries simultaneously but typically achieve this over a period of time (often decades), so too they do not make all their localization efforts at the same time. Typically, there are three critical drivers of localization:

1. Length of time the company has had a presence in the country.
2. Extent of customer differences between the local country and the home country of the firm.
3. Size of the local market.

Put simply, the longer the firm has been in a given country, the greater the differences in what customers in that country want from the products and service the company offers compared with the firm's home market, and the greater the size and potential revenues that would come with increased localization in that market, the greater the actual localization. In most cases this process of staggered localization and unequal localization investment is driven by the fact that the cost of simultaneous (i.e., non-staggered) and equal localization across many countries is simply beyond the financial resources of any company. As one executive put it,

"The world is just too big a place to localize all your activities all at the same time and to the same degree. Even if we wanted to, we just don't have that much money. No company does that I know of."

Thus, as a company pursues greater localization of products and processes in five countries, the individual and aggregate costs are not that big; they are not that noticeable. However, as the scale and scope of your localization efforts grow, so too do the costs of doing things differently in various countries. However, these costs creep up over time—not all at once. As a consequence, they can build below the radar screen for some time. When a firm reaches the point that it is localizing not just products and packaging but performance management practices, IT platforms, finance systems, quality control measures, branding, sales approach, etc., across not just five countries but across 50 countries, the costs start to add up. However, as we pointed out, like a slow boiling frog, executives may take a long time to notice the inefficiencies, redundancies, duplications, etc. Then finally, when they are large enough, or when a shock wakes people up, the costs of having 59 small factories, 17 different finance systems, 11 different IT platforms, 21 different performance appraisal forms, 4 job grading systems, and the like are just too great to ignore anymore.

Stage 5: borderless global business focus

This realization of the large costs and inefficiencies that grew out of success—localization efforts across products and processes—is typically the catalyst for borderless globalization—movement from Stage 4 to Stage 5. The transition into and the dynamics of borderless globalization in Stage 5 are marked by the reemergence of two dynamics that separately played leading roles in Stage 2 (exports) and Stage 4 (localization). In Stage 2, the economies of scale and benefits of standardized exports pushed companies to focus on making something one way at home and then selling it largely the same way around the world (i.e., global integration). In Stage 4, the differences across regions and countries pushed companies to localization and to modify and adapt to the local differences (i.e., local adaptation). In the borderless global stage both forces—the forces for global integration *and* for local adaptation—hold sway. As a consequence, companies struggle with but eventually must master a complex process of determining which things to globally integrate (e.g., IT platforms), which things to locally differentiate (e.g., sales promotion), and which activities and products need to have a unique blend of both. While it is easy to say that Stage 5 involves getting the right configuration of globally integrated, locally responsive, and hybrid activities, it is very hard to figure it out in practice. As a consequence, there is a lot more to say about Stage 5, but we will dive into these details a bit later in this chapter and in Chapter 5.

What's new?

With this background set, we can now look more closely at the question of what is new about globalization today compared with the past. It should be obvious that the pattern of globalization we just highlighted is, in a technical sense, *not* new. No doubt you can think of different companies, perhaps your own, that have gone through this pattern some time ago. However, if there is nothing really new about global business today compared with a few decades ago, let alone a few centuries ago, then there is really no justification for our writing this book or for your reading it. Fortunately for both you, the reader, and for us, the authors, even though the pattern we discussed is not new, there are at least two things that are new and different under the globalization sun today compared with the past. While we separate them in this chapter for ease of discussion, you will soon see that they are quite interrelated. The first difference is what we call the *pervasiveness* of globalization, and the second is what we call the *interconnectedness* of globalization. In combination, they provide some powerful reasons to care about globalization and global leadership, which we will discuss in Chapter 2.

Pervasiveness of globalization and global focus

Even though you could argue that globalization has been going on for 500 years or more, over that period, it has been a daily reality and concern for a very small minority of leaders. Quite simply, global customers, competitors, suppliers, employees, strategic partners, and the like were not very pervasive for most executives across most of the last 500 years. However, that has changed dramatically in the last 10–20 years as globalization's pervasiveness has exploded.

To examine this last statement, let's take a look at the pervasiveness of globalization through a few different lenses. We want to start with the lens of company revenues. We choose to start with revenues because they capture the focus and attention of virtually every leader of every commercial enterprise on the planet. They capture their attention for one simple reason: If you cannot generate revenues, no matter how well you control costs, enhance quality, run logistics, inspire people, or anything else, you can't sustain a commercial enterprise. As a consequence, it should be no surprise then that top executives give the most time and attention to what they perceive as the strongest drivers of revenue. In the context of globalization, the more that global customers, global competitors, global suppliers, global employees, global strategic partners, etc. find their way into revenues, the more executives pay attention to those global factors. Conversely, the more domestic customers, domestic competitors, domestic suppliers, domestic employees, domestic strategic partners, etc. find their way into revenues, the more executives pay attention to those domestic factors.

In our work with companies and executives around the world, regardless of industry, country of origin, or anything else, most executives simplify this revenue picture in a similar way. They simply divide revenues into two categories: domestic and international. With this simple split, you will likely not be surprised that our research shows that the higher a company's international revenues are as a proportion of total revenues, the more executives pay attention to globalization. In general, executives see domestic factors having their biggest impact on domestic revenues and global factors having their biggest impact on international revenues. As we will discuss later when we examine the interconnectedness of globalization, this simple view is not a completely accurate reflection of reality, and we predict that it will break down over time, but for most executives today, it holds true.

Although the split of revenues into two simple categories is common for most executives around the world, the relationship between the source of revenues and the overall global focus of executives is not a simple linear one. Our research finds that the relationship between executives' global focus and degree of international sales forms an "S-curve" (see Figure 1.3).

Specifically, as international sales increase as a total percentage of sales and move from zero to about 15 percent, there is very little increase in how salient executives see global customers, competitors, suppliers, employees, and so on; executives' global focus does not increase much and remains low. Instead at that level they still primarily focus on domestic customers, competitors, and the like. A comment from one executive we interviewed captures the essence of this relationship. When we asked him why he seemed almost entirely focused on domestic competitors, employees, and the like, when 20 percent of his firm's sales came from outside the home country, he asked a rhetorical question, "Why should I spend 80 percent of my time where I get only 20 percent of my sales?"

However, as international sales move from 20 percent to about 50 percent, there is a sharp increase in how salient executives see global issues. As we already indicated and as we will explore later in this section, part of this is because the interconnectedness of business is not perfectly reflected in the source of a firm's

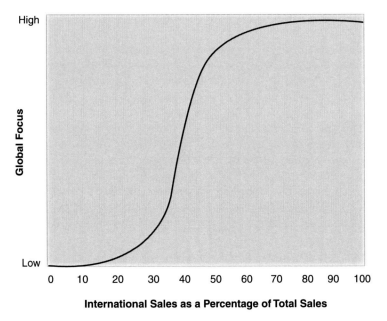

Figure 1.3 International sales and executive global focus

sales. For example, a firm might have only 30 percent of its sales outside its home borders but 60 percent of its supply chain might be international and 80 percent of its largest competitors might be foreign companies.

Nonetheless international sales move from 50 percent to 100 percent, our research suggests that there is only a gradual increase in executives' global focus. Again, without yet diving into the issue of interconnectedness, you can likely appreciate that once 60, 75, or 90 percent of your sales are international, many other aspects of your business are also likely to be at or above that level of globalization, and thus, executives' level of global focus is already high. As a consequence, as the level of international sales moves from 50 percent to 90 percent, executives' global focus increases but is already so high that the rate of increase diminishes.

Our research also suggests that the shape of this curve changes somewhat as you look at not just the absolute level of international sales but also its composition. In terms of the composition, we divide international sales into two categories: exports and non-exports. Our definition of exports is simple. Exports are products or services that are made in the company's home market and then sent to foreign markets for sale. Non-exports are products made somewhere other than the company's home market and sold somewhere other than the company's home market. The proportion of exports in international sales has an important impact on the shape of the S-curve relationship between global focus and international sales. A higher proportion of exports shifts the curve to the right, which means that it takes a higher level of international sales to generate the same level of global focus in executives. A lower proportion of exports shifts the curve to the left, which means that it takes a lower level of international sales to generate the same level of global focus in executives. These shifts are illustrated in Figure 1.4.

The reason exports as a proportion of the international sales affect the relationship curve is because of the fundamental difference between export and non-export sales. By their nature, exports allow executives to make products utilizing existing assets at home with employees they know and understand in a linguistic, cultural, regulatory, governmental, and societal context that they know and likely have mastered. Thus, by their nature, exports do not force top executives to look outside their home market and understand the world the same way that non-export international sales do. Non-export sales typically require firms to manufacture products outside their home market and with employees in linguistic, cultural, regulatory, governmental, and societal contexts that they may not understand well and quite likely have not mastered. This naturally increases executives' global focus. As a consequence, as we already mentioned, a high proportion of exports shifts the curve to the right, while a low proportion shifts the curve to the left.

While it is somewhat secondary, our research also suggests that this "S-curve" relationship between international sales and global focus applies not just to top executives but to managers as well. However, unlike top executives whose global focus is most influenced by the company's overall level of international sales, lower-level managers' global focus is most influenced by the international sales of products that they are personally involved in or affected by (what academic

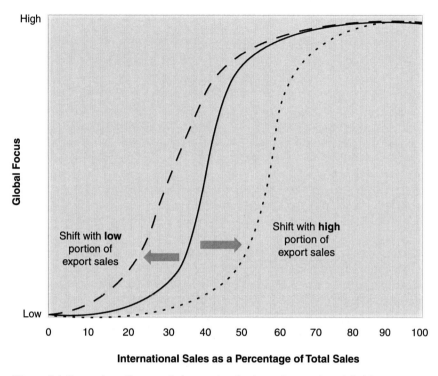

Figure 1.4 Proportion of exports in international sales and executive global focus

researchers call "proximity"). Thus, even if overall international sales account for 50 percent of total sales, if international sales account for only 10 percent of sales for Product A, then the managers working with Product A will have a much lower global focus than the company executives overall. Conversely, even if overall international sales account for only 20 percent of total sales, but account for 60 percent of sales for Product B, then the managers working with Product B will have a higher global focus than the company executives overall.

One final finding from our research concerns the global focus of functional managers (e.g., human resources, supply chain, legal, etc.). Functional managers also have a global focus "S-curve," but the curve is most directly influenced by factors that are more proximate to functional managers' jobs. For example, for HR managers, the proportion of international employees rather than international sales has the strongest impact on their global focus. Or for supply chain managers, the proportion of the supply chain that is outside the home market, rather than international sales, has the strongest impact on their global focus. Thus, the overall proportion of international sales to total sales is a good but not perfect proxy for top-executive global focus but is a less strong proxy for lower-level managers and for functional managers. In the end, while we recognize that the proportion of international revenues is not a perfect proxy for the pervasiveness of globalization in the minds of executives and a driver of their global focus, it is not too bad either and is a good place to start to examine the extent to which the pervasiveness of globalization has changed over time.

Pervasiveness of globalization and international revenues

If we use the proportion of international revenues as an imperfect but reasonable proxy for the pervasiveness of globalization, then a key question to examine is how the percentage of international sales has changed for companies over time. Sadly, there is no reliable data set to answer this question on a global scale. However, for the United States, there are reasonable data on the S&P 500 stock market index that go back far enough in time to give us some good perspective. Before we present the data, we of course recognize that these companies are not representative of all companies (large and small) in the United States. In addition, even if they are a good representation of large companies in the United States, we also recognize that the United States may not be representative of the world. Nevertheless, given the realities of reliable and available data, the S&P 500 seems to us like a reasonable place to start.

With the S&P 500, we can reliably go back to 1950 to look at the average percentage of sales that came from outside the United States (i.e., foreign or international sales) and then examine how much and how fast it has changed over time. In 1950, the average international sales as a proportion of total sales were just 6 percent (see Figure 1.5).

On the basis of our previous discussion, you can appreciate that with international sales at just 6 percent in 1950, company executives had a very low

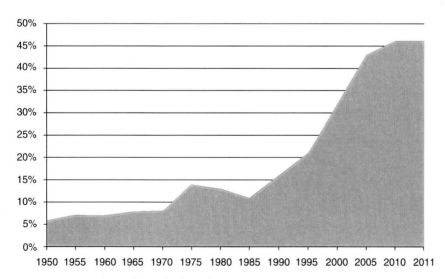

Figure 1.5 Percentage of S&P foreign sales, 1950–2011

Sources: U.S. Bureau of Economic Analysis; UNCTAD World Investment Report 2013

global focus. Today, with the benefit of hindsight and knowing where things have gone since then, we might argue that even with international revenues at only 6 percent executives should have had a higher global focus. However, if you put yourself back in 1950 and 94 percent of your sales were from your home or domestic market, where would most of your focus be? It is quite logical that it would be on domestic customers, competitors, suppliers, and the like, and it was.

No doubt you can think of some exceptions. For example, in 1950 international sales for Coca-Cola were more than four times the S&P average. As a consequence, you would rightly expect Coca-Cola executives to have a higher global focus than executives at the average S&P 500 firm. But that is our point; in 1950 Coca-Cola and the handful of firms like it were the exceptions that proved the rule. After all, if the average level of international sales in 1950 for the largest 500 firms in the United States was 6 percent, that meant that for every Coca-Cola with international sales higher than 6 percent there were many firms with international sales that were much lower. In fact, even companies that today we think of as relatively global were quite domestically focused in 1950. For example, today we think of GE as a global company, but in 1950 it was more than 90 percent focused on doing business in the United States. The bottom line is that for U.S. companies in 1950 globalization was not very pervasive and executives' global focus was quite low. In that sense, the pervasiveness of globalization and therefore executives' global focus in 1950 was not much different from 1850, or even 1750. Globalization was just not on the radar screen for most executives.

Over the next 25 years, the percentage of international sales of the S&P 500 doubled from 6 percent to 12 percent. While this was an important increase, the absolute level of 12 percent and the composition of that 12 percent were such that, even in 1974, globalization was not very pervasive. Again, our earlier discussion provides insight as to why this was the case. In terms of the absolute level, 12 percent international sales was still a small number compared with 88 percent coming from domestic sales. In this sense, size matters. To paraphrase our earlier quote, "Why should an executive put 88 percent of her focus on only 12 percent of sales?" In addition, as we previously discussed, the export versus non-export sales proportion of total international revenue also mattered. In the case of the S&P 500, much of the increase in foreign sales between 1950 and 1974 came from greater export sales, not from non-export sales. For example, from 1950 to 1974 U.S. exports increased 133 percent; they went from 3 percent of gross domestic product (GDP) to about 7 percent (largely because of lower tariffs, which we discuss later). As a consequence, for the vast majority of S&P 500 executives at the time, globalization and global focus were not very pervasive because total international sales were low (i.e., 12 percent) and the proportion of international sales coming from exports was high. As strange as it may sound to say, for most U.S. executives, 1974 was not that much different in the level of global focus from 1954 or 1904.

In pointing to the role of exports in the low level of global focus at the time, we are not criticizing exports in general or executives who pursued them in particular. As we discussed earlier in this chapter, executives had a natural incentive to pursue exports. However, it is worth a reminder that even if exports helped the proportion of international sales' relative increase, its nature deflected at least some executive focus away from globalization and back toward domestic issues. As a consequence, even though from 1950 to 1974 exports were an important driver of the doubling of international sales from 6 percent to 12 percent, they partially dampened executives' global focus.

It is important to note that U.S. firms were not the only ones to add international sales disproportionately through exports in the 1960s and 1970s. For other companies in other countries the trend was the same, though the numbers generally were higher. Specifically, global exports as a percentage of world GDP increased from 9.6 percent in 1960 to 16.2 percent in 1974 and reached a peak at just over 18 percent of GDP in 1981, as Figure 1.6 illustrates. Thus, exports' dampening effect on global focus compared with non-export sales was true not just for U.S. executives through the mid-1970s but for executives globally.

Japan was a classic case in point. In Japan, exports as a percentage of GDP increased from 7.8 percent in 1960 to 12.1 percent in 1974 and continued to grow, reaching 14 percent by 1984. The relatively lower percentage of international sales overall and the high percentage of exports' share of international sales were common across most Japanese firms at the time. For example, in 1983 Toyota produced almost 100 percent of the cars it sold worldwide in just one country— Japan. A staggering 64.2 percent of all the cars Toyota produced in Japan were produced for exports. Even in 1983, exports were nearly 100 percent of all of Toyota's international sales.[3] In this context it is easy to understand how exports

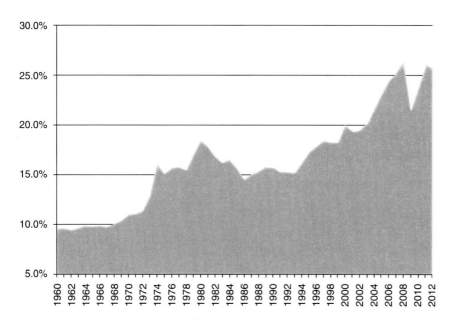

Figure 1.6 Exports as a percentage of world GDP, 1960–2012

Sources: WTO; World Bank; UNCTAD World Investment Report 2013

as a high percentage of total international sales dampened Japanese executives' global focus. In fact in a recent book (*Sunset in the Land of the Rising Sun*) we argue that Japan's strong focus on exports made it difficult for their executives to move to Stages 3, 4, and 5 and has been one of the reasons that Japanese firms' share of the Global Fortune 500 has dropped by over 50 percent between 1995 and 2012.[4]

Beyond the natural economic incentives we mentioned earlier for exports, it is natural to ask why we see an increase in exports for U.S. companies, as well as for companies around the world, over this 35-year period from 1950 to 1984. While we mentioned the role of reduced tariffs earlier, we want to dive into the details a bit deeper now.

In beginning this examination, it is important to appreciate that the same economic incentive to seek exports existed before this period of rapid growth in exports (1950–1984) and therefore highlights the question of why exports grew so much during this period. While there is no single cause and a full explanation is beyond the scope of this book, we want to highlight one driver of exports during this period—reductions in tariffs. Reductions in trade and tariff barriers achieved in the Kennedy Round (1964–67) and Tokyo Round (1973–79) of the General Agreement on Tariffs and Trade (GATT) were important drivers of the subsequent increase in exports around the world. For example, the Kennedy Round reduced tariffs about 35 percent and eliminated or reduced approximately $40 billion of tariffs, which was ten times that achieved in the previous Dillon Round of the GATT. As a consequence, exports from the end of the Kennedy Round in 1964 until the beginning of the Tokyo Round in 1973 increased from $176 billion (9.8 percent of world GDP) to $580 billion (12.9 percent of world GDP). The subsequent Tokyo Round amplified this increase in exports by reducing tariffs by nearly $200 billion. As a consequence by 1980 exports had risen nearly four times to $2 trillion and from 12.9 percent to 18.5 percent of world GDP. Again, while tariff reductions alone did not cause this surge in exports globally, they were important and their influence is easy to understand. After all, all other things being equal, reducing tariffs makes exports more affordable and more attractive to foreign customers.

Referring back to Figure 1.5, you can see that for the S&P 500 the next major surge in foreign sales as a percentage of total sales began in the mid-1990s. In a period of about 15 years, international sales as a proportion of total sales exploded threefold from around 15 percent to 45 percent. As before, to understand the impact of this increase on executive global focus, we need to examine both the absolute level and the composition of this increase. For top executives, an absolute level of 45 percent is very significant and drives a high level of global focus. Again to paraphrase the earlier executive quote, "It makes little sense to put *only* 10 percent of your focus on 50 percent of your sales." As a consequence, the pervasiveness of globalization increased dramatically.

This sudden and massive increase in the pervasiveness of globalization and global focus was amplified by the lower proportion of exports within firms' international sales compared with the past. For example, during this period, while international sales as a proportion of total sales tripled, U.S. exports as a percentage of GDP rose from only 8 percent to about 10 percent. Thus, as U.S. companies moved through this period, the proportion of export sales declined and the proportion of non-export sales increased to the point that in 2012 the vast majority of international sales for S&P 500 firms were non-export sales. From an S&P 500 company senior executive's perspective, this meant that the majority of 45 percent of total sales was coming from products created in foreign locales, purchased by non-domestic customers, competed for against global competitors, using international suppliers and foreign employees in linguistic, cultural, regulatory, and societal contexts that were relatively new to the executives. Given this, it is only natural that executive global focus would also dramatically and quickly increase. Suddenly, 2012 was not only different from 1812, or 1912, but it was different even from 2002.

Recent explosion in pervasiveness of globalization

As we explained, for most executives the pervasiveness of globalization only becomes a reality as the firm experiences the limits of exports, increases its foreign direct investments, and moves into Stage 3. While firms follow their own individual timing in terms of this transition, a significant number of firms around the world, not just in the United States, made significant moves into Stage 3 as is evidenced by a tripling of FDI as a percentage of world GDP from 1997 to 2012, as Figure 1.7 illustrates.

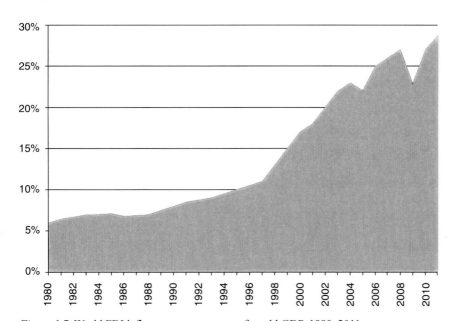

Figure 1.7 World FDI inflows as a percentage of world GDP, 1980–2011

Sources: World Bank; UNCTAD World Investment Report 2013

To get an idea of what this was like for companies from five of the largest developed economies, we present data on the United States, Germany, France, the United Kingdom, and Japan in Table 1.1. From the table it is easy to see the significant increases in outflows of FDI made by companies in each of these countries. In examining Table 1.1, as we mentioned earlier, you can see that Japanese firms stayed with an emphasis on exports (Stage 2) longer and began outward foreign direct investments and the move into Stage 3 later in comparison with U.S., German, French, and British companies. As a consequence, Japanese FDI stock as a percentage of GDP in 1997 was only 6.4 percent. By 2011 it had risen to 17.6 percent, which, while an important increase, was still significantly lower than its peers.

No doubt you can think of companies such as Coca-Cola, Nestlé, Shell, and others that had made major investments outside their home country long before 1997 and therefore had moved into Stage 3 much earlier. This is of course the case. However, the data in Figure 1.7 and Table 1.1 illustrate that these firms were again the exceptions, not the rule.

Where was all this investment going? While the popular press would have everyone believe that virtually all of this investment was going into the BRICs (Brazil, Russia, India, and China), this was actually not the case. Table 1.2 shows the top 15 countries and the total in dollars invested in each country between 2006 and 2011. As Table 1.2 illustrates, the United States was the number 1 targeted country. China was number 2, but received 30 percent less investment over this period than the United States. The UK was number 3, and Belgium was number 4. Of the top 15 countries, 70 percent of FDI flowed into developed economies and 30 percent flowed into developing economies. This is not to say that developing economies in general or the BRICs in particular were not important. In total, the BRICs received $1.7 trillion of investment, which was $335.3 billion more than went into the United States. It is worth noting that the lion's share (60 percent) of the FDI into the BRICs went to China during this period, and that despite all the media attention regarding India, it received only 11 percent of the BRICs' total.

Pervasiveness and the leadership challenge

What we have tried to illustrate up to this point in the chapter is that for the vast, vast majority of firms and their top executives globalization was not a visible,

Table 1.1 Increases in FDI, 1997 and 2011

Country	1997 FDI Stock as percent of GDP	2011 FDI Stock as percent of GDP
United States	10.5	31.2
Germany	14.3	43.1
France	16.6	58.2
UK	27.2	74.3
Japan	6.4	17.6

Source: World Bank

Table 1.2 FDI inflow, 2006–2011

Rank	Country	Total FDI inflow 2006–2011
1	United States	$1,364,670,000,000
2	China	$987,100,000,000
3	UK	$625,870,000,000
4	Belgium	$578,116,000,000
5	France	$328,021,000,000
6	Canada	$317,331,000,000
7	Russian Federation	$292,443,000,000
8	Germany	$255,433,000,000
9	Spain	$252,613,000,000
10	Australia	$251,601,000,000
11	Brazil	$239,581,000,000
12	India	$184,952,000,000
13	Netherlands	$182,153,000,000
14	Switzerland	$140,207,000,000
15	Mexico	$135,134,000,000

Sources: World Bank; UNCTAD World Investment Report 2013

daily concern until the late 1990s or early in the twenty-first century. As a consequence, for most executives on a practical level globalization is a relatively recent phenomenon. Specifically, executives did not see their overall international sales move above the 25 percent level until about 15 years ago. Most did not see a majority of these sales come from investment directly into foreign markets rather than exports until the last 10 years. Most executives did not see their international sales get close to the 50 percent mark until the last 5 years. For the vast majority of companies and executives, the serious move from Stage 2 into Stage 3 has been over the last 15 years and the move into Stage 4 over the last 10 years. The move into Stage 5 for most of the executives we interviewed was just beginning or was within the last 5 years.

We stress this because of the practical challenge it presents to many top executives. To understand this, we need to do just a little math. The majority of the corporate top executives we interviewed were in their fifties and had on average a 30-year career up to that point. Thus, this globalization surge we have highlighted happened in just the last third of their career. In most cases, neither they nor their firm had the foresight 30 years ago to plan out a global leader development roadmap so that they built up the needed global leadership capabilities in order to have them when they were needed. As a consequence, executives described to us the need to develop global leadership capabilities in themselves "on the fly." One executive put it this way:

> It's like for your first solo flight being given the controls of a 747 full of passengers with no live flight instructor and only a Cessna Piper Cub instruction

manual to read and flying through turbulence especially in 2000–2003 and then 2008–2010 that even the most experienced pilots had never experienced before.

When we probed deeper into this feeling, which another executive described as "drinking from a fire hose," two drivers emerged. The first was the fact that many of these top executives' careers had largely been in their home market. As a consequence, many had *not* spent significant time in various markets learning in depth the different countries and cultures, regulatory systems, politicians, or deeply understanding foreign customers and the like. Given all the differences from country to country and region to region, trying to learn the world in just 10 years of one's career is a heck of a challenge, especially without living in the various countries.

When we pressed a bit further and pointed out that they must have traveled to various countries over the course of their careers—long before the last 10 years—most nodded and smiled and then talked about the "executive cocoon of comfort" that usually accompanied their business travel. (Actually none of them used the term "executive cocoon of comfort"; we coined the term.) The executive cocoon of comfort starts when the executive's assistant coordinates all the details for the trip—the flights, the hotels, the office visits, etc. The executive flies in on the company jet or in the comfort of a first-class seat (or at worst a business-class seat) on an airline on which he or she has Platinum, Gold, Ruby, Diamond, Emerald, or some other elite status. Typically local staff meet the executive at the airport or at least arrange for a car and driver to meet the executive. Almost never does the executive have to hassle with trying to hail a local taxi and then have to get the driver to understand where to go. The executive arrives at a five-star hotel. Often they stay at a hotel whose headquarters is in the same country as the company headquarters. For example, you find a lot of Americans staying at the J.W. Marriott, Japanese at a Hotel Nikko, and French at a Sofitel wherever in the world they are traveling. The next day, staff pick up the executive in the morning and whisk him or her to the office. There is almost never any standing in line for buses, trains, or the subway in an effort to get to the office. The executive works at an office that in most ways on the inside looks and functions quite like the one he or she just left back home. At the end of the day, the executive is taken to a nice dinner and back to the hotel. How much of the real smell, taste, grit, grime, nuance, and nature of the country and culture does the executive really encounter? By their own admission to us, not much. This would not be a problem if the FDI decisions in Stages 3, 4, and 5, ranging from small plant upgrades to major acquisitions, could be made effectively with a passing, superficial "executive comfort cocoon" understanding of the local factors and dynamics. Unfortunately, again by executives' own admission, these critical decisions require a much more in-depth knowledge, understanding, and insight into the local situation.

The second reason executives commonly cited for why their sudden emersion into globalization has felt like drinking from a fire hose was that the FDI decisions and the global integration and local responsiveness decisions not only required in-depth knowledge of and experience with a whole variety of countries and cultures but it required a conscious effort to *not* simply approach the factors and decisions as one would "at home." Virtually all of the executives we interviewed understood at an intellectual level that they needed to take a more globally broad and a locally sensitive perspective and approach than was required and had been successful for them "at home." However, understanding this at an intellectual level and putting it into action at a practical level are two different things. As the head of a large French retailer admitted, "I've spent most of my career in France and I've been successful. It is hard for me not to think like a Frenchman."

Again we pressed a bit further and pointed out that they must have had lower-level managers in the countries and regions where these investment decisions had to be made who should have had the requisite knowledge and experience to properly inform the decisions. Invariably the executives admitted that "yes, there were locals" who had this experience and knowledge. However, what followed in more than half the cases we interviewed was an interesting confession. The quote below captures the essence of these confessions:

> Of course you are right. There were local people who knew the markets, the players, etc. But quite often I didn't know these people personally or well. That matters because at the end of the day, even if I delegate some of the decision authority to them, the overall [decision] responsibility stays with me. I'm the one recommending to the management board, or if it's big enough to the board of directors, that we make the investment. That's hard to do based on the knowledge and judgment of people on the ground that I don't know well. If things don't work out well, I cannot go back [to the board] and say, "Yes, but so and so on the ground advised me that this was a smart move." No. It's my decision and if I don't know the guys on the ground well, then there is a long and steep learning curve I have to try to get up before I'm going to recommend that we go ahead with a $300 million investment in China or wherever.

So while the shifts from Stages 2 to 3, or 3 to 4, or 4 to 5 are natural, logical, and common ones, there are several things that make them challenging on a practical level. The reality in many cases is that firms and their executives do *not* have the anticipation of the "Great One"—Wayne Gretzky. The Hall of Fame hockey player was famous for his ability to look well ahead of where a teammate was at a given moment and anticipate where he was going to be and then pass the puck to that currently open space and have it arrive just as his teammate filled the gap. Companies and executives should be like this, but, by their admissions to us, they are not. As a consequence, most of the executives dealing with the recent surge in globalization were not preparing themselves years and years ago, nor were their companies providing systematic developmental experiences requisite for today's global challenges.

To bring this simple dynamic to life, let us walk through the career of one of the executives we interviewed and whose career history was typical. John (not his real name), age 56, started his career in 1979 after graduating with an engineering degree at age 22. He joined U.S. manufacturing in the Midwest. The engineering group he joined was focused on hydraulics used in large construction machinery. In 1980, 57 percent of the company's sales were international, though the majority of these were export sales.

Objectively, the company was in Stage 2 and moving into Stage 3. However, John's unit and John's personal focus were domestically oriented (Stage 1). When he was promoted after several years to engineering manager, the company was moving more into Stage 3 but still more than 60 percent of all its international sales came from exports. For certain products, up to 80 percent of the products made were made at home and exported abroad. It was little surprise then that John's focus was largely still on Stage 1. When John was subsequently made a project manager for one of the core products for the company, his global focus expanded somewhat but, given that more than 70 percent of the products affected by his project were made domestically and then either sold domestically or exported, his focus was still largely domestic, even though by this point (mid-1990s) more than 60 percent of the company's overall sales were international sales.

Then in early 2003 John was promoted to the head of one of the core products for the company. The product was sold in four different regions and nearly 70 percent of its sales came from outside the United States. Still, over 80 percent of the product sold was produced in the United States. Nevertheless, even though final assembly was done largely in the United States, more than 50 percent of the product's supply chain was outside the United States. As a consequence, though John was located in the United States he had to travel to meet with key suppliers in about 12 critical countries. So far, so good. John described his global focus as moderate and, although he felt challenged, he was not overwhelmed.

When he was named as the head of the division of the company's large construction machines, life changed dramatically. Suddenly, John now had to decide whether the company would build a manufacturing and assembly plant in China and whether he should encourage key suppliers in the United States to set up shop in China or to replace those U.S. suppliers with Chinese suppliers or other suppliers in Asia, at least for the products made in China. All this required more than an "executive comfort cocoon" understanding of China and the countries in the region to make good decisions. However, up to that point, John's career had been entirely in the United States.

In fact, part of his career success had come from *not* being on an international assignment and being "out of sight and out of mind" like a couple of people. Unfortunately for them, their careers suffered when they were sent on international assignments and especially when they repatriated back to the United States and there was really no planning for this move and no good position in which to place them. In fact, several colleagues he knew left the company within 18 months of repatriation.

So while John's career in one sense had benefited from being "in sight and in mind," this had prevented him from developing in-depth relationships with the people on the ground abroad to really trust them with the decisions. In addition, his firm had not been so farsighted as to identify and send up-and-coming leaders from places like China to headquarters (what is often called "inpatriation") so that they could get to know people like John and he could get to know them. In John's case one of the specific decisions he faced involved over $250 million in investments and would affect more than $3 billion in sales. To quote him, "You don't just make these sorts of decisions based on some Power-Point presentations and Excel spreadsheets. You have to know and trust the people behind the presentations and projections."

John confessed that ideally he would have been sent to China or Japan about 10 years before his promotion to division head so that now he could have a first-hand and in-depth understanding of the factors and dynamics of the region, as well as the players on the ground. His company had not anticipated the benefit or need of this sort of move; nor had he. The Stage 3 globalization hockey puck was streaking toward the open spot and John was having to lunge through the air with his arm and hockey stick fully extended to try to meet it. His fear was that he would miss the puck, crash down on the ice, and only have a concussion and scrapes and bruises for his trouble.

On a personal note, John confessed that even though he knew he lacked the personal in-depth experience to inform the decisions he was making and even though he simply did not have the in-depth personal relationships with those who might have the direct experience, he was not letting his boss or subordinates in on this secret. He was putting up a bold and confident front, while keeping all the anxiety of these two shortfalls bottled up inside. As a consequence, on a personal level his internal stress compounded the challenge of drinking from the fire hose or jumping directly from the seat of a Cessna Piper Cub to the captain's chair of a 747.

This example illustrates what was often confessed to us. On the one hand, executives were trying to get quickly up the learning curve of all sorts of countries and regions to make intelligent investment decisions, and, at the same time, they were trying to get quickly up the relationship curve with all sorts of people who had the experience, knowledge, and judgment to help inform those investment decisions. If the executives and their firms had been farsighted and anticipated this, they might have made the investments five to seven years in advance that was needed so that the capabilities and relationships were in place when needed. Generally this did not happen, and what one described as "drinking from a fire hose" another said was more akin to "waterboarding."

Consider the problems of a new factory in Vietnam that was designed to play a significant role in a major European manufacturing firm's global strategy. This European firm needed a low-cost manufacturing base from which it could ship products throughout the Asian region in order to compete with its major Japanese competitor, which was about to begin delivering product manufactured in its new factory in Indonesia. Since most of the Japanese competitor's raw materials were sourced in Indonesia, the recent and dramatic depreciation of the Indonesian rupiah actually gave the Japanese competitor an even greater cost advantage.

> We just opened up operations in Vietnam—a joint venture with the government. Guess what we found when we went to inspect our new greenfield factory site: a green field all right—of rice, flooded with water. We have no usable road out there, no electricity, no sewer, no city water. We're supposed to be turning out product six months from now. We'll be lucky if we can figure out how to get the field drained and construction started six months from now.

This executive and his team were sailing in uncharted waters. For example, how do they get a sewer line extended out to the factory site? Contact the local sewer department? There is no sewer department. Build a separate septic tank and leach field system for the factory? The problem here is that there are no specific regulations or specifications to comply with and no formal procedures to follow for getting such a plan for a self-contained sewer system approved. And while the firm struggles for a solution, the company cannot afford to let its main global competitor gain a significant advantage in Asia—a major strategic battleground.

Future pervasiveness of globalization

So where will globalization go from here? How much more pervasive will it get? If pervasiveness increases, what will be the effects and who will feel it the most?

Let's take the first question first. How much more pervasive can globalization get? Are we at the peak of globalization, or is there more to come? Today world exports of goods account for 30–40 percent of world GDP. Can it rise to 80 percent? World FDI is about 30 percent of world GDP. Can it double to 60 percent? Quite frankly, it is hard to say. However, there is at least one way to speculate about how much more globalization may be coming at us in the future. Suppose that a firm's mix of domestic and international activity were similar to the ratio of the firm's home country's economic value relative to that of the world. How much more globalization could we expect?

To illustrate this general point of speculation, let's take a concrete example. Let's examine the relative mix of domestic and international activity of a company most would agree is fairly far up the globalization curve and compare that with the relative ratio of its home country's economic value relative to the rest of the world. Let's look at Nestlé and its home country of Switzerland. In 2013, approximately 98 percent of Nestlé's total revenue came from outside its home country of Switzerland. You say, "OK, but Switzerland is a small country. You would naturally expect domestic sales for Nestlé to be small." However, this is potentially the point. Nestlé's domestic and international revenues match fairly closely the size of Switzerland's domestic economy in the context of the global economy.

Specifically, Switzerland's share of world GDP is about 1 percent and the other 99 percent comes from other countries. Nestlé gets about 2 percent of its total revenues from Switzerland and about 98 percent comes from other countries. From this concrete example, it is interesting to speculate about how much further firms' globalization could or would progress if other companies' domestic and international sales matched the relative value of their home country's economy compared with the global economy.

To illustrate this, let's take the case of U.S. companies. According to the World Bank, the U.S. economy in 2012 was about $15.7 trillion. The world economy was about $71.7 trillion. Thus, the U.S. share of the world economy was 21.9 percent. If the 500 largest firms in the United States had domestic and foreign sales similar to the U.S. domestic economy relative to the global economy, foreign sales would need to rise from 46 percent to 78 percent on average (a 67 percent increase). Domestic sales in relative terms would need to decline from 54 percent to 22 percent. For some U.S. companies this would involve little change, but they are the exception. For example, Coca-Cola gets approximately 75 percent of its annual revenues from outside the United States, as does Caterpillar. However, for many of the largest U.S. companies, such as Walmart, GE, General Motors, Ford, AT&T, HP, Costco, and even P&G, they would have to increase the percentage of sales they received from outside the United States by non-trivial amounts to achieve 78 percent threshold. For many mid-sized companies, the change would be monumental.

Let's take Japan as another example. According to the World Bank, the Japanese economy in 2012 was about $5.96 trillion. Thus, Japan's share of the $71.7 trillion world economy was 8.3 percent. If the 500 largest firms in Japan had domestic and foreign sales similar to the Japanese domestic economy relative to the global economy, foreign sales would need to triple and increase from about 30 percent to 91.7 percent of the total. If the magnitude of this change surprises you, let's take as a concrete example the largest and most global Japanese company on the basis of rankings by *Fortune* magazine and the United Nations Conference on Trade and Development (UNCTAD)—Toyota. In 2011 approximately 61 percent of Toyota's sales were international. Thus, even for Toyota, a move from 61 percent to 91 percent international sales is a very big change. It is even bigger when you consider that in 2011 a staggering 88.9 percent of all its passenger vehicles sold were exports *from* Japan. For many of the other large Japanese firms, such as Toshiba, Panasonic, Sony, NTT, and Hitachi, the increase from their current level of international sales to a 91.7 percent level would be monumental.

Whether a firm's domestic and international sales should approximate the relative size of its home country's domestic economy in the context of the entire world economy is easy to debate but hard to prove. Still, it is an interesting way to speculate about how far globalization could yet go in the future.

Assuming for a moment that there is room for global pervasiveness yet to run, the key question we asked in our research was what might be the impact and who will feel that impact the most? As we illustrated in Figure 1.3, for top executives once international sales are above the 50 percent threshold, their global focus is already high and increases only incrementally as international sales rises above 50 percent. However, there is a bit of a delayed cascade effect down through the organization. This is because quite often an overall percentage of international sales of 50 percent is not distributed evenly across all the firm's products, lines of businesses, or even divisions. Thus, while the global focus of all the top executives might be similarly high, it is not uniform as one moves across and down through the organization. There the uneven distribution of international sales across products, services, etc. is reflected in varying levels of global focus across and down the leadership ranks.

However, as the overall percentage increases above 50 percent toward 70 percent, it often means that its distribution becomes more even across the organization's products, services, lines of business, and the like. Obviously, at 100 percent, the distribution of international sales is completely uniform. But that is not the point. The point is that, as international sales overall approach 70 percent and exhibit little impact on executive global focus, it does increase the global focus and required global capabilities of more and more people across and down the firm's leadership ranks.

Because of this process we consistently encountered top executives who were surprised by and disappointed in the lower-level leaders who did not have the same global focus as senior executives. Channeled correctly, this surprise and disappointment can be quite functional. Otherwise it can be rather misguided and dysfunctional.

As an example of the latter, we were working with one company where the chief executive office (CEO) and other leaders were so disenchanted with the lower than desired and more uneven than expected global focus of its mid-level leaders that the top team was beginning to think that they needed to replace most of these mid-level leaders. Once a few were replaced and this layer of the organization felt the top management's lack of faith in them, these mid-level leaders' efforts and performance deteriorated. One mid-level leader put it this way, "I'm working my (tail) off and yet it's clear that the top team thinks that I'm too parochial and not 'global' enough. If they are not going to recognize my efforts, why should I bust my butt?"

In contrast, if channeled correctly, top executive surprise and frustration with inadequate and uneven global focus of lower-level leaders can result in development efforts such that, when really required, these leaders have the global leadership capabilities they need. For example, we worked with a major financial firm to design and execute a significant global leadership development effort that was applied to several levels of leaders regardless of the degree of global revenues currently in their job or business. Later, as globalization increased and as the global financial crisis of 2008 hit and lingered, they had leaders capable of meeting these demands rather than splashing about trying to keep their heads above water. Naturally, one of the key question we address later in this book is what firms can and should do to ensure they have the right number and quality of global leaders when they need them so that like an experienced surfer they are paddling soon enough and fast enough to catch the wave rather than missing it or being smashed by it.

Interconnectedness of globalization

The second thing that is different today about globalization compared with 500 or 50 or to some extent even 5 years ago is the interconnectedness of the world. To get a sense of this interconnectedness, we only need to look at some recent illustrations.

First let's look at the financial crisis of 2008. While a variety of scholars have examined this issue, few have produced visual images that better capture the increased interconnectedness, especially financial interconnectedness, than Dion Harmon and his colleagues (see Figure 1.8).[5] Figure 1.8 shows the growing interconnectedness of the financial markets from 2003 to 2008. These tighter interconnections are in large measure what allowed the significant problems in a few organizations to ripple through the global financial systems. It also helps us understand why those ripples and the negative economic impact have lasted another five years after the crisis.

A different way to look at financial interconnectedness over time is to examine how correlated the movements of different markets have been with each other. Figure 1.9 shows data gathered from reports by Quinn and Voth[6] and Société Générale and Thompson Reuters across more than two dozen markets over more than 100 years. As Figure 1.9 illustrates, from the late 1980s there has been a dramatic and sustained increase in the correlation of stock markets from an

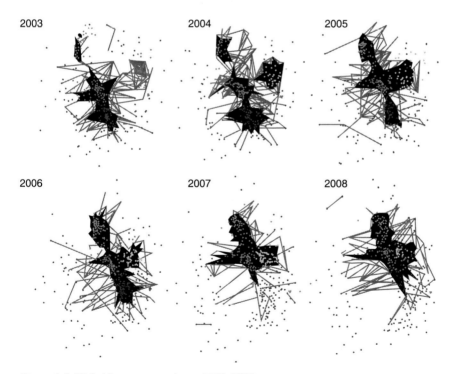

Figure 1.8 Global interconnectedness, 2003–2008

Figure 1.9 Correlations of global stock returns, 1893–2010

average of around 0.25 to a high of 0.85. Thus, at least in terms of finances, the world is significantly more interconnected now than just 20 years ago.

The second area to examine is the interconnectedness of countries and companies in terms of their value chains or supply chains. Perhaps no recent event has highlighted how interconnected these have become than the tsunami in Japan in 2011. At the time, Japan was a major supplier of intermediary components for a variety of industries, especially automotive. Japanese automotive companies such as Toyota and Honda had to shut down production at several plants because they could not get parts from plants in the affected areas. These automotive plants produced not only for Japan but for other countries as well.

But it wasn't just Japanese suppliers that were affected. For example, Bosch, a German company, is a supplier of components such as fuel injectors, pumps, and electronic control systems for virtually every automotive company in the world. Because of the tsunami, Bosch found itself unable to meet demand because of its own and its supplier operations in Japan. It couldn't get GM or BMW the components they needed.

The impact of this was amplified by the movement of the entire auto industry over the last several years to "just-in-time" inventory and other elements of "lean manufacturing." This meant that GM, BMW and other original equipment manufacturers (OEMs) did not have more than a few days or usually a few hours of inventory of Bosch's critical parts on hand. The tightness of the system also meant that the OEMs were not able to quickly get inventory from other suppliers. As a consequence, vehicle manufacturers like GM and BMW simply had to suspend vehicle production because, while components like fuel injectors are small (in size and cost), their cars could not run without them.

But the impact went far beyond automotive components. At the time Japan had 57 percent share of image sensors produced in the world, 60 percent share of silicon wafers, 49 percent share of optical components, and 40 percent share of microcontrollers. As with the automotive companies, because of firms' tightly integrated supply chains and "just-in-time" inventory management, the disruption caused by the tsunami resulted in a number of firms having to temporarily shut down production. This was especially true in Asia, where dependence on Japan as an intermediary supplier was on average twice as high as for firms based in the United States, Germany, France, and other western economies.

The third area to illustrate the interconnectedness of the world is that of health and wellness and the spread and impact of diseases. One of the most salient examples of this was the 2003 incident of severe acute respiratory syndrome (SARS). The epidemic started in Guangdong Province, China, in November 2002. The first patient, a farmer, died soon after being admitted to hospital. However, the Chinese government officials did not inform the World Health Organization (WHO) of the outbreak until February 2003. In the meantime, air travel accelerated the spread of the disease beyond China. WHO physician Dr. Carlo Urbani identified SARS as a new disease in 2003, when he diagnosed a 48-year-old businessman who had traveled from the Guangdong province of China, through Hong Kong, to Hanoi, Vietnam. The businessman and the doctor who first diagnosed SARS both died from the illness. SARS quickly infected thousands of people around the world, including people in Asia, Australia, Europe, Africa, and North and South America. Schools closed throughout Hong Kong and Singapore. The 2003 outbreak resulted in an estimated 8,000 cases and 750 deaths.

The effect of SARS on Asia's important travel and tourism industries was dramatic. More than 40 percent of flights into Hong Kong were canceled in the several weeks that followed the official announcement of the outbreak in early 2003. Cathay Pacific, Hong Kong's flag-carrier, lost $3 million per day for the first month after the outbreak. Singapore Airlines had to ask all of its 6,600 cabin crew members to take unpaid leave and cut capacity to just 29 percent of normal levels. Airlines with headquarters far from Asia were also affected. Lufthansa announced that demand on its Asian routes fell by 85 percent and had to ground more than a dozen planes. The decline in travel had a knock-on effect on demand for fuel. The Organization of Petroleum Exporting Countries (OPEC), the oil-producers' cartel, estimated that SARS reduced Asian oil demand by 300,000 barrels per day.

If people weren't flying, they were also not staying in hotels. For example, five-star hotels in Beijing registered occupancy rates of around 20 percent. Rates were similarly low in Hong Kong. Whereas airlines could ground planes and simply not fly them, hotels had almost no way to cut capacity. In the aftermath, five major hotels in Hong Kong experienced such financial distress that they went up for sale: the Regal Oriental Hotel in Kowloon City, the Regal Riverside Hotel in Sha Tin, the Winsor Hotel and the Kimberly Hotel in Tsim Sha Tsui, and the Majestic Hotel in Jordan.

Tourist arrivals in Singapore declined by two-thirds. Worries were so high that on May 1, 2003, the Singaporean government announced it was canceling two major technology trade fairs. The next day, Taiwan announced the postponement of that year's Computex—the world's third-largest computer trade show—until later in the year. Even L'Oréal announced that its sales in 2003 were hurt by SARS because of the impact on sales to domestic consumers in Hong Kong and Singapore and the fall in the number of tourists visiting airport duty-free outlets. Like L'Oréal, luxury goods companies such as Louis Vuitton and Burberry experienced sales decline as their key clientele in Hong Kong simply feared to venture out of their homes and shop. In general, consumers' decision to stay at home in general hurt a variety of companies' sales in Asia from McDonald's to Coca-Cola.

Interconnectedness summary

While it seems global interconnectedness has increased, especially when compared to historical statistics regarding international sales, exports, or FDI, it is more difficult to quantify the change in global interconnectedness. However, Figure 1.9 suggests that in terms of financial market interconnectedness the vast majority of increase has happened in just the last 20 years. Both empirically and on the basis of our interviews, it seems that in comparison with the pervasiveness of globalization, the interconnectedness of the world has happened a bit more gradually and a bit more off the daily radar screen of most executives until specific events such as SARS in 2003, the financial crisis of 2008, and the tsunami in Japan in 2011 vaulted interconnectedness to the front and center.

Unlike the scenario with the pervasiveness of globalization, the future level of interconnectedness is hard to project, let alone predict. What we can say for sure is that virtually none of the executives we've worked with or interviewed believes that the interconnectedness of the world is going to go backwards.

Conclusion

So what can we conclude from all this? First, whether you argue that globalization began with Magellan's expedition or some other event is less important than recognizing that globalization as a general phenomenon has been around for a long time. However, there are at least two things that are different about globalization today than the past.

First, globalization is significantly more pervasive today than it was even 15 years ago. This has profoundly increased the global awareness and focus of top executives. In relation to this, there are some examples that suggest the pervasiveness of globalization could go a lot further still. If pervasiveness increases, globalization's relevance to and impact on managers down the line, not just top executives, is highly likely to increase. If so, rather than be caught scrambling, it may be wise for companies to get their people on the development path in advance so that they have the required capabilities when they are needed.

Second, globalization is significantly more interconnected today than it has been in the past. It is perhaps easiest to measure this interconnectedness in finances and financial markets, and while they are important, they are by no means the only domains of interconnectedness. We can see the interconnectedness in everything from supply chains to pandemics. How much more interconnected the world will become is hard to predict. However, the technologies that facilitate this interconnectedness—communication, the Internet, containerization, air travel, etc.—and their declining real costs seem unlikely to move backwards and therefore unwind the current level of interconnectedness. Therefore, the interconnectedness will likely only move forward, though how much and how fast is anyone's guess.

But even if we have made a compelling case that globalization is today different not only from the distant past but even from the recent past, and even if you believe that the pervasiveness and interconnectedness of globalization will rise in the future, it all still invites the question, "So what?" How does all this affect you and why should you care about it?

That is the focus of the next chapter.

Notes

1 Morrison, A. J. and Roth, K. (1992). "The Regional Solution: An Alternative to Globalization." *Transnational Corporations*, 1(2), 37–55.

2 Ghemawat, P. (2005). "Regional Strategies for Global Leadership." *Harvard Business Review*, December, pp. 98–108.
3 Toyota-global.com (accessed August 7, 2013).
4 Black, J. S. and Morrison, A. J. (2010). *Sunset in the Land of the Rising Sun: Why Japanese Multinational Corporations Will Struggle in a Global Future.* New York: INSEAD Business Press.
5 Harmon, D., Stacey, B., Bar-Yam, Yavni, and Bar-Yam, Yaneer. (2010). Networks of Economic Market Interdependence and Systemic Risk. arXiv:1011.3707, November 16.
6 Quinn, D. P. and Voth, H. J. (2008). "A Century of Global Equity Market Correlations." *American Economic Review: Papers & Proceedings*, 98(2), 535–40.

2   Globalization's relevance
to you

At this point you might be saying to yourself, "OK, these are interesting facts and figures, but why should I care? What does this mean for me?" Perhaps an easy way to illustrate some of the implications is to walk through three interrelated company case studies.[1] The first case begins with Motorola in the early 1990s. On the basis of key technology invented at Bell Labs along with its own key innovations, Motorola produced the very first commercial portable phone in 1983 after more than ten years and $100 million of investment. From that point on, Motorola was not only the leader in its home market for mobile phones (or what were called cell phones at the time), it was also the global leader and by 1991 had nearly a 40 percent global market share. Quite simply, Motorola's mobile phones were the ones to own. However, in the early 1990s there were rumblings of a new technology and a new competitor. The new technology was digital signals versus Motorola's analog technology and the new competitor was Nokia.

In terms of the threat of the new technology, early on it was not clear how superior digital signals would be for voice transmissions. While this may seem crazy today, at the time there was a very sound logic for questioning the superiority of digital technology for voice transmission. After all, voice was a sound; sound was a wave; and analog was a wave-based technology. In addition, at the time the new digital technology would require literally billions of dollars of new infrastructure investment. Most U.S. carriers, such as Sprint and Verizon, did not seem to want to make this investment, and it would make little sense to produce a phone that would not work on the carriers' systems. Perhaps this is why none of the other U.S. mobile phone makers leaped in this new digital direction at first. Even though European carriers did seem as though they would embrace the new technology, any individual country such as Germany or France paled in comparison to the market size of the United States. With that in mind, put yourself in the shoes of a Motorola executive. In 1991, how worried would you be about Europeans embracing this new digital technology? Perhaps you would worry, but Motorola executives didn't.

In 1991, Nokia looked like an even smaller threat than the new technology. After the unfortunate suicide of its CEO in 1990, in 1992 Nokia installed Jorma Olilla, a former banker, as its new CEO. In addition to having a non-technologist as CEO, Nokia had virtually no standing in mobile communications. In 1992, mobile communications represented less than 2 percent of the company's total revenue. At that time, the vast majority of Nokia's revenue came from forest products, as it had for over 130 years. If you were an executive at high-tech Motorola at the time, how worried would you be about a company that had been chopping down trees and grinding them up as their main business for over 130 years? How high-tech does that sound to you?

Ah, but chopping down tress and grinding them up was not the only thing Nokia did at the time. It also was one of the largest makers of rubber boots in the world, especially rubber fishing boots. Again, if you were a Motorola executive how worried would you be about a company that made rubber fishing boots taking you on in the high-tech business of wireless communication, especially when you created some of the key technologies and owned some of the critical patents?

But perhaps Nokia would leverage or sell major assets to fund its push into mobile communications. So if you were a Motorola executive, you might naturally want to know how big Nokia was at the time. What assets could it sell to fund its move into mobile communications? In 1992 Nokia had total sales of approximately $3.4 billion. In contrast, at Motorola you had annual revenues four times that at $13.3 billion. The difference in terms of profits was even greater. In 1992 Nokia lost $134 million and Motorola made $453 million. Given this, if you were a Motorola executive, how worried would you be about Nokia?

But perhaps at the time Nokia was sitting within an amazing ecosystem that would enable it to come from nowhere and take you on if you were Motorola. It turned out that Nokia was coming from nowhere—the middle of nowhere in frozen Finland. Nokia's origins and name trace back to 1868, when one of its earliest pulp mills was built on the Nokianvirta River near the town of Nokia. Even in 1991, Nokia, the town, had only about 30,000 people and the entire country had only around 5 million inhabitants. The total population of Finland was less than that of the city of Chicago near where Motorola was based. At the time, the only ecosystem for Nokia seemed to be one of snow and ice in frozen Finland, where reindeer outnumbered people. As an executive in Motorola, how worried would you be about an upstart from frozen Finland whose name you were not even sure how to pronounce? Probably not too worried, and initially Motorola turned a bit of a blind eye toward this unlikely competitor from far off Finland.

The financial results concerning sales and profits of Motorola and Nokia in 1991 may explain the lack of worry. Figure 2.1 shows the comparable levels of Motorola's and Nokia's market capitalization, revenues, and profits (losses). Nokia was nothing compared to the mighty Motorola.

But then, in just five short years, Nokia's revenue increased threefold from $3.4 billion to $9.8 billion. By then, all of Europe adopted digital second generation (2G) cellular networks launched on the Global System for Mobile communications (GSM) standard. This convenience drove greater demand throughout Europe. In the meantime, the fragmented U.S. standards meant that one phone would not necessarily work in every state, which caused a dampening

In Millions

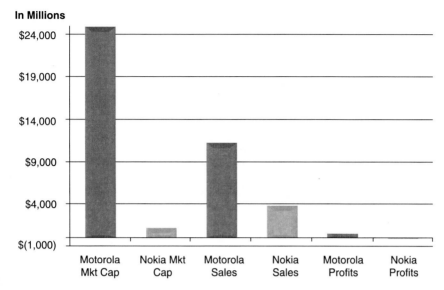

Figure 2.1 Motorola and Nokia, 1991 (*Source*: Motorola and Nokia Annual Reports 1991)

effect on growth. Still, if you were a Motorola executive, why should you worry? While Nokia had grown fast and had $9.8 billion in revenue in 1997, you had also grown and at $29.8 billion in revenue. You were nearly three times larger than Nokia. Perhaps what should have been more worrying was that, while Motorola made $1.18 billion in profits in 1997, at only one-third the size, Nokia made almost as much ($1.15 billion).

As Nokia pushed headlong into mobile phones and sold other businesses to fund its new strategic direction, it also decided to emphasize brand and brand management as much as technology. It focused on seemingly innocuous items like making the user interface intuitive (such as a green key for "send" and red for "end call") and making interfaces consistent across all its models. In 1998, just six years after it decided to enter the global mobile phone market, Nokia moved from not even being in the race to taking over the number 1 position and passing Motorola in terms of units sold. Between just 1997 and 1998 Nokia's revenues shot up from $9.8 billion to $14.8 billion. Motorola's revenues on the other hand declined slightly from $29.8 billion to $29.3 billion. More importantly, Nokia's profits increased in one year from $1.15 billion to $1.96 billion (a 70.4 percent increase), while Motorola went from making $1.18 billion to losing $962 million. In terms of market cap it was even more dramatic. Even though Motorola's sales increased by 159 percent between 1991 and 1998, its market cap increased only 30 percent from $25 billion to $32.5 billion. In the meantime, while Nokia's sales grew 289 percent, its market cap exploded 6,581 percent from $0.9 billion to nearly $59.8 billion. Motorola's sales were

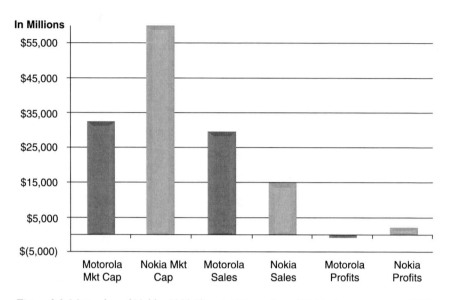

Figure 2.2 Motorola and Nokia, 1998 (*Source*: Motorola and Nokia Annual Reports 1998)

Note: Market cap is calculated by multiplying the number of outstanding shares as indicated in the firm's annual report multiplied by the firm's average price stock.

twice as big as Nokia's but its market cap was only a little better than half as large, as Figure 2.2 illustrates.

What happened over the next six years from 1998 to 2003? Motorola's global share of mobile phones plummeted from a peak of 45 percent to 15 percent. Revenues declined 27 percent to $21.3 billion. Conversely, Nokia's revenues soared threefold to $37.1 billion. However, it was not just revenues that were rising for Nokia; so were profits. In 2003, Nokia made $4.5 billion, while Motorola made only $893 million. Perhaps more interesting was that in 2003 Nokia made more money in that one year than Motorola had made in the previous ten years (partly because Motorola had big losses in 1998, 2001, and 2002). In essence, one year of Nokia profits beat one decade of Motorola profits.

However, Motorola was not going to go quietly into the night. Nokia had knocked it down but not out. In 2004, Motorola came roaring back with the introduction of the RAZR line of phones—slimmer, lighter, more stylish than anything it had produced before. The market loved them and Motorola's revenue rocketed up by more than $8 billion in one year to $29.7 billion. The ascent continued in 2005 and Motorola's revenues rose to $35.3 billion compared with Nokia's $40.5 billion. On the profit front, Motorola actually moved past Nokia. Motorola made $4.6 billion in 2005, while Nokia made only $4.2 billion.

At this point, if you were a Nokia executive and you were determined to preserve your number 1 position, who would you focus your attention on? A resurging Motorola, of course.

To distance itself from Motorola, Nokia pressed heavily on the new model gas pedal. In 2006 Nokia introduced the 1600, 1650, 1661, which, combined, sold over 130 million units in the first year alone. In 2007, Nokia launched the 1200 and 1208, which together sold over 250 million units in one year. As a consequence, Nokia's revenues skyrocketed 84 percent to $74.6 billion. Profits exploded 150 percent to $10.5 billion. Nokia was now the undisputed king of the mobile phone world. In fact, in 2007, four out of every ten mobile phones sold in the world were Nokia phones. More impressive still was the fact that eight out of every ten dollars (euro, yen, etc.) in profits made in the entire global industry went to Nokia. That's right: Nokia's "profit share" was double its "market share."

If only the story ended in 2007, but it didn't. While Nokia was busy taking over the world and dethroning Motorola, a company that had never before made a mobile phone announced that it would—Apple. In summer 2007 Apple announced the iPhone. But if you were a Nokia executive, how worried would you be about Apple (especially with its silly name)? In 2006 Apple had total sales of $19.3 billion compared with Nokia's $54.2 billion. Apple had profits of only $2 billion compared with Nokia's $5.6 billion. If you were a Nokia executive, how worried about Apple would you be?

Besides, what did Apple know about mobile phones? It sold silly little gizmos that played music. What did it know about Code Division Multiple Access (CDMA) or GSM or packet switching? Even if its computers were somewhat more complicated than its music gizmos, in 2007 Apple's computer market share was just over 3 percent. At that level how good could the company really be? On top of all that, despite all the media hype, from its introduction in July 2007 until the end of the year, Apple recorded only 1.4 million iPhones sold. If you were a Nokia executive, how worried would you be?

Fast forward just five years to 2012 and as a Nokia executive you would have had plenty to worry about. In that short time, the market shifted from the phone as a tool you used to talk to other people with to a personal hub for communication, entertainment, and information via the new world of apps. In July 2008, a year after it launched the iPhone, Apple launched its iPhone apps store with 8,000 apps. One year later, it had more than 100,000 apps on its site. By October 2010, it had 300,000. By October 2011, it had 500,000. By October 2012, it had over 700,000 apps. More impressive were the number of downloads. By the end of 2012 Apple announced it had passed the mark of 40 *billion* unique downloads (excluding re-downloads and updates), of which half had occurred in 2012 alone.[2]

Nokia tried to react, but it was too little, too late. Its sales declined 48 percent from $74.6 billion in 2007 to $38.9 billion by 2013. It went from making $10.5 billion in 2007 to losing $4 billion in 2012. In just five short years from 2007 to 2012, Nokia saw its market share drop by more than half from 40 percent to 19.1 percent and its market cap shrink by 85 percent from $102 billion to $14.8 billion. In fact, what took Nokia about a decade to do to Motorola Apple did to Nokia in half the time.

In the meantime, life for Motorola was also not so great. Between its peak in 2000 and its low in 2010, shareholders saw the market cap of Motorola drop 98 percent. In 2011 Motorola had to split itself into two different companies (Motorola Solutions and Motorola Mobility), because its mobile phone business was doing so poorly. Its mobile phone business continued to decline and in 2012 Google bought Motorola Mobility for $12.5 billion. By the end of 2012, Motorola Mobility had only a 1.9 percent global market share. Without question Google has its work cut out for it. Only time will tell whether Motorola can be revived or given a new name and life under Google.

During this five-year period, Apple's revenues soared from $24.6 billion in 2007 to $156.5 billion in 2012 (a 536 percent increase). Its profits went from $3.5 billion to $41.7 billion—a 1,191 percent increase. Interestingly, Apple had more profits in 2012 than Nokia had in *total revenue*. Yes, we said that correctly. In 2012, Nokia had $38.9 billion in sales and Apple had $41.7 billion in profits. Not only that, but Apple made more profits in that one year (2012) than Nokia had made in the previous ten. Once again, one year beat one decade, but in half the time. Figure 2.3 provides a graphical comparison of Motorola, Nokia, and Apple for the full year 2012.

What will happen to Apple? Will some competitor from some far off part of the world and/or from some other industry that Apple has not noticed emerge and inflict on it the fate that Nokia inflicted on Motorola and then Apple inflicted on Nokia? It is hard to know. But part of the purpose of this three-part case study is to illustrate that, in today's global world, threats and opportunities are pervasive and interconnected. As a consequence, they can come at you and to you from any corner of the world at any time with little warning. The days of looking across the street to domestic competitors, home market customers, local technology, etc. are going, going, gone.

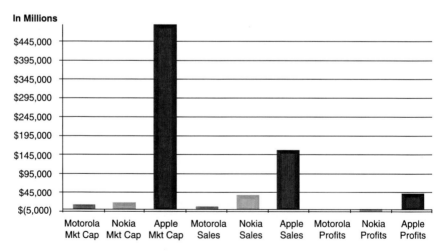

Figure 2.3 Motorola, Nokia, and Apple, 2012 (*Source*: Motorola and Nokia annual reports 2012)

Note: Market cap is calculated by multiplying the number of outstanding shares as indicated in the firm's annual report multiplied by the firm's average price stock.

The personal challenge

As international business consultants and professors, 15 or so years ago it used to be that we worked with a small and specialized group of managers within a company who had responsibility for international operations. Now prefixes such as Worldwide and Global are being added to standard titles such as Product Manager, Vice President of Marketing, Director of Quality, and so on. For many executives, it is not just the titles that are unfamiliar:

- I've got competitors now coming out of Peru, Hungary, and Taiwan that I didn't even know existed two years ago. They have cost structures that I have no idea how to compete against.
- I'm responsible for a worldwide product launch that requires me to bring people together who lie far outside my direct lines of authority. In some cases, I'm not even sure where the help I need is in the organization.
- I've been given a mandate to lower our costs by 20 percent and to scour the earth for the highest-quality, lowest-cost components for our products. The world is a pretty big place when you've been using local suppliers for the last 25 years.
- I'm in charge of a task force that has people on it from France, Germany, Italy, Canada, the United States, and Mexico. Even though we all speak English, it's clear to me that we do not speak the same language.
- Sometimes I think I'm going nuts. How do you listen to "the voice of the customer" when they speak a hundred different languages and don't all want the same thing?
- The company wants a worldwide standard of ethical conduct, but I'm losing business in some countries because it's against company policy to pay for things such as a golf game when we take out government officials.
- It used to be that foreign exchange was something that the finance folks worried about. Thanks to the financial crisis, now I have to worry about it. Should I keep our prices in Asia the same to protect our profit margins and risk our market share dropping like a rock, or should I lower our prices to maintain share and take a hit in profits?
- Sometimes I feel almost overwhelmed. I've got seven major competitors from five different countries; 42 tier-one suppliers representing 25 different currencies; governments ranging from dictatorships to open democracies; local customers in every major region of the world that want my services tailored to their needs; global customers that want my services standardized and delivered to all of their worldwide operations. I've never dealt with anything like this before and neither has anyone else in the company. No SOPs [Standard Operating Procedures] exist for the challenges we face today.
- I just returned from my first trip to China. It was a joint-venture negotiation. People have asked me, "Well how did it go?" I have to say I'm not sure. I couldn't get a direct answer or commitment from them. I sensed that something was going on in the background with their team but I have no idea what it was.

As these quotes demonstrate, many managers today have to navigate with no mapped-out answers. While the media make international business seem glamorous, for managers who need new skills both to survive in their current positions and to prepare for future promotion opportunities, globalization feels more like a giant wave about to crash down on top of them. Managers who are not trained to deal with international government relations, cultural issues, and global market uncertainty will not produce the results expected by the home office and will not achieve their own desired level of personal success.

Sailing in uncharted global waters

Today you have the unprecedented opportunity and challenge of leading organizations into the new, unmapped frontiers of the global marketplace. In that sense, global leadership has many parallels with Magellan's voyage nearly 500 years ago. These excerpts from the ship's log convey the enormity of the three-year journey:

> The captain general Fernandez Magellan had resolved on undertaking a long voyage over the ocean, . . . a course as yet unexplored by any navigator. . . . On Monday morning the 10th August 1519 foresail was set. . . . On Wednesday 28th November, we . . . entered the ocean to which we afterwards gave the denomination of Pacific and in which we sailed the space of three months and 20 days, without tasting any fresh provisions. The biscuit we were eating no longer deserved the name of bread; it was nothing but dust and worms, which had consumed the substance. The water we were obliged to drink was equally putrid and offensive. . . . In the course of these three months and 20 days in the Ocean denominated by the Pacific . . . we saw no fish but sharks and if God had not granted us a fortunate voyage, we should all have perished of hunger in so vast a sea. . . . We reckoned to have sailed upwards of 14,600 leagues, having circumnavigated the globe from east to west. I do not think that any one for the future will venture on a similar voyage. . . . On 8th September 1522, I presented to His Sacred Majesty Don Carlos neither gold nor silver . . . but a book written with my own hand, in which by day and day, I had set down every event on our voyage.
>
> (Ship's log August 1519 to September 1522, as kept by Antonio Pigafetta during Ferdinand Magellan's voyage around the world)

Imagine what it must have been like for explorers such as Magellan as they scanned the horizon of the great Pacific Ocean for days on end—no reliable charts, the stars of an unfamiliar hemisphere often blocked from view by clouds, waves crashing over the ship's bow, wind howling threats of potential destruction, a crew losing confidence with each passing day of nothing but sea and sky, ravenous sharks ready to devour unfortunate sailors who slipped from the deck.

Now fast-forward to the present. These descriptions may have a familiar ring. The global business opportunities today are vast, both for you personally and for your company. There are new markets to be developed, new territories to be explored. But just as the Pacific Ocean was for Magellan, our global marketplace is a shark-infested sea of danger. It is filled with brutal storms of competition, endless seas of change, contradictory winds of customer preferences, and hidden shoals of disruptive technology. Like Magellan, the global executive of today must display unwavering leadership in the face of all these challenges.

While there are important similarities between then and now, there is one great difference—a difference that to you as a leader makes all the difference. In the Old World, once the seas and islands were accurately charted, once the rivers, valleys and mountains were properly mapped, the coordinates didn't change. The static nature of geographical landmarks allowed pioneers, and later settlers, to follow the maps of early explorers and move with confidence into the new territories. The first inquisitive footprints of the early explorers became well-beaten paths of settlers. Lands that were once hazardous and strange became safe and familiar.

Today's global business world is in a constant state of flux: markets, suppliers, competitors, technology, and customers constantly shift, which means that as quickly as the territory is mapped, it changes. As soon as the map's ink is dry, it's useless. The result? The New World of global business requires all leaders to constantly upgrade their capabilities and to be ever learning.

The tsunami of globalization

Increasingly, you do not have to seek out global business opportunities nor can you hide from global threats. Whether we like it or not, the tsunami of globalization is inescapable. Given the devastating effects of the tsunami in Japan in 2011, we are cautious in using this metaphor but tsunamis have features that are instructive when it comes to thinking about globalization. The largest waves are caused by volcanic eruptions or earthquakes far below the surface of the ocean in deep waters of 20,000 feet or more. The amount of water displaced is enormous but because it happens in such deep waters, tsunamis appear at the surface as merely one- to two-foot swells. However, they travel faster than a commercial airliner at over 600 miles per hour. They reveal their true force and size as they near shore and shallow water. At that point the massive amount of displaced water rises into waves sometimes towering 50 or 100 feet high. Interestingly there is usually a "lull before the storm." An hour or so before the wave hits, the waters along the shore actually recede, usually to a point much lower than the lowest tide. Then the water rises and just when things seem to have returned to normal, the tsunami hits with mind-boggling force.

This proves to be a revealing analogy for businesses as they encounter the New World of global commerce. For example, consider the calm before the storm for a private yacht building and refurbishing company in Southern California. Growth and profits were good, and competition was moderate and local. Competition was so local in fact that West Coast players rarely if ever competed with East Coast companies. In fact, in terms of refurbishing, Southern Californian companies rarely competed with firms next door in Oregon or one state away in Washington.

For West Coast Yachts (WCY is a disguised name), with about 90 employees, and its owner, life was great, and global business concerns were about as far away as icebergs from the company's home in San Diego Bay. Then, the U.S. government put a 10 percent luxury tax on boats, even as the national economy took a nosedive. The company's workforce shrank to about 30 employees. Suddenly they found that their customer base was turning to Korean, Indonesian, and Brazilian competitors that they never even knew existed. To survive these stormy seas, WCY reached out to customers in Japan and Saudi Arabia. It took advantage of the America's Cup's return to the United States in 2013 to help boost its international contacts. Expecting that the U.S. economy would continue to rebound in 2014 and beyond, the company prepared to make the most of it. But the business will never be the same. It is now a global business. Never again can the owner afford to take his eye off foreign competitors or ignore potential clients from throughout the world. The company is still not large (less than $20 million in annual revenue) but now the owner tracks the movement of foreign exchange rates for the euro, pound, dollar, Swiss franc, won, rupee, and others on a daily basis in order to know where he stands on both his prices and his costs in the context of global customers and competitors.

Driving forces of globalization

So what are the driving forces behind the dramatic rise in the pervasiveness and interconnectedness of globalization? What are some of the factors that global leaders need to understand and pay attention to? As with real tsunamis, we need to look far below the surface at the underlying tectonic plates of technology, costs, consumers, global customers, governments, and competitors in order to comprehend the powerful forces giving rise to the tsunami wave of globalization. Effective global leaders understand the power and dynamics of these tectonic plates of global business. Other recent books have been wholly devoted to explaining the drivers behind globalization; our purpose here is served with a brief review of them.

Technology

Technology is a wonderful and wicked thing. It is wonderful in what it can save you and the productivity it can bring. It is wicked in terms of what it can cost and how fast it can change. For example, consider that today there is more computing power in a leading-edge personal computer than there was in the entire world in 1950! Sixty years later, a new fabrication plant that manufactures the computer's microprocessor costs over $4 billion dollars to build. Consequently, chip makers, such as Intel and AMD, have no choice but to "go global." There is no single market large enough for them to recoup this level of investment. Consequently, their strategy is all about going after global sales.

The same is true for Airbus. Development costs for Airbus's new A380 double-decker jumbo jet were between $14 and $16 billion. This doesn't even take into account subsequent manufacturing costs. How will Airbus recover this investment? Even if every airline in Europe fell in love with the new A380 and ordered one for every possible route for which the A380 were appropriate, Airbus still could not recover its investment, let alone make enough money to fund the next generation of planes. Consequently, Airbus had no choice but to go after sales in Europe, in Asia, in the Middle East, in Africa, in South America, and in North America.

The simple conclusion? As technology becomes an increasingly critical lever for competitive advantage and as its development costs rise, the market required to recoup the investment must stretch beyond domestic shores and out into the world.

In addition to high technology costs driving the search for global revenues, technology has also facilitated access to the world. For example, containerization (i.e., the standardizing of shipping container size and structure), which began in the 1950s and achieved global integration in the mid-1970s, facilitated not only the less expensive shipment of goods by sea but the intermodal shipment of goods by sea, rail, and truck without ever opening the container.

More recently, the impact of the Internet on global business in terms of creating new businesses, integrating global supply chains, sharing competitive intelligence, reaching far-flung customers, etc. is incalculable. Yet, its role in driving globalization is without question.

The bottom line is that technology advancements from communication to shipping to information and beyond have both driven and facilitated globalization.

Costs

Costs are another tectonic plate driving the wave of globalization. As we mentioned, thanks in large part to technology, industrial customers, as well as consumers, increasingly have access to information that helps them compare product quality and price. To survive, companies must keep their costs competitive so that they can remain competitive on price. To keep costs down, purchasing executives have no choice but to scour the earth in search of suppliers with the best products at the lowest possible prices. In Europe alone, GM saved over $1 billion through global sourcing. This saving is equivalent to GM buying a company with $15–$20 billion in annual revenues and good profit margins.

Consumers

Successful global leaders also understand the growing convergence of consumer preferences. Maybe everyone doesn't need a "2-in-1" shampoo that lets you shampoo and condition your hair at the same time, but the successful launch of Pert shampoo in 36 countries in 18 months suggests that at least some consumer preferences are converging.

Just look at the numbers and you can see the enormous potential for global success. By 2050, there will be only 1.28 billion people in developed countries and 6.2 billion in developing countries.[3] KFC, for one, is very aware of these numbers. At the end of 2012 it had almost as many restaurants in China (4,260) as in the United States (4,618), where it began. Or consider MTV, the Viacom division that now has more viewers in developing countries than in the United States. From Beijing to London, from Montreal to Milan, Coca-Cola, Levi Strauss, Toyota, Kodak, Sony, and Swatch products are everywhere. While it would be a mistake to say that consumers have identical preferences around the world, global leaders recognize that those preferences are converging and consumers' capacity to buy products is rising.

Global business customers

As certain firms go global in response to technology, cost, and consumer drivers, they in turn pull many of their suppliers with them. Savvy suppliers recognize this as a tremendous opportunity to grow their businesses by following their leading customers overseas. For example, when GM committed billions to China, Bosch recognized that expanding into China would enable them to continue to be a leading supplier to GM and would grow Bosch's global business. In fact, not following key industrial customers may actually hurt the firm's domestic business with that customer. Similarly, as Toyota set up operations in China, it made it clear to its suppliers in Japan that if they did not follow suit, Toyota might look to "more committed" suppliers for some of its domestic (i.e., Japanese) purchases. Similarly, if you are a major supplier to Fiat or Daewoo or Shell, you may have no choice but to go global.

Governments

Global leaders also recognize the power of governments in today's global economy. Despite claims of "a borderless world," savvy global leaders recognize that national and local government officials the world over have no intention of meekly giving up their power to "transnational" companies or any other type of corporation. Governments can and do create both threats and opportunities. For example, the government of Mongolia threatened in 2011 to renegotiate its ownership agreement of the Oyu Tolgoi mine with Rio Tinto and knocked off more than $500 million in market cap from the company in one day. While the government later withdrew its threat in part because of an aggressive response by Rio Tinto and the international community in general, the government renewed its pressures to get enhanced benefits in 2013.

Competitors

Today, competitors can come at you from virtually any country. Effective global leaders keep a vigilant watch on current and future competitors. The best global leaders recognize that they cannot afford to simply defend their home turf. For example, 20 years ago, no one predicted that virtually every major U.S.

TV manufacturer would be out of the business by 2010. Would Zenith executives have predicted that they would have to sell 58 percent of the company to LG Group of Korea in order to survive? In turn, would LG executives have predicted that, a few years later, competition would have forced them to sell off major components of their conglomerate in order to stave off bankruptcy?

Who would have predicted the company that (a) launched the first commercial camera in 1888, (b) controlled 90 percent market share on film and a 65 percent market share on cameras sold in the United States in 1975, and (c) produced the first digital camera and by 2013 had more than 1,100 digital image patents would have had to file for bankruptcy? And yet, Kodak was forced not only to seek protection from creditors in bankruptcy but to sell off its digital patent portfolio in order to emerge from bankruptcy.

The lack of global leaders

Globalization creates new opportunities that require new leadership capabilities. However, these capabilities are not acquired or developed overnight. Consequently, in nearly every firm, the demand for global leaders far outstrips the supply, as Figure 2.4 illustrates.

Interestingly these results were somewhat worse than those in a survey we conducted nearly 15 years ago. This suggests that either demand has risen faster than supply, or that supply has somehow lagged behind demand, or both. To better

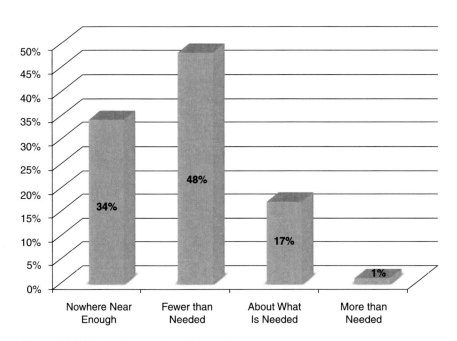

Figure 2.4 Global leader supply and demand

understand this shortage of global leaders, we conducted in-depth interviews with over 40 global HR executives. This research led to four main conclusions that suggest there are issues both with rising demand and lagging supply:

1. The global leader supply–demand shortage is largely driven by fast-growing demand as the percentage of international revenues has surged in the last ten years.
2. The demand is growing fastest in developing markets where leaders have to be able to respond both to local needs and to integration requirements for the global enterprise.
3. Supply lagged because firms failed to anticipate the need for a diversified pipeline of global leaders and started much too late to identify potential global leaders outside their home market.
4. Supply lagged because firms failed to fully appreciate how much time, training, and deliberately designed experience it took to develop global leaders.

Given these results, we asked HR executives how long they found it took to develop a global leader. The average answer was around ten years, assuming that the firm had properly identified someone as having leadership potential. In the majority of cases, this general leadership potential was not confirmed until individuals were in their mid-thirties, which meant that even if a company had begun an individual's global development in 2000, that individual would not be ready to handle global leadership positions until he or she were in their mid-forties in 2010. HR executives pointed out that this meant that *if* an individual by his or her own fault or because of corporate neglect missed the development window by as little as five years and therefore received their first global responsibilities at age 50, the individual might miss out on top global leadership positions altogether later in their career.

To a large extent, we have already examined why and how fast global leadership demand has grown. Given that the surge in globalization has taken place largely in the last 15 years, if you did not start identifying and developing high-potential leaders from your home market as well as foreign markets at least ten years ago, you would be with the majority of companies and have fewer or nowhere near enough global leaders today. To paraphrase the great Wayne Gretzky, between 1995 and 2005 many companies passed the puck to where the other player was at the moment, not to where she was going to be. Similarly, if a firm is going to have a sufficient number (let alone quality) of global leaders five years from now, it would have needed to have identified and started those individuals' development five years *ago*. Companies and their leaders are starting to get more systematic about this, but our research indicates that only about 17 percent of top executives feel their firm has a fully developed and well-integrated global leader identification and development system.

In terms of developing sufficient quantity and quality of global leader supply, as you progress through this book, you will see why the required global leader capabilities are not acquired overnight. No one can come along, sprinkle global leader dust over you or your people and magically bestow these global leader capabilities. Unfortunately, few corporations have systematically and proactively sought to provide their employees with the experiences and training needed to develop global leadership capabilities. As we discussed in Chapter 1, for many years most companies succeeded and grew without moving into Stage 3. As a consequence, many managers developed into provincial rather than global leaders. For example, even today the vast majority of Japanese managers deal primarily with other Japanese—bosses, subordinates, customers, suppliers, regulators, politicians, etc. As a consequence, they have provincial Japanese mental maps of leadership to help them captain their businesses. The same is true, though to a lesser extent, for U.S., French, German, Italian, British, and other managers.

While supply of global leaders is essentially flat, demand is growing almost exponentially. Many people say that the world is getting smaller. However, it is actually getting larger. Think about your own company. Go back 20 years in time and ask yourself how many countries did your company operate in then? Ten years ago? Five years ago? How many countries does it operate in today? What about five years from now? Or consider how big those operations were 20 years ago? Ten years ago? Five years ago? Today? How big will they be five years from now? Clearly most firms are operating in more places today than ever before and are running much bigger operations than ever before. For most executives, the world they have to think about and understand is getting larger, not smaller. Countries that didn't even show up on anyone's radar screen ten years ago present major market opportunities today. As a consequence, more global leaders are needed now and in the future because globalization means greater revenues, lower costs, and even corporate survival. Demand is also rising because there is no way to plot a reliable, lasting map of global business. The terrain is constantly changing. Consequently, it is not possible to simply develop a few global leaders and then have the masses follow the trails these leaders blaze.

Globalization demands a new leadership model

None of us can escape the tsunami of globalization. Consequently, if you have aspirations of leading any organization or significant business unit in the future or if you need to ensure that there are sufficient numbers and quality of global leaders to succeed you, there is an exciting but significant challenge ahead.

Provincial leadership models worked in the past

Leadership models that were effective in the past now fall short and will increasingly miss the mark in the future. These old models were based on a strong belief in hierarchical command and control structures, and focused on the domestic environment. Executives who exemplified these models in turn hired and promoted others who shared this orientation. However, what worked in the past will not work in the future. For example, research shows that U.S. multinationals with CEOs who have substantial international assignment experiences perform better than firms whose CEOs are without such experiences.[4]

Recently, we met with a senior human resource manager at a primary division of Philip Morris. He had just returned from a tour of duty in Europe. From his comfortable New York office, he recalled the difficulty of trying to apply old models to the New World. "We wanted to get some consistency of direction in how we develop our people around the world," he explained. "So we developed a competency model for leadership. I think this was a good idea." But he went on to reveal that the company had made the error of assuming that the leadership model developed for North America could be reapplied everywhere else. "I was in Europe at the time as an HR director," he continued, "and thought this was just crazy. The words meant nothing to the Europeans." He was expected to measure his people in Europe against standards that had little meaning in their context. He shook his head, his voice still edged with frustration: "I could hear my European colleagues say, 'Psst, it's American!'"

However, Americans are not the only ones guilty of taking a rather ethnocentric approach to leadership. Japanese, Korean, German, French, Swedish, British, and other managers have the same tendency.

In one sense, this tendency is both natural and functional. It is natural, because values across countries and even regions within countries do differ. The importance of relationships, short-term profits, hierarchies, ethics, and risk aversion and other factors varies from culture to culture. For example, the Japanese adage "The nail that stands up gets hammered down" reflects a culture that places a priority on the group rather than on the individual. Consequently, consensus decision making rather than individual accountability prevails. Every country has a somewhat different leadership model, which in turn dictates different leadership practices. These models work fine as long as the leaders deal primarily with individuals from within the culture of the model. This has largely been true in the past but will not be in the future.

Global leadership models work in the future

Globalization is a major challenge to provincial leadership models. For a company to become more global, its leaders must look beyond familiar, provincial approaches. If becoming a global company means overcoming national differences, then becoming a global leader means the same thing. Yet most of us are threatened by any change to the status quo. When facing new challenges, we tend to rely on what has worked well in the past. We work harder, put in longer hours, or try to think smarter; but, in the end, we usually come back to doing what we have always done, because what we've done is what we know and it has worked— right up until it doesn't. When faced with a new challenge, most of us try to meet that challenge by doing what we know a little bit better. Provincial leadership models of the past worked precisely because the past business environment was more provincial.

The wave of globalization requires something more than an American or European or Asian leadership model. It demands a global model that applies around the world, a model that transcends national perspectives and delivers a powerful tool for recruiting, developing, and retaining a company's future leaders.

For many corporations, this global leadership gap is a growing crisis. For you as an individual, it is an enormous opportunity. Global leaders are needed and are in short supply. If you have the interest and capabilities, you will be in great demand. It can also be a threat. If you have significant leadership aspirations but no interest in things global, you may face more career limitations in the future than at present. For companies, this global leadership gap also presents both opportunity and danger. In an increasingly knowledge-based, global economy, having great global leaders today and a good bench strength for tomorrow is likely to provide significant competitive advantage. From our research, less than 20 percent of firms have the quantity and quality of global leaders that they need. If ever statistics painted a picture of competitive white space, these do. Put another way, there are very few firms with first mover advantage in the area of global leadership. However, the current and future global leadership gap represents a significant threat to companies as well. It represents literally billions of dollars wasted in mistakes and bad decisions and even more in lost opportunities because of inadequate global leadership capabilities.

Having sketched the basic terrain of globalization, we now want to turn to a discussion of the key drivers behind what makes a successful global leader, and then turn to in-depth discussions of those capabilities and how you can develop them.

Notes

1 The material on Motorola, Nokia, and Apple has been adapted with the author's (J. Stewart Black) permission from *It Starts with One*, New York: Pearson, 2013.
2 http://www.apple.com/pr/library/2013/01/07App-Store-Tops-40-Billion-Downloads-with-Almost-Half-in-2012.html (accessed 7 April 2013).
3 United Nations Population Fund (2013). http://www.unfpa.org/pds/trends.htm (accessed 21 October 2013)
4 Carpenter, M. A., Sanders, W. G., and Gregersen, H. B. (2001). "Bundling Human Capital with Organizational Context: The Impact of International Assignment Experience on Multinational Firm Performance and CEO Pay." *Academy of Management Journal*, 44(3), 493–511.

3 A framework for global leadership

As we mentioned earlier, our joint research agenda on globalization and global leadership started about 20 years ago, when the first signs appeared that companies and their executives were headed for an unprecedented surge in the pervasiveness and interconnectedness of globalization. In the late 1990s we launched a major study and over two years conducted interviews with over 130 senior executives in 50 firms based in Europe, North America, and Asia. We also interviewed managers who were identified in their firms as exemplars or role models of the future global leader. Since that time many of the young exemplars we interviewed have gone on to rise to very senior positions. For example, Steve Burke, one of the exemplars identified in our interviews with Disney in 1997, later left Disney and became chief operating officer (COO) at Comcast and then in January 2011 became CEO of NBC Universal, when Comcast purchased the unit from GE. Burke also now serves on the Board of Directors at Berkshire Hathaway and J. P. Morgan Chase. Another example, Steve Holliday, was identified in our interviews at Exxon. He later joined National Grid in 2001 and was made CEO in 2007. He has served on the Board of Directors of Marks and Spencer since 2004.

In revisiting our initial study, we again interviewed top executives—more than 100 across 50 firms based in all the major regions of the world. In addition, in the intervening years we have had the opportunity to work closely with a wide variety of companies and executives on substantial consulting engagements on issues of globalization and global leader development. Throughout this time, our driving interest has been to understand what is different about effective global leadership compared with just good leadership in a domestic context. Though our early pioneering investigations were at the beginning of the globalization wave, we have been impressed and surprised how consistent the data and findings have been over time as to what capabilities drive effective global leadership.

Part of this consistency has come from diving below the wind-tossed waves at the surface and examining the deep ocean currents that make global leadership different. What we originally discovered and what has been reconfirmed is that effective global leadership is driven by two sets of dynamics: situation-specific and global. While the situation-specifics matter and constitute about one-third of overall leadership success, we touch on them only lightly and leave their detailed research and discussion to others. Rather we want to focus primarily on the global dynamics and the required leadership capabilities they drive.

Situation-specific dynamics

In terms of situation-specific dynamics, our research has identified three situation-specific dynamics that account for about one-third of successful leadership: the industry in which leaders operate, the dominant national culture of the company in which it is situated, and the specific company culture in which leaders work. Across time, space, nationality, and everything else executives have consistently conveyed to us that these three situation-specifics matter and that leaders need particular capabilities that match these situational differences in order to be successful.

Industry effects

The first situation-specific dynamic is that of industry. Its importance came out in our interviews more than any of the other situation-specific factors. Within the topic of industry, three main issues emerged as to why industry drives certain needed global leadership capabilities. The three underlying differentiating elements of industry were business life cycle, technology, and competitive intensity.

Business life cycles

Repeatedly executives talked about the impact of industry cycle times or life cycle on everything from strategy to decision making to stakeholder management. For example, in the mining industry investments are made in mines that are expected to have 20–50-year life cycles. The upfront investments for a single mine can be in the billions and involve discovery and feasibility assessment which can go on for 7–10 years in advance of the actual start of production. Given these high investment costs, breakeven points can reach out farther than a decade after actual production starts.

For example, Rio Tinto invested an estimated $7 billion into its Oyu Tolgoi mine in Mongolia and spent nearly ten years of development work before a single ton of copper or gold was commercially produced. Even though the first commercial shipment was made in 2013, it will take until 2020 before the mine (a) moves past its breakeven point, (b) pays back the investment, and (c) starts to make money from a net present value (NPV) perspective. However, the mine will likely continue to produce until 2050 or even longer. As a consequence, it is almost certain that the executive who will have to close the Oyu Togoi mine had not entered the workforce at the time of its first commercial shipment and may not have even been born then. With this in mind, it is easy to see how the long life cycles could influence effective strategic planning, financial analysis, decision making, and even requisite patience of effective global leaders in the mining industry.

In contrast to Rio Tinto, Google measures product life cycles in days, not decades. They can know in days and sometimes hours if a new product or service is a hit with customers. As a consequence, leaders often have no time or sometimes no need for detailed pro forma calculations or business plans. Therefore, the level of detailed planning, checking, and double-checking that would make a Rio Tinto global executive effective would make a Google executive a disaster.

Technology

Industries differ rather dramatically in terms of technology intensity. One easy measure of this is the percentage of revenue invested in research and development (R&D). For example, many of the large pharmaceutical companies, such as Pfizer and AstraZeneca, spend 13–18 percent of sales on R&D. For fast moving consumer goods (FMCG) companies, it can be as low as 1 percent. In addition, in many industries the details of the technology can matter, and strategy, financing, and investment decisions cannot be made in the absence of a solid understanding of the technology or science. Often there is an interaction between technology and industry cycle times, such as the long cycle times in pharmaceuticals and the relatively high R&D investment. As a consequence, the "fast-second" strategic thinking and mentality that can be very effective in the retail industry would be a disaster in the pharmaceutical industry, where patent protection can make a fast second be the same as a slow twenty-second.

Competitive intensity

As Michael Porter and others have demonstrated over the years, industry structures, competitive intensity, and therefore profitability vary dramatically from one industry to another. For example, one of the poorest-performing industries consistently over the last 20 years has been the commercial airline industry. In fact, in the largest and one of the most deregulated markets in the world, the United States, since deregulation in 1979 the industry has lost about as much money as it has made. This stems from a variety of structural factors including:

- Relatively lower barriers to entry that bring new entrants into the industry at a regular pace.
- High fixed costs that create an incentive to use price to ensure that capacity is utilized (i.e., to fly the plane as close to full as possible).
- High elasticity of demand that causes customers to fly or not fly and to switch carriers because of price.
- Low switching costs that allow customers to easily switch to different carriers.

As a consequence of the industry's structure, competition on price is very intense and margins are thin to negative. It is no surprise then that it takes different capabilities to be an effective leader in the airline industry than in the software industry.

Birth country effects

As we mentioned previously, virtually all of the large multinationals today were born and spent their early years in a particular country. Research over the last 50 years has demonstrated that there are important and systematic differences in values and behaviors from country to country and that these differences influence what leadership capabilities are required to be successful within that cultural context.[1] For example, in some cultures, such as the Netherlands, effective communication is very direct. You say what you mean and you mean what you say. If you don't, you are not trustworthy. In other cultures, such as Korea, such explicit communication would not be viewed favorably and instead would be considered very immature and self-centered and cause people to not trust you. Instead, in Korea effective communication is implicit and what is said is not necessarily what is meant and what is meant is not necessarily said. Thus, for a leader in a Dutch company, it is easy to understand why certain capabilities such as speaking very explicitly and directly would be associated with effectiveness, while the same capability in a Korean company would be associated with ineffectiveness.

Sometimes in bringing up this issue with executives we hear comments such as, "Yes, that was true when you started your research years ago, but that's just not true today. We live in a borderless world where those sorts of cultural differences are disappearing." This is a nice sentiment but the empirical evidence does not support it. As we mentioned, the work by scholars over the years shows relatively little homogenization or harmonization of fundamental cultural values. So while you might see people wearing Nike sneakers all over the world, it does not at all mean that they are converging on fundamental values or deep cultural norms.

In addition, we can simply look to the national composition of top executives of some of the largest multinational corporations in the world today to test how "passport-blind" companies are or how little national culture matters. On this point, if you take the largest company by revenues in France, Carrefour, approximately 50 percent of the top 25 executives are French. If you take the largest Japanese company, Toyota, about 97 percent of the top 25 executives are Japanese. If you take the largest British company, BP, more than 50 percent of the top 25 executives are British. If you take the largest German company, Volkswagen, more than 65 percent of its top 25 executives are German. If you take the largest U.S. company, Walmart, more than 75 percent of its top executives are Americans. We could go on, but you get the point.

To be clear though, we are not saying that cultural differences across countries are bad or that some cultural values are better than others. We are also not saying that the influence of national culture on what are successful or unsuccessful leadership capabilities is undesirable. The empirical evidence over the last 50 years makes it clear that different cultural orientations can be equally successful.

Korean firms and leaders are successful with their implicit communication and Dutch firms and leaders are successful with their explicit orientation. However, to be clear, the evidence is also consistent that differences in successful leader capabilities have been and continue to be heavily influenced by national borders and history. Finally, the evidence is quite compelling that these differences and their impact on successful leadership are not going to go away any time soon. Therefore, our point is that, in addition to having leadership capabilities that fit with the industry, having leadership capabilities that fit with the national culture in which a company might be embedded also matter.

Corporate culture effects

The third situation-specific dynamic is a company's culture. Even in the same industry and within the same country, two different companies can have different cultures. These differences are often most evident when two companies in the same industry from the same "birth country" merge or when one is acquired by the other. For example, the recent acquisition of the New York Stock Exchange by Intercontinental Exchange (ICE) highlights these potential differences. In confidential interviews, several executives who left the merged entity cited vast differences across a variety of leadership activities from how decisions were made to conflict was resolved. Again, it is not the case that one company's culture is necessarily superior or inferior to another's, but failure of a leader to understand and fit a company's particular culture can result in that leader's failure.

As we mentioned at the beginning of this section, our research suggests that the unique leadership capabilities that arise as a function of these three situation-specific dynamics account for about one-third of the complete set of capabilities required of successful global leaders. The remaining two-thirds arise from global dynamics (see Figure 3.1). The important point here is that two-thirds of effective leadership is a function of dynamics and capabilities whose relevance and impact transcend situational differences. They are truly global. Therefore, ultimately

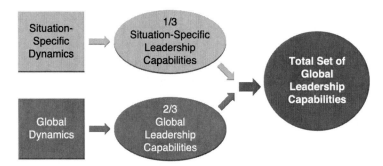

Figure 3.1 Situation-specific and global dynamics

successful global leaders must do two things simultaneously. On the one hand, they must pay attention to and develop capabilities that fit with situation-specific dynamics, and at the same time they must develop a set of global capabilities that are independent of situation-specifics.

Global dynamics

In our research, in order to determine what leadership capabilities were truly global, we asked executives what aspects of leading in a global context were different from leading in a non-global or domestic context. Consistently executives brought up two issues or dynamics that were different. We labeled these the dynamics of dispersion and duality.

Dispersion dynamic

Executives most often described what we label the dispersion dynamic by contrasting it to a domestic dynamic that has played a starring role in leadership almost regardless of the country from which the executive originated or the industry in which he or she worked. The domestic dynamic with which they made the contrast was "command and control." Command and control has been a dominant principle of effective leadership around the world for more than 100 years. While perhaps not the father of command and control, Henri Fayol laid out the key elements of command and control in his book *Administration Industrielle et Générale* published in 1916. His concise, logical approach had a monumental influence on management thinking and practice for nearly 100 years. For Fayol, to command meant that a leader should provide direction and a plan and then bind together, unify, and harmonize all activity and effort toward the plan. For him, to control meant ensuring that everything conformed to the plan and to the command. If mistakes were made or if actions deviated from the plan, then control involved pointing out those mistakes and deviations, rectifying them, and ensuring that they didn't happen again.

Some might suggest that Fayol's notions, or similar ones by his contemporaries at the beginning of the twentieth century, were good for their times but have simply become outdated for our day. While this is true, it invites two questions:

- Why did command and control work so well and get so widely adopted that we heard about it from executives regardless of where in the world they were from?
- What has changed that makes command and control less effective today?

In answer to the first question, command and control was so widely adopted for a very simple reason—it worked. It worked so well because the reach of command and control matched the scope in which it was applied—a single country. Although we tend to take this for granted, it is important to keep in mind that the vast majority of even the largest organizations through most of the twentieth century focused

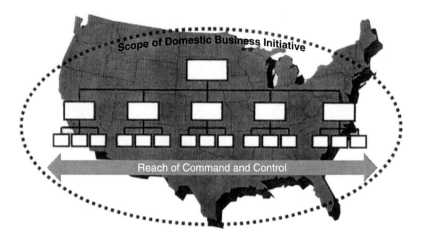

Figure 3.2 Match between reach of command and control and scope of domestic
business initiative

almost all their activities on and within the borders of one country. As one executive put it, "Command and control worked for me and others because even though
Canada is a big country and spans multiple time zones, I could literally reach out
and touch someone if I needed to." Another executive put it this way, "If you stay
within one country, you can understand the customers, competitors, suppliers,
employees, regulations, politicians, etc. You can wrap your mind around one
country; you can wrap your arms around the organization."

This match between the reach of command and control and the stretch of one
country is illustrated in Figure 3.2.

So why is it less relevant and less effective today? Were the leaders of 1910
or 1950 or 1990 less evolved and enlightened than today? Have we just matured
and marched on to a higher level of being? Hardly. What has happened is
globalization. The simple fact is that the world is a very big and diverse place. It
is so big and diverse that you cannot command and control it, nor can you command and control your organization across it. Put differently, the reach of
command and control has been exceeded by the stretch of the world. And that is
why command and control has barely a cameo role on the stage of globalization.

In particular, as companies moved from Stage 2 to 3 and beyond, command and
control stopped being effective—again not because we humans had somehow
evolved beyond it but because we had stretched our organizations beyond command and control's effective reach. The mismatch between the reach of command
and control and the stretch of global business is illustrated in Figure 3.3.

One executive described it this way:

It is almost like in the past you had a can on a shelf and if you stretched,
you could just extend your arm, hand, and fingers far enough to reach it.

Figure 3.3 Mismatch between reach of command and control and scope of global business initiative

Now the can you want is much higher up and simply exceeds the reach of your arm. As long as you didn't need that can, your arm was sufficient. [Your arm's] deficiency only came out when you needed that can that was a "reach too far."

Fundamentally this dynamic of dispersion revolves around the extension of organizational resources, particularly people, across the world—their dispersion. This dynamic gains its power from the sheer scope of the global environment—a scope that is so great that no single domestic business environment's scope comes even close to it. For example, though Russia is a large country and spans 11 different time zones, and has different ethic and linguistic groups within its borders, its diversity, however remarkable, cannot begin to approach the enormity of the cultural, linguistic, political, regulatory, and societal differences that exist across the entire globe.

In making this point, we do not want to create the impression that domestic environments are somehow "simple" or even internally homogeneous. Clearly they are not. However, there is simply no comparison with the global environment. And this is what has changed—not in an absolute sense, but in a relative one. In 1916, when Fayol published his book in French, the world was a big and diverse place. Arguably the linguistic, cultural, political, and societal differences were as big then as they are today. But in a relative sense or as a matter of everyday executive concern, the size and complexity of the world were not relevant because the vast majority of businesses were domestic and logically that was also where executives placed their focus. This was not just true in 1916, when Fayol wrote his book, but it was the case in 1926, 1936, 1966, and to a large extent even in 1996, as we demonstrated in Chapter 1.

While in hindsight this makes sense, in setting up our hypotheses and organizing our research, we had not anticipated this finding. Fayol's notions of command and control were so engrained, including within ourselves, that we were actually somewhat skeptical when we first heard executives talk about the limits of command and control in a global context and the implications of dispersion. For example, we listened to a senior executive at IBM lament his inability to get a specific global initiative effectively implemented. When we asked what the problem was, he responded, "People are just not going along with it."

Since we had known the executive for several years, we pressed him a bit more, "But you have authority over 99.9 percent of the employees. How can it be that they are not going along with it? Besides IBM is a somewhat hierarchical place and when you say 'jump', people ask 'how high' on the way up!"

The executive laughed but then proceeded to educate us. "Guys, you don't understand. The world is a big place. I can't be everywhere at once. Someone in China, India, or Russia could sidestep me for months. I can shout out orders but by the time I found out that they're not following, it's too late. I could try to force compliance, but the world is big and there are lots of places to hide," he responded. This type of comment was typical of many we heard from executives all around the world on the topic.

Consistently, the most senior executives—those who in theory have formal authority over virtually every employee in their companies—reported that they needed the cooperation, goodwill, and trust of employees in order to successfully implement global initiatives. The world is just too big, with too many time zones, languages, governments, traditions, customs, political systems, values, and miles, for executives to directly command and control it all.

Dualism dynamic

The second global dynamic that came out of the interviews was dualism. Dualism revolves around the dual pressures that executives simultaneously face for global integration on the one hand and local adaptation on the other. As we discussed in Chapter 1, during Stage 2 executives focus primarily on the integration pressures and standardization, which fit very nicely with a domestic focus plus exports. During Stage 4, executives focus primarily on the localization pressures, which fit very nicely with efforts to more deeply penetrate into local markets. In Stage 5, executives are trying to figure out what for them is the best configuration and balance of global integration *and* local responsiveness.

As we described in Chapter 1, the push for global integration of activities is tremendous. There are economies of scale that can come from the consolidation of manufacturing sites, from integrating purchasing and leveraging volume discounts, from having a common IT platform, etc. Pressures for global integration can also come from the high development costs that then push companies to amortize those costs across a global revenue base. For example, if you are

Airbus and you have spent €14 billion on the development of the A380, you cannot afford to customize the wings, the length of the plane, etc. to different customers' preferences. In addition, you have to go after customers everywhere in the world. Similar global integration pressures apply to the development of a new engine for a car. While the development investment is smaller, it still can cost more than $2 billion to design and develop a new engine. As a consequence, you need to utilize this engine in cars all around the world with as few modifications and adjustments as possible in order to make back your investment.

At the same time, there are pressures for localization. For example, while you might be able to keep the engine of a certain model of car basically the same around the world, the significant differences in road conditions mean that the suspension is likely to need more variation and adjustment. You might even have to make cosmetic changes in the exterior styling of the car because, despite some convergence of preferences, consumers around the world still do not universally aspire to or prefer the same styles and looks. In addition, not everyone demands the same level of precision engineering and safety and even if they wanted the highest level, not all can afford it. So at least during our lifetime, the pressures for localization from customers and conditions will continue.

Likewise, despite the global trend toward deregulation over the last 50 years, governments still impose different standards, regulations, and statutes on companies. State sovereignty and the right to set laws and regulations in accordance with a given country's system, values, preferences, etc. is arguably the most fundamental tenet of international relations that exists. In addition, it is not something that countries are likely to relinquish any time soon. Therefore, to the extent that laws and regulations require local adjustments, firms will have to make them, even if they go against pressures to be more globally integrated.

In our research most executives reported that they simultaneously experience both pressures to globally integrate and locally adapt (see Figure 3.4). However, there were some executives in some industries in which one of these dual pressures was stronger than the other.

For example, semiconductor industry executives reported to us that the global integration pressures were much greater than the local responsiveness pressures. Part of the reason for this we have already discussed in terms of the high minimum investment for just one new fabrication plant. In addition, atoms moving around circuits on a microprocessor do not care about language differences, time zones, cultural differences, political systems, and the like. Electrons, neutrons, and protons behave as they behave. This is not to say that AMD or Intel do not face local responsiveness pressures, but only to say that executives within companies in this industry reported that the global integration pressures were much stronger than the local responsiveness pressures.

Conversely, perhaps the most local industry that we encountered across the entire world was the funeral home industry. Sadly people pass away in every country of the world, and in every country, there are customs, rituals, and norms for how the event is handled. However, in all our interviews and travels, we have

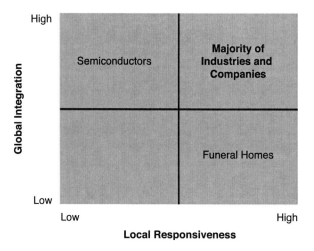

Figure 3.4 Dynamics of duality

failed to find a single global company in this service industry. In fact, there are very few national companies in any country. In the vast majority of cases, companies that look after the services related to dearly departed loved ones are small and operate at the local, almost neighborhood level. This is in large part because the local responsiveness pressures are extraordinarily high virtually everywhere in the world.

As we discussed in Chapter 1, companies typically move through five stages of global development as the incentives to lean in the direction of trade or investment change. In Stages 2, the incentives lean in the direction of trade and global integration. In Stage 4, the incentives lean in the direction of investment and local responsiveness. As we also pointed out, in Stage 5 the incentives for investment and localization remain high and the incentives for trade and global integration re-emerge and result in a "high–high" configuration. Figure 3.5 illustrates that the complement of "Trade" in terms of the dual dynamics is "Global Integration" and the complement of "Investment" in terms of the dual dynamics is "Local Responsiveness."

However, the nature of the trade pressure is different in Stage 5 compared with Stage 2. Whereas in Stage 2 the incentives were primarily in terms of products and exporting them from the home market, where existing assets and capabilities could be leveraged, in Stage 5 companies have the incentive to move components, products, activities, knowledge, and people around as seems optimal.

For example, in Stage 2, GE tried to export medical equipment from the United States to places like China. However, they discovered that the equipment was too expensive, too fragile, and too bulky for China's needs. In Stage 3, they invested in the ability to make products that better fit the needs of those markets. They

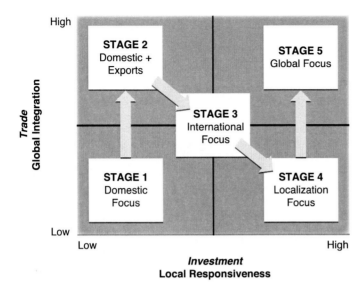

Figure 3.5 Correspondence of five stages and dualism dynamics

de-featured and discounted products that they had developed in and for the U.S. and other developed markets. GE modified this in Stage 4 and focused even more on adapting products for China. As GE moved deeper into Stage 4, they even had a slogan "In China for China." In Stage 5, GE discovered that the optimal configuration of globally integrated and standardized and locally responsive and different was not easy to figure out. For example, in terms of ECG machines, it was not just about making great ones in the United States and then exporting them to China. Neither was it merely making ECG machines in China for China. What it discovered was that for portable ECG machines, the best cost and know-how intersection for GE *globally* was China. Its engineers in China were able to design and deliver a portable, highly accurate, and affordable ECG machine that could be sold not just in China but in the U.S. and other markets as well. Thus, in Stage 5, GE might decide to move ECG knowledge from the United States to China and might do this by moving people there or by bringing Chinese scientists to the United States and then transferring them back to China. They might invest in being able to make a component in India and then ship that component to China to be incorporated into the final product assembled there to sell in the United States. However, because of tariff or trade agreements between France and Vietnam, it might be more cost-effective to ship the same product from a plant in Vietnam to France instead of from the one in China, and so on and so forth. As this example illustrates, in Stage 5, trade and investment are not mutually exclusive mechanisms but are flexible and can be configured in an almost infinite array of possible combinations.

The reality is that for most companies entering into or moving through Stage 5 is a bit more complicated than Figure 3.5 would suggest. As we have talked with executives and consulted with companies, it is clear that often when you examine the dual pressures carefully, while they might be equal at an aggregate level, they actually differ when you dive deeper and look at the picture at the activity level. It is not just about "Thinking Global and Acting Local" as was popular a few years ago. Rather it is "Thinking Global and Acting Global" on some things and "Thinking Local and Acting Local" on other things. Probably the best way to illustrate this is with an example. Let's take a simple product like Coca-Cola and look at just four activities: brand management, concentrate production, bottling, and sales promotion.

Effective *brand management* primarily experiences the pressures of global integration. To be effective, the color, logo, and other visible aspects of the brand need to be integrated and consistent around the world. And they are. For example, what is the brand color of Coke? Red. However, it is not just any red. The exact hue, saturation, chroma, and brightness are all specified and largely controlled out of headquarters in Atlanta. Suppose you say, "Red is nice but, in Spain, yellow is the color we should use. Let's make the brand color yellow. Trust me, Spaniards love yellow!" What are the odds that you will get to use the color yellow as the brand color in Spain, even if you are correct and Spaniards will love it? If you said "zero," you are correct. Brand management is globally integrated.

Concentrate production or the secret syrup from which Coke is made is carried out on a regional basis. For example, in 2011 Coca-Cola opened a new concentrate production plant in Singapore for the Asia region.[2] Irial Finan, President of Bottling Investments and Executive Vice President of The Coca-Cola Company, said:

> This is an investment for growth. Asia is one of our fastest-growing markets and across the region we see high demand for our wide range of beverages. The decision to locate in Singapore took two years of review. Factors that were taken into account included infrastructure and connectivity, proximity to key markets, quality control with a target of zero defects, and the availability of skilled manpower. Singapore scored very highly on our key considerations and we were particularly drawn to the country's world-class infrastructure and global connectivity.

Thus, syrup production is managed at a regional level.

Bottling is done at a country level, in part because, when it comes to shipping bottled Coke, much of the volume and weight is water. Water is heavy and its weight-to-value ratio is not so great. Consequently, as the shipping distance goes up, so too do the transportation costs to the point where it just doesn't make economic sense to bottle on a scope larger than a country basis. In addition, by bottling at the country level, the exact mix of carbonation and sugar can be adjusted to fit better local preferences. In January 2013, Coca-Cola announced the opening of a new bottling plant in Myanmar after a 60-year absence from the country. CEO Muhtar Kent commented, "As we grow as a local business in Myanmar, we are committed to creating economic value and building sustainable communities."[3] After the lifting of sanctions and the implementation of Myanmar's new Foreign Investment Law, Coca-Cola became one of the first U.S. companies to receive an investment permit. The company announced plans to invest $200 million from 2013 to 2018 in production capacity, logistics (including sales and distribution operations), and in improving marketing and people capabilities. The investment was projected to create more than 22,000 job opportunities across the entire value chain. The plant would initially bottle Coca-Cola and Sprite in 425ml plastic bottles with uniquely scripted Myanmar labels. Subsequently, the plant was intended to bottle beverages in aluminum cans and in Coke's iconic glass contour bottle (300ml).

Finally, *sales promotion* for Coke is done almost exclusively at the local level so that adjustments in channel, type, extent, and target of sales promotion can fit the local need. This degree of localization is needed for sales promotions because there are significant differences not just country to country but region to region within a country. For example, in the U.S. promotion, coupons are put in the newspaper, which customers then cut out and take to the market to get certain discounts. Such coupons are unheard of in Japan. However, sales promotion doesn't just differ between countries; it can differ significantly within a country. For example, even within the United States you might have significantly hot weather in the southeast in Atlanta and very cool weather in the northeast in Boston in the same week. As a consequence, a promotion to drink an ice-cold Coke in Atlanta might be very effective and the same promotion in Boston would not be.

Figure 3.6 provides an illustration of how Coca-Cola's different activities corresponded to places on the continuum from high global integration to high local responsiveness. In Chapter 5, we explore in more detail the specific global leader capabilities and challenges that grow out of the fact that, for most companies, even when they face dual pressures at roughly equal levels at the aggregate level, they typically vary, and can vary dramatically, at the activity level.

When you focus on competitiveness at the activity level, you can develop far greater precision in determining the optimal level of globalization integration and local responsiveness for your company. Clearly, globalization does not produce scale or scope advantages for all activities. In the final analysis, you may optimize some activities at the global level with resulting global scale and scope advantages, and optimize others at the local level.

A model of global leadership

As we mentioned previously, our model of global leadership is based on rather extensive research. The global leadership characteristics that emerged from our interviews were largely driven by the dynamics of dispersion and duality. However, not all the leadership characteristics were equally related to both dynamics. Consequently, as we introduce each characteristic, we will also briefly

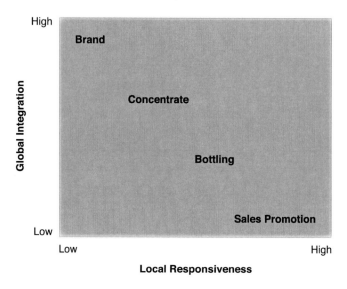

Figure 3.6 Coca-Cola's configuration of activities

describe how each one relates to the dynamics of dispersion and of duality. Figure 3.7 illustrates the characteristics of global leaders. Here we just want to briefly introduce each aspect; we devote chapters 4–7 to exploring each in greater depth: inquisitiveness, perspective, character, and savvy.

Inquisitiveness is at the core of our global leadership model. Although inquisitiveness is a central characteristic of effective global leaders, it is more an attitude than a skill. Someone can be quite inquisitive without having well-honed skills or knowledge. For example, healthy babies are at the same time incredibly inquisitive and essentially devoid of skills. Inquisitiveness is a state of mind and a vital characteristic of global leaders, providing the nourishment and sustenance required to keep the other three global leader characteristics at full strength. In many ways, leading a global organization is like leading a crew on a great voyage. And just as curiosity drove explorers to sail great distances through uncharted seas and trudge through dangerous, unmapped lands, inquisitiveness drives leaders to understand and explore new international markets. This is the core element of successful global leadership.

In our framework in Figure 3.7, inquisitiveness is the core; perspective, character, and savvy comprise a set of triangles around the core. This triangle represents the observable and measurable characteristics of successful global leaders. Each of the corners represents a different set of skills and knowledge, and each has two subsets.

Perspective is all about how leaders look at the world. It has two subcomponents: embracing uncertainty and balancing tensions. In Chapter 5 we explore both of these dimensions in greater detail. Duality dynamics are the main driver

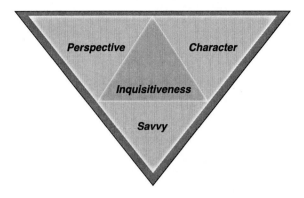

Figure 3.7 Model of global leader capabilities

behind the significance of perspective. The pressures for global integration and local adaptation each create tremendous uncertainties. While most managers shy away from these uncertainties, global leaders embrace them and are invigorated by them. In addition, the duality dynamics create tensions that have to be balanced. Successful global leaders do not have the luxury of simply ignoring one pressure in favor of another. Once again, while many managers are paralyzed by the opportunity to find innovative solutions rather than to settle for mediocre compromises, global leaders are driven to search for innovative ways to balance competing demands.

Character is the second corner of the model and has two subcomponents: emotional connection and unwavering integrity. Both are thoroughly explored in Chapter 6. This portion of the model is driven primarily by the dispersion dynamic. Successful global initiatives require the goodwill and trust of people outside leaders' formal lines of authority—people who have different cultural paradigms from the global leader and often from each other. Consequently, connecting with them emotionally and exhibiting unbending integrity are critical to engendering their goodwill and trust. These things cannot be commanded or controlled. They are freely given, not surrendered on demand.

Savvy represents the third corner of the model. Just as the great explorers displayed enormous skill in accessing money and provisions, effective global leaders demonstrate both exceptional business savvy and organizational savvy. They have a clear sense of what needs to be done and know how to access the resources to make it happen. Just as the great explorers enjoyed the confidence of their crews, effective global leaders have the full support and commitment of their employees. This is crucial, because unlike yesterday's sailors who had little choice but to stay with their ship, employees today have many more options when it comes to abandoning the team or deserting their leader. The need for organizational savvy arises primarily from the dispersion dynamics. To successfully implement global initiatives, you need to know who to tap and what organizational resources

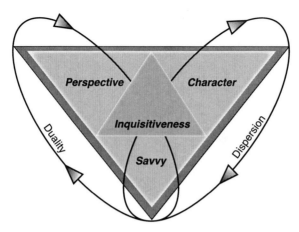

Figure 3.8 Alignment of global leadership capabilities and global business dynamics

are available in order to successfully reach beyond the limits of ordinary command and control. Business savvy, on the other hand, arises primarily in response to duality dynamics. Great global leaders have to be able to figure out which activities need to be globally integrated and which need to be locally adapted, as well as how to simultaneously satisfy both demands, to maximize your firm's moneymaking opportunities.

Figure 3.8 provides a graphic representation of how the global leadership characteristics relate to the two central global dynamics. As you can see, inquisitiveness is equally related to both dynamics. As we have already pointed out, inquisitiveness is not only the core of the leadership model but it is also the primary means by which global leaders transcend mere coping strategies and actively engage with the dynamics of dispersion and duality. Perspective is critical in responding to duality dynamics, while character issues arise primarily because of dispersion dynamics. Savvy relates to both dynamics: organizational savvy to dispersion, and business savvy to duality.

Mapping your global leadership profile

Before the sixteenth and seventeenth centuries, mapmakers relied heavily on travelers' tales and explorers' rough sketches to construct their maps of the world. With the invention of more accurate measuring instruments and better mathematical techniques, mapmakers became increasingly precise. In fact, most sailing charts after the 1600s usually include an interesting series of connected triangles, which literally crisscross the entire map.

These patterns result from applying the cartographic principle of triangulation, which early explorers relied on to map their journeys. With some mathematical manipulation, they could figure out the exact dimensions of each side and angle in these triangles and then chart where they had been, where they were, and where they were going.

This whole process was facilitated by the use of control points. Control points are distant objects that allow cartographers to determine an exact position on the map. For example, by knowing the height of Mt. Everest beforehand, by incorporating angle and distance with the control point, mapmakers can easily determine via triangulation the exact height of adjacent peaks. When mapping your world of global leadership, you should create similar control points by comparing your leadership skills with others'. We have created a simple Global Leader Survey to help you do that (see Appendix).

Balance is critical for your success

As you examine your global leadership characteristics, keep in mind that while some raw aptitude is necessary, exemplar global leaders must work hard to develop all four characteristics to ensure success. They know that success depends on a strong and balanced set of characteristics. In contrast, executives who are weak in one or two areas will find themselves significantly handicapped at some point in their careers. Thus, whether you are working on your own development or advising individuals or designing systems for developing large groups, assessing the current balance and working toward creating the appropriate balance is critical.

For example, managers who lack proper perspective and have difficulty embracing ambiguity and balancing tensions will not be effective global leaders. Without those skills, they can never achieve the proper medium between timidity and brazenness when acting in critical markets. They become paralyzed, incapable of making the types of decisions that set one apart as a global leader. Managers without character are similarly ineffective. They may be savvy and talented at spotting moneymaking opportunities, but without empathy and integrity, they become self-serving and lose the goodwill and trust of valuable employees. Managers who lack savvy are also ultimately of little use as global leaders. While employees may perceive them as warm people, their lack of savvy makes them prone to costly business mistakes that eventually undercut their ability to lead.

Global leadership profiles

Just as centuries ago each part of a triangle played an essential role for cartographers in charting unknown lands and waters, inquisitiveness, perspective, character, and savvy are equally important in effective global leadership. Building on the mapmakers' triangle, you can determine where you are or the leaders for whom you are responsible and where you or they need to go as a global leader.

The journey to mapping leaders' profiles starts with inquisitiveness. How curious are they about the world? Next, examine how they look at ambiguity and how well they balance tensions. Similarly, take a look at how well they connect emotionally with people and how consistent they are in their ethical behavior. Do they inspire goodwill and trust in others? Finally, examine their organizational and business savvy. Do they know where critical resources are in the global organization and do they know how to tap into and leverage them? Do they recognize business opportunities amidst the chaos of the global marketplace?

Assessing your global leadership characteristics

To help assess your global leader potential, consider your responses to the following questions:

Inquisitiveness

- Do you read everything you can get your hands on?
- Do you love to travel to new parts of the world?
- When in a foreign country, do you try to immerse yourself in the local culture?
- No matter where you are in the world, do you really enjoy talking to customers or potential customers?
- Do you really enjoy learning and wish you had more time for it?

Perspective

- Are you comfortable with uncertainty?
- Do you enjoy not being told what to do?
- Are you good at differentiating between the policies and products that should be globally standardized and those that should be locally determined?
- Are you comfortable with applying company policies in different ways in different circumstances?

Character

- Do you fully understand and embrace your company's ethical code of conduct?
- Do the people you work with, both inside and outside the company, think you are an honest person?
- Do you genuinely like people—your employees, your customers, other people you work with?
- Do people find you easy to talk to?

Savvy

- Do you have a solid understanding of how money is made in your industry?
- Do you have a strong track record of making money for your company?
- Are you familiar with your company's strengths and weaknesses on a world-wide basis?
- Do you know who the key decision makers are throughout the company's worldwide operations?

Your responses to these questions can help you better understand your strengths and weaknesses, map your global leadership triangle, and guide your development as a global leader. Of course, these questions we provide here do not represent scientific measures of your potential as a global leader. Nor are they intended to assess how well you may or may not perform on an international assignment. They are, however, a valuable step toward a deeper understanding of your global leadership strengths and weaknesses. Much more comprehensive global leadership and international assignment assessment tools are available.

A few organizations have recently begun developing instruments to measure global leadership potential. On the basis of the research presented in this book, we have developed through the Global Leadership Institute a broad assessment tool (Global Leadership Inventory™) to help individuals and companies assess global leadership potential (a small sample of the instrument is presented in the Appendix). This instrument helps you get an idea of how balanced or unbalanced your characteristics are and what your personal strengths and weaknesses are relative to each of the four global leadership characteristics. For example, some individuals are strong in business and organizational savvy but weak on emotional connection. While this unbalanced profile may work for a time, at some point all the savvy in the world will not engender the goodwill and trust that comes with emotional connection. The feedback report not only gives individuals a profile of their global leadership characteristics but also what they can do to bolster weak areas and develop a more balanced profile.

Perhaps you are fortunate and your global leadership triangle is not only well balanced, but quite large, suggesting significant strength in all areas of global leadership. More likely, though, your triangle is somewhat unbalanced, with a mix of strong and weak areas. In any case, each of us as global leaders still has room for improvement.

As we pointed out earlier, global leaders are in high demand, but in short supply. Consequently, competent global leaders are very valuable assets. While companies can find country experts, they find very few who are capable of effective leadership across multiple borders. One senior executive explained that it was "easy to find country-competent people who can master a single market, but it is almost impossible to discover managers who are masters at multiple markets."

We saw this shortcoming again and again around the world. From Europe to North America to Asia, top managers had a difficult time identifying more than a few individuals in their own companies who could be counted on to effectively lead anywhere in the world. While European companies tend to have proportionately more leaders who are effective outside their home countries than firms in America and many Asian countries, many of these European leaders are focused on Europe and not the rest of the world. Their skills and knowledge base beyond Europe are not appreciably different from those of Americans outside the United States.

Because there is a severe global leader shortage and because the needed characteristics cannot be developed overnight, the sooner you launch full sail into the development of your global leadership characteristics, the sooner you will find yourself in a position to fill this leadership gap. Perhaps you lead a functional team like accounting, marketing, or purchasing; maybe you manage a business—small, medium, or large; perhaps you manage a particular geographic unit in your company or are in a corporate leadership position. No matter the position you hold, if you lead, the message is clear: Your inquisitiveness, perspective, character, and savvy will have an enormous positive impact on the value you create for your company. The stronger your competencies, the deeper and wider your impact will be on your firm's bottom line. And while the imperatives to develop these competencies are greater if you are a top manager, they will give you a personal competitive advantage no matter what your leadership position in your company.

Notes

1 Hofstede, G. (2001). *Culture's Consequences*. London: Sage Publications; Trompenaars, F. (2012). *Riding the Waves of Culture*. New York: McGraw-Hill.
2 http://www.coca-cola.com.sg/news/localnews.asp?NeID=380 (accessed 13 November 2013).
3 http://www.coca-colacompany.com/press-center/press-releases/coca-cola-starts-local-production-in-myanmar (accessed 4 December 2013).

Part II

The essence of global leadership

4 Inquisitiveness

Inquisitiveness lies at the heart of global leadership. The reason is simple. The world is a big, diverse, complex, and changing place. If you are not curious about all the differences, complexities, and changes, then global business and global leadership are draining. They suck the life out of you. In contrast, if you are curious and inquisitive, the same differences, complexities, and changes are invigorating, not draining. They breathe life into you.

We understand that this first element of global leadership seems simple, and it is. Quite frankly, it is not what we expected to be the core of our findings, but it was. In fact, we thought that in the second wave of our interviews, which occurred several years after the first, since the world had changed so much, this finding might change as well; it didn't.

The power of inquisitiveness and its role in driving and sustaining global leadership came up consistently during our most recent interviews. One of the things we did in the latest wave of interviews was to ask executives to review with us their calendars going back one to three months just to get a concrete feel for what their life was like as global leaders. You can imagine all the travel, meetings, discussions, negotiations, presentations, etc. involved in a global executive's schedule over that time period. In addition, you can probably imagine all the time zones, cultures, regulatory frameworks, political systems, languages, personalities, and so on that the executives had to deal with over this time. In talking through a typical sample of their schedule, the details and specific issues were of course different from executive to executive, but the general level of diversity, complexity, and challenges was essentially the same. What was interesting and what was very telling was what happened to executives' energy levels as they recounted their recent schedule to us.

For those who had low levels of curiosity, you could feel and see in their faces and hear in their voices the energy drain as they recounted all the differences and complexities that they had to navigate over the last one to three months. Their pace of speech would slow, their voice would lower, their gaze would drop, their shoulders would hunch as they slogged their way through a recounting of their schedule. They would often complain about the difficulties and challenges they encountered and lament that things were so different and complex in the world they had to navigate. After one particularly poignant interview, one of us commented to the other, "I thought we were going to need some defibrillation paddles so we could shock him back to life." The other replied, "If he is so drained by what he has to do, why does he do it?"

In contrast, for those executives who had high levels of curiosity, you could feel and see in their faces and hear in their voices the energy build as they recounted all the differences and complexities that they had to navigate over the last one to three months. Their pace of speech would quicken, their voice would rise, their gaze would intensify, their shoulders would straighten as they breezed their way through their schedule. They would often comment on and explain the difficulties and challenges and extoll the differences and complexities of the world they had to navigate. After one particularly energizing interview, one of us commented to the other, "I'm ready to hop on a plane right now and travel with this lady. Think of what you could learn just hanging out with her."

From our research it is clear that exemplar global leaders are constantly curious and eager for knowledge. They actively seek new information, investigate the world, and challenge what other people generally take for granted. As A. L. Flood, chairman and CEO of the Canadian Imperial Bank of Commerce, maintained, "Global leaders acquire new knowledge and skills precisely because it is something done *by* rather than *to* them."

In our research, the importance of inquisitiveness was not much different in companies with long and deep global histories than in companies that were just beginning to internationalize. Consider International Flavors and Fragrances (IFF), a company whose international origins go back to 1833 and that today gets over 75 percent of its nearly $3 billion in annual revenues from outside the United States. The fragrance division develops scents and fragrances that are a key component in many of the world's finest perfumes and best-known consumer products brands, including beauty care, fabric care, home care, and personal wash products. The flavors division is a leading creator of flavor solutions for beverages, sweet goods, and savory and dairy products around the world. Given that the company has such a long history and has ingredients that go into literally thousands of products across nearly two hundred countries, it is safe to say that IFF has both deep and broad experience with globalization. This global depth and breadth is also reflected in the diversity of its senior leadership, who come from around the globe. All this is to say that IFF knows from experience something about global leadership. As a consequence, we were impressed when IFF's CEO and Chairman, Doug Tough, stressed the importance of curiosity. "Our best leaders are always looking around at competitors, customers, suppliers and asking questions. As a consequence of asking questions, they listen more than they talk. There is always more to learn. When I see an executive who thinks he or she know it all, I get very nervous, especially in a company like ours, where innovation is our life-blood." Reflecting on IFF's leadership development, Angelica Cantlon, senior vice president of human resources, confided, "Our best leaders are curious about the differences in consumer preferences around the world, as well as commonalities. Curiosity for us is a key competency. The world is changing too much for knowledge to be static."

Not surprisingly, IFF puts its leadership development money where its executives' mouths are. IFF runs, over a period of about six to nine months, a three-module development program that includes one module in which participants spend time in a key developing market to ensure that they are building their knowledge base and learning about markets in which they may never have worked. Just as a specific fragrance becomes the essence of a perfume and works in harmony with the other elements of that particular perfume's brand, inquisitiveness constitutes the *essence* of global leadership *effectiveness* and works in concert with the other key global leader characteristics. It is not only the essence, but *inquisitiveness is the fundamental driving force behind global leadership success.*

Inquisitiveness is a mindset

Are inquisitive global leaders born or made? When we put that question to Duncan Niederaure, CEO of NYSE Euronext, his answer was, "Yes." We agree. Anyone can enhance their level of inquisitiveness. As we will discuss later, there are certain behaviors that inquisitive leaders consistently demonstrate. Behaviors can be learned and the skills at exhibiting them can be built. At the same time, we want to stress that in our interviews it became clear that, for the vast majority of leaders with high levels of inquisitiveness, it was for them a mindset—a natural way of being. For the vast majority, they could not really remember not being curious or inquisitive. Most had parents or other key people early in their lives who encouraged their curiosity.

For our purposes here, we do not need to determine how much of inquisitiveness is due to genetics and how much is due to environment. We just want to stress that, for those who enjoyed and were invigorated by the challenges, complexities, and dynamism of globalization, inquisitiveness was so strong that it was a mindset more than conscious or deliberate acts. Part of the reason we stress this is one never knows where or when the global learning opportunities will arise. Often they happen in an unexpected instant. If you have an inquisitive mindset, you are much more likely to catch that learning moment than if inquisitiveness is less engrained and is more of a conscious, deliberate act.

Consider for a moment the following incident that happened to a good friend and global leader, J. Bonner Ritchie. For decades, Bonner has engaged in extensive international consulting, ranging from organizational development issues at Exxon to Middle East peace negotiations. The incident we want to reference is actually a non-business incident but we think it still gets at the essence of an inquisitive mindset. The incident happened a few years ago, when Bonner was driving with his wife and children along a French highway. Everything was progressing nicely but ahead he saw flashing lights and realized that traffic was stopped. He slowed down and then stopped. He waited. He waited some more. Traffic did not move and, despite being toward the front of the traffic line, he could not really see any reason for the delay. After some time, he grew impatient. There seemed to be no accident, no construction, no clean-up of a spill, really no need for the delay. Bonner considered two options. On the one hand, he could continue waiting but with no official seemingly in charge, who knew how long they might be there waiting? Or he considered another option. Between the highway lanes was a grass median. Bonner thought that he could pull onto the grass median and then go around this whole scene and get on his way.

He was positioned on a long straightaway and so he could see that the median was clear. With things looking safe, Bonner pulled over on the left shoulder near the median strip of grass separating the highways. With everything clear, he drove onto the grass to go around the situation. However, unbeknownst to Bonner, what looked like a solid grass median was really a large ditch or U-shaped gully with all the grass cut level at about the height of the road. As a consequence, when Bonner accelerated and turned the Volvo he was driving on to the apparent median, the car quickly leaned and then rolled over, leaving Bonner and his family suspended by their seatbelts upside down in the hidden gully.

Just imagine yourself in this situation. Your car just rolled over and is upside down; your family is dangling by their seatbelts; kids are shouting and crying; blood is rushing to your head. What would be the first words out of your mouth? (Could we repeat them in a family setting?) Bonner's first words were not: "Is everyone OK?" or "Is anyone hurt?" Instead, the first words to his family were: "This is interesting. What can we learn from this?"

Now that's an inquisitive mindset! When your family is dangling from their seatbelts in an upside-down car and your first instinct is to ask, "What can we learn from this?", then you know you have an inquisitive mindset. This is a bit extreme, but it illustrates the point. Those that have an inquisitive mindset naturally and reflexively want to learn. Bonner lives to learn. His attitude of constant, almost boundless inquiry mirrors what we see again and again in our work with exemplar global leaders around the world.

This inquisitive mindset does not need to be extreme, but it all pushes in the same direction. Consider the observation by Pat Canavan, a former senior executive at Motorola:

> They [exemplar global leaders] usually bring along something interesting to read when they travel, not to act smart at cocktail parties when they arrive, but because they want to be better able to perceive and understand the world around them wherever they are. If they are going to India for the first time and notice an Indian in the corporate cafeteria at headquarters, they sit down by them and ask questions. If they travel to Europe, they read the *International Herald Tribune* instead of *USA Today*. If they land in Hong Kong, they buy the *Hong Kong Standard*, not the *Asian Wall Street Journal*.

Global leaders are the exact opposite of those whose lives revolve around how many points they collect in frequent flier and hotel programs. Global leaders find rewards in the experience itself, where learning replaces consumption as the chosen mode of personal enrichment. Here is what a senior manager at GE Lighting remarked:

One key to our global success has been developing leaders who see their work as a learning adventure both on and off the job. While they push hard to drive the bottom line of business—and ours is a cost-driven business—they are equally committed to sitting back, listening, learning, and understanding what's going on in the local environment. As a result, these global leaders thrive on the fundamental tension between a strong desire to make money today and an incredible interest in the immediate world around them.

Global leaders make the wisdom of Henry David Thoreau a habit of their hearts. Thoreau said, "I wished to live deliberately. To learn what life has to teach me, and not, when I came to die, realize that I had not lived or learned." Instead of hunkering down in hotel rooms to watch cable movies after arriving in a new place, they take a walk, they observe, they immerse themselves in the local culture. On business trips, they avoid limousines like the plague. Instead, they take taxis, talk to the drivers if they can, walk the streets, venturing out into markets, stores, and museums. They read local papers and pose penetrating questions to people about their culture and history. Put simply, global leaders love to discover new things and their curiosity drives them to see and experience all that they possibly can.

Take for example John Pepper, twice CEO of Procter & Gamble. Pepper had a practice that, when he traveled, he would visit five local families, even before heading to the office, in order to learn about and better understand how locals did their laundry, washed their dishes, cleaned their kitchen, and so on. He wanted to understand firsthand customers' needs, what their space constraints were, what their budget limitations were, what their aspirations were, and so on. He felt that these direct experiences gave him a much better idea of how P&G products might be developed and adapted to meet those needs. Global leaders are content with nothing less than learning the texture of any place they work in, any country they visit. They live the lifelong credo of Jacques Cousteau, the famous undersea explorer, whose ship *Calypso* carried the motto "Il faut aller voir" ("We must go and see [for ourselves]").

Global leaders know that the best answer is a question

Naturally, as global leaders travel, employees in the various offices, plants, labs, etc. want to hear from them. They get this. This also know that even though the importance placed on hierarchy varies from country to country and culture to culture, some emphasis is placed on it in all cultures and, therefore, they realize that if they talk, other people won't. One leader put it this way:

If I'm talking, I'm not learning. I already know what I think and what I'm going to say. Yes, I understand that people want to hear from me. And there is a place for that. But if I'm not careful, that place will grow too large. People will sit there and just let me talk. The temptation [to talk too much], if I'm honest, is also my fault because it's a bit of an ego boost to have people sit and listen. So I've learned to first ask a lot of questions, to answer some questions with questions. Otherwise, there's the temptation to fall in love with the sound of my own voice and to think others have [fallen in love with it] because they seem to be listening.

Inquisitive global leaders not only ask provocative questions, but they also encourage them and field them from people both inside and outside their organizations—even though such questions can often pose challenges to deeply held beliefs. Successful managers perceive others' tough questions as starting points for dialogue and understanding, rather than for argument and persuasion. They pay careful attention to probing questions from customers and employees at home and overseas. As Philip LaChapelle, recently corporate controller at Otis Elevator Company, observed:

> Global leaders know how to observe; they make a conscious effort to learn. When they visit, they invite me to talk and then they listen. When going overseas or when meeting someone new, I try really hard to focus on asking questions and listening carefully. Ask questions; field questions—that is the key to discovering a part of their world that just might impact mine.

Global leaders create a culture around them that treasures inquisitiveness, that considers tough questions far more valuable than pat answers. At the very core, inquisitive global leaders work from an assumption that neither they nor their company have a corner on all the answers. As a result, they listen carefully to others' questions that may well challenge strongly held views on strategies, policies, or practices.

Global leaders not only ask and field tough questions, but they also command the courage and the intellect to doggedly pursue those questions. They don't take "no" for an answer, at least not until they are convinced that "no" is the only answer that makes sense. Put simply, global leaders never give up in the face of extreme adversity. They are personally committed to gathering data—about markets, competitors, best practices, internal organization, cultures, people, and technologies—and to seeing how those data interconnect.

For example David Neeleman, the founder of JetBlue airline in the United States, looked at the Brazilian market and asked, "Why do two firms have to control 80 percent of the market?" When others tried to explain that was just the way things were, he refused to accept it. Brazil was deregulated and there was no law legislating that the two firms, GOL and TAM, were entitled to control 80 percent of the market at prices that were more than 50 percent higher than in the U.S. The fact that they had done so for a long time was not an acceptable answer for Neeleman. As a consequence, in 2008 he put in several million dollars of his own money, gathered a record amount of external investment, and started Azul. Neeleman brought JetBlue pricing and high customer focus to Brazil because he was convinced that Brazilians were also sensitive to price and cared about a quality experience. He discovered that he was right; you could significantly stimulate demand with price, and with high quality you could make repeat customers out of first-time fliers. In addition, Neeleman pushed innovations that made sense specifically for Brazil. For example, in Brazil, getting to airports, which tend to be far outside the city centers, was inconvenient and costly. Neeleman created a *free* bus service that would pick people up at certain points in the city and then whisk them to the airport in a new, air-conditioned, wifi-enabled bus. Customers loved the service. In five short years, Azul went from 0 percent market share to 17 percent and TAM and GOL's combined share dropped to 75 percent. David Neeleman, like all effective global leaders, did not accept "This is the way it has been" as an answer to his question. There may be reasons why something is the way that it is, and there may be reasons why it cannot be changed or will be very difficult to change, but simply saying "This is the way it has been" explains exactly nothing.

Box 4.1 provides a list of practical ways you can change your own level of inquisitiveness.

Box 4.1   Ten steps to increasing your inquisitiveness

1. Seek out the unexpected, unknown, or novel. Surround yourself with people, books, ideas, and movies with perspectives different from your own.
2. Maximize the number of experiences at work and home that create contrast in your head. When confronted by disconfirming information, don't discount it—savor it.
3. Actively challenge your own perspectives. Engage in regular self-debate. Seek opinions inside *and* outside both your company *and* your industry—especially on key decisions.
4. Make the time to learn; don't leave it up to chance. Provide a resource margin for making little mistakes today to avoid making big ones tomorrow. Celebrate failure in your world as much as success.
5. Regularly check whether you are approaching life with a learning assumption ("I need to learn") or a knowing assumption ("I don't need to tell").
6. Construct head-jerking questions—ones that challenge core assumptions of yourself or others: individuals, groups, or organizations.
7. Model question-asking; then foster question-asking in those around you.
8. Respect and value others' questions as much as your own.
9. Never accept "It's just the way things are" as an answer. Seek a deeper understanding of the situation individually or collectively.
10. Maximize your question–answer ratio. In other words, contribute more questions than answers to each hallway conversation, conference call, memo, or team meeting you engage in.

Global leaders understand the terrain

To know the terrain, or competitive context, at home and abroad, inquisitiveness drives global leaders to challenge the outer edges of individual and organizational limits and to dig into and understand what they don't know.

Early in his career, current CEO of NBCUniversal, Steve Burke, worked for Disney and was responsible for growing part of Disney's consumer products business. It was a mature and slow-growing business. He posed difficult questions to people throughout his unit but he also encouraged questions from the people in his unit. One day when talking with a number of employees, one of the junior employees asked, "Why do I have to go to Disneyland to buy certain merchandise? Why can't Disney have retail stores outside of theme parks, in regular places like shopping malls and airports?" On the one hand, it had always been this way. Disney stores had only ever been inside Disney theme parks. For all Steve knew, the great man himself, Walt Disney, wanted it this way. But Walt had passed away nearly 20 years earlier, and even if he had wanted it that way then, should it be that way now? Not satisfied with "It's always been that way," Steve pursued the concept. Rather than just licensing Disney characters and the like to toy makers and other retailers, he repeated to himself and others the employee's simple question, "Why couldn't Disney have their own stores outside Disney theme parks?"

Steve admitted that at the time he was not a big shopper and was not that personally acquainted with or interested in retailing. As a consequence, he knew that there was much he didn't know. As a consequence, he spent hours upon hours at the local mall and other stores watching the customers, the store employees, and the whole retail experience. In the process he discovered that while he was not so fond of shopping, lots of people were. He observed that a good retail design could make customers feel welcomed into the store and help them find what they're looking for. He observed that sometimes people's greatest pleasure was when they discovered a pleasant surprise of something they weren't looking for but fell in love with once they saw it. He saw people happy to pay for what they bought and talk about it with friends long after they left the store. Steve was convinced that Disney could make a store outside its theme parks create a feeling of fun and fantasy just as the ones inside the parks did. He pursued the issue for two years until the concept of a chain of Disney stores became reality. He began with a series of test stores in southern California and eventually expanded the concept at a swift pace around the world. In short order, Disney Store became a $1 billion profitable business. Its success was one of the early career boosters that put Steve on a lofty trajectory that led to later opportunities in Disney and beyond at ABC, then COO at Comcast, and CEO of NBC, Universal.

Global leaders accept that "They don't know what they don't know"

To some extent the Disney Store experience also illustrates in Steve what we consistently observed in the best global leaders—the humility to recognize that they "don't know what they don't know." With that recognition comes a hunger to learn and discover. Conversely, we encountered some leaders who assumed that their prior experience was always 100 percent of reality irrespective of the new environment or situation, or who didn't want to appear to others as though they had some knowledge deficit even if they knew in their heart it was there. This sort of person is typified by one manager we met recently who was traveling throughout South America. At his first stop in São Paulo, he was introduced by his boss from corporate headquarters as "the man who thinks he knows everything." As one might expect, the moment was sobering, yet essential: he heard for the first time that his all-knowing style—as politely as he might be pulling it off—was not the best approach. Compare this unfortunate experience with the counsel of a particularly insightful marketing executive at GE who advised: "You have to work to know that you don't know what you don't know. Whenever you enter any new environment, *you enter with a learning assumption that you always have something to learn,* rather than a knowing assumption." Global leaders overcome the arrogance of a knowing assumption through unbridled curiosity.

To illustrate the antithesis of an inquisitive nature, consider the plight of several senior marketing managers and engineers from a Fortune 50 firm. These men lived in upstate New York. They scheduled a three-day business trip to Montreal. Upon arriving at the airport, they were stunned to hear French, having simply assumed that all Canadians must speak English. After fumbling around, they hired an interpreter to help them conduct business in Montreal. Next stop, Toronto. Upon arrival at the Toronto airport, they met their potential clients by calling out a hearty "Bonjour!" To their embarrassment, they realized that people in Toronto generally do not speak French (and may not particularly care for those who do). The entire business trip was an expensive disaster. It had not occurred to these executives that perhaps they didn't know some important things about Canadians before they ever began their journey to Montreal and Toronto. They came to a foreign country operating on automatic pilot, entered "thought-less," and paid the price.

Jon Huntsman Jr., former vice-chairman of the Huntsman Corporation and U.S. presidential candidate, presented to us an alternative:

> The most important valuable asset that someone can derive from an overseas experience is learning what not to do. When you're doing international business, as important as knowing what you want to do is knowing what you shouldn't do. You can only learn that from experience. For example, we learned through experience in parts of the world that we simply could not maintain the high safety standards that are required in chemical production facilities. As a result, we decided to place fewer production facilities in those areas. After having been burned a few times here and there, the real value-added of overseas experiences is knowing how to react when inevitable surprises come along.

Global leaders crush curiosity killers

A famous Yiddish proverb suggests that a person should live if only to satisfy his curiosity; yet from our experience we observe the opposite in business: too many managers live to kill the natural curiosity of people. Business managers are not alone. Studies show that children in the United States discover at a young age how not to learn in school. It becomes clear that giving the "right" answers—meaning the answers that the teacher wants to hear—is rewarded far more than asking the best questions. When these children reach adulthood and begin their careers, they face a hauntingly similar dilemma with managers who too frequently seek self-confirming information, acting like classic "confirmatory hypothesis testers."

Even the best companies can struggle with this challenge. When it comes to razors and shaving, Gillette (a brand owned by P&G) is a king in its home market with a share of close to 80 percent in the United States. More impressive still, it achieves market share without sacrificing profitability, in part because many of its products carry premium pricing. For example, its Fusion ProGlide retails for around $4.

Such prices in developing markets would not yield high market share. Gillette was no dummy and did not try to sell its expensive products in India. It tried to sell its lower-end products, like the Mach 3, with simpler packaging. However, its efforts were not very successful. The thinking was, "We know shaving and people in India just don't have enough money for our product. As they get richer, more will be able to buy our products and our market share will grow." Because that attitude kills curiosity, P&G sent in a team to go and learn how Indians shave—to observe them shopping and at home shaving.

They discovered that an Indian customer was much more price-sensitive than they had ever suspected. The target price point was probably about $0.12 not $4, not even $2. They discovered that, rather than standing at a sink with water running looking into a large mirror with bright bathroom lights, they were more likely sitting on the floor, with a small bowl of water with a small mirror in low light. They were likely using a double-edged razor, and experiencing frequent nicks and cuts from this.

These insights led to the Gillette Guard.[1] The Guard contained about 80 percent fewer parts than a traditional Gillette razor and provided a superior shave compared with the traditional double-edged shaver. The Guard contained an enlarged "lubrastrip" to provide more soothing lubrication. On the front side of the razor head before the blade they created a "micro-comb"—a slotted guard that "automatically manages bulges on the face by flattening the skin for increased safety." This reduces the irritation, as well as providing a more consistent shave, because it "allows the user to press the razor on to the skin while shaving without having to worry much about cuts." The blades are a lot thinner, finer, stronger (reinforced with carbide steel), and contain a low-resistance coating compared with traditional double-edged blades which therefore allows the blade to easily cut courser hair. Hair that can get stuck and clog the housing on traditional double-edged razors, but the Guard can be easily rinsed clear with just a swish in a bowl of water. Once the blade starts to dull after several shaves, it can be easily replaced with simple squeeze of the thumb and forefinger near the neck of the razor to detach the old head and by inserting the razor in the docking of the new blade.

Interestingly, P&G did not just design a razor to meet the needs of India; they redesigned the business model as well. They moved manufacturing to India to ensure that the razor and the cartridges were affordable (about $0.30 and $0.10 respectively). Given the fragmented nature of India's retailing structure, they focused not just on large stores and retailers but on the millions of Indian kiranas, or local shops. Finally, they used well-known Bollywood actors to endorse and be spokesmen for the Gillette Guard. The result? Around 74 percent of users reported fewer nicks and cuts and about 75 percent claimed that they felt safer with Gillette Guard as compared with the double-edged razor. Its market share has been equally impressive and stands at about 50 percent. At the end of the day, people who were not curious enough to really understand the Indian shaving market were pushed out of the way and those who wanted to learn and respond (including, of course, leaders within India) were given the mandate and resources to deliver this outstanding success.

More personally, we recently traveled to China to facilitate a global leadership program for a client. The company, a diversified U.S. multinational company, sent 20 senior executives on the excursion. The goal was to orient these senior managers with emerging markets. Many in the group had neither lived abroad nor done much international traveling. The most remarkable part of the entire experience for us was the different attitudes reflected by the people in our group.

To our chagrin, most of these executives had little international exposure and seemed quite uninterested in learning anything about China beyond the Great Wall and the Forbidden City. They were constantly on the phone to offices back in the United States. They spent evenings eating Western food in a Western hotel, and topped the day off with CNN International. These managers acted as if the China trip was simply an irritation; it interfered with what they believed were more important responsibilities. Even though they were in China physically, their minds were back home.

In stark contrast to the globally inexperienced, the more seasoned international executives created a much different experience for themselves in China. They actively sought out local street markets, as well as unique cultural sites off the tourist trail. They initiated, set up, and followed through on appointments with potential customers and suppliers. It seemed as though they had one primary goal on the trip: to stay as far away as possible from the hotel. For these highly inquisitive executives, the relatively brief time they had in which to experience China firsthand was of far more value than any task they might have left undone back home.

In contrast to sedate, routine-loving managers, inquisitive global leaders often ask questions about things that they don't know, believe, or understand, provoking interesting and enlightening responses. For example, David Ogilvy, co-founder of the global advertising agency Ogilvy and Mather, used to run several ad campaigns each year that his colleagues thought would be winners, though he was fundamentally convinced that they would be losers. He consciously chose to run a few of these campaigns to challenge, or disconfirm, his personal beliefs about what constituted a successful ad campaign. As one might expect, some failed, but just as many succeeded. David Ogilvy learned from those successes (that he thought would fail) and built a better decision-making framework for developing successful advertising campaigns. He was inquisitive enough to challenge his own perspectives on how to do business.

Global leaders master the terrain

Exemplar global leaders not only gather facts and gain experience, but they master the application of facts and experience in the global marketplace. They consciously seek out a sophisticated understanding of how complex data fit together, an understanding that has to be lived, not taught. Norm Merritt, an executive at Warner Brothers Studio, articulated this opportunity and challenge quite well:

> Out there you have to be smart; you must have the gray matter to manage the complexity and ambiguity. The last six months have been an incredible learning experience figuring out how international activities fit together, how wholesale relates to domestic markets, and how that relates directly to the consumer. Underneath it all, there seems to be a complex algorithm of how all these things fit together in a very sophisticated pattern, and you must have a strategic mind to recognize what really matters.

To capture these complexities, global leaders observe, deliberate, and ponder. They consistently commented to us that pondering and reflecting on experiences was in a fast-paced world the hardest. They had to carve out specific time and had to mentally push out distractions, emails, and interruptions in order to think on their experiences and distill the learnings. It would be great if we could just pile on experiences and count on gravity to somehow pull the learnings down through the morass and have them emerge as pure and distilled insights like a fresh spring that emerges at the base of a mountain after its long and contorted journey through the cracks and crevices, but unfortunately for the vast majority of people it isn't like that. Illuminating insights take deliberate reflection, and effective reflection takes time and effort.

But as we said, today's fast-paced world works against this. One executive put it to us this way:

> I believe in the power of reflection. I really do. But imagine if, after a series of experiences, I was at my desk, leaning back in my chair, eyes closed, reflecting, and my boss walked in. 'Jack, what are you doing?' he would ask. If I answered, 'Reflecting,' he would likely say, 'Reflecting? We don't have time for that. Get back to work.'

But to their credit, many leaders we met recognized that reflecting was part of their job and despite the pressures against it, they create time and space for it. For example, one global leader we interviewed just itched to get from one place to the next on his business trips but also built in self-financed side trips to places like Vietnam and Turkey—countries where his company had no formal business activities. These excursions gave him the chance to step back and contemplate the places he had just visited and what he had learned there. When describing these reflective moments, this executive reiterated a favorite quotation from Albert Einstein: "No problem can be solved by the same consciousness that created it." We could tell that he lived by those words.

Often global leaders are at a loss when asked to describe the rich, complex knowledge that results from reflective learning, or explain precisely how they developed it through experience, because "the greater the master (of any skill or art), the more completely his person vanishes behind the work."[2]

For example, when Tony Wang brought Kentucky Fried Chicken (KFC) to China for the first time, he had no accurate market entry data and felt that collecting it through traditional marketing tools would prove unproductive. As a Taiwanese native who had traveled extensively in China, Tony turned to his own experience and pulled together various tidbits of information to predict how the Chinese would likely respond to KFC products. He had watched their buying habits in small shops, observed their use of spices in food, and noticed their liking for chicken in general. By combining these data points with his extensive fast-food industry experience, Tony could confidently forecast how KFC would fare in China. When we asked Tony to articulate why he was convinced that KFC would prosper, all he could say was, "I just knew the Chinese would like it. I can't exactly say how I knew this, but I could *feel* the Chinese would love us." In fact, his years of fast-food industry experience combined with astute observation and probing of local customer preferences and habits gave Tony Wang an instinctive mastery of the competitive business terrain that concluded by the end of 2012 with KFC having 4,260 restaurants in China—nearly as many as its 4,618 in the United States.

Having this kind of "feel" for markets and employees is key for global leadership. There are times when one simply knows what to do. While it takes a lot of work to acquire the necessary depth of knowledge, it is not impossible. It reflects years and, at times, decades of business experience combined with an inquisitive nature that refuses to let prior experience sediment over present reality. This is where inquisitiveness plays a remarkably powerful role: helping global leaders build on past experience to make better sense of the present without letting the past dictate the future.

Learning to know *and* feel these complex interrelationships may be no easy task at first for young global leaders, especially as they crisscross a growing number of international borders. Yet the exemplar global leaders we interviewed move with ease from one paradigm to another. They are "zigzag people" who switch the angle of their point of view from one cycle to the next, like a sailboat tacking in the wind. Their ability to change, adapt, and truly embrace what works helps them piece together the complexity and master the chaos.

Developing this kind of mastery is a real challenge. As one senior executive in our study warned:

> You can find cross-cultural people a dime a dozen, but they're single market managers. If you wanted me to, I could easily grab fifteen people from our company who could work extremely well between the U.S. and Japan. But don't send those same people to Korea, and never send them to Europe. It is far more challenging to ferret out people who can move through multiple markets and master a much trickier and far more valuable world.

Precisely because these skills are relatively rare, global leaders not only actively seek out learning experiences for themselves, but they also create opportunities for subordinates to learn through exposure to a broad range of cultures and markets. At a major consumer goods firm one senior executive whom we interviewed practices this principle regularly for himself and his team, as exhibited in the following example:

> I just itch to get to the next new place and learn what it is like. In fact, my work is like living in a big theme park and the theme park is the world. For example, I have taken a personal side trip to Vietnam after a business trip to Japan—just because I was dying to learn more about Vietnam. I did not have anyone meet me at the airport. I simply did it on my own. On another trip, I went to Turkey because it was a convenient place to visit for two days before going home. Most of my team doesn't take diversions, but if I'm along, they have to. Recently we had some business meetings in Munich, Germany. I knew that it was not that far to visit Salzburg, so we finished our three o'clock meeting, rented a car, and I said, "I am going and if anyone else wants to come along, that's great." We made the trip and created an important learning experience.

Global leaders not only embrace experience, they make sense of it. They know the difference between, and the relative impact of, watching someone else exercise and exercising oneself. They create experiences for themselves and others in order to magnify their understanding and ultimately master the local or global competitive business terrain. Box 4.2 provides some concrete steps you can take to master the territory.

Cultural baggage destroys our capacity to see and make sense of new terrain

To illustrate the challenges associated with learning and unlearning the layers of core assumptions, or worldviews, that we all carry around in our heads, consider this historical example. For centuries, Europeans were entranced by legends of far-distant islands endowed with unimaginable wealth and resources. In 1541, Hernando Cortés and a group of adventurers set sail from Spain to discover such

Box 4.2 Action steps for mastering the terrain

1. Identify and gain the knowledge base required for mastering your territory—functional, organizational, industry, and geographical. Carve out the time to master each knowledge base. Do this by relying on "to learn" lists more than on "to do" lists.
2. Find a regular time and place for reflection. Construct your own version of a Japanese rock garden where you can sit, ponder, and make sense of things without interruption.
3. Seek out opportunities to test your mastery of the terrain by applying your knowledge in real-time profit-and-loss settings.

an island. Cortés—at least as interested in his own glory as he was in that of Spain—sailed across the Atlantic, portaged through Mexico, and then set sail again up the Strait of California. Eventually, his provisions low, his crew close to mutiny, he was forced to an unhapppy decision: to turn back, having apparently failed in his goal. For Cortés, failure was unacceptable, and so, with a little wishful thinking, he created a success. To the east and west, land was in view; to the north and south, water. Cortés reached a conclusion that seemed perfectly logical: he was in search of an island, and an island he found—La Isla de California. Cortes returned to Spain and reported to the king and queen exactly what they wanted to hear (and what he wanted to believe): *California is an island* (see Figure 4.3).

Shortly after Cortés's discovery, another expedition was sent to confirm the find. This one traveled far up along the Pacific coast, past present-day San Francisco. This over-ambitious expedition also ran low on supplies, and by the time they reached the mouth of the Mendocino River on the coast of northern California, the crew was stricken with scurvy. With no inclination to dispute Cortés and no absolute proof that he was wrong, they concluded that the river was really a strait that separated the northern part of the island of California from the rest of the continent. This cartographic myth persisted throughout Europe for over two centuries—in spite of overwhelming evidence to the contrary collected by numerous other leaders—until a royal proclamation from Spain finally declared that California was not an island.

For the monarchies and mapmakers alike, paradigms took a great amount of time and a great many challenges to change. The experiences of those who held such worldviews so deeply only served to confirm them, since for these true believers contrary evidence was simply invisible. In fact, they lived the reality of Machiavelli's oft-quoted observation:

There is nothing more difficult to carry out or more doubtful of success than to initiate a new order of things. For the reformer has enemies in all those who profit by the old order, and only lukewarm defenders by all those who can profit by the new order. This lukewarmness arises from the incredulity

Figure 4.1 Map of the Island of California (*c.* 1656)

of mankind who do not truly believe in anything new until they have had experience with it.

Once the belief that California was an island became established, reports from later leaders were filtered to fit the reigning paradigm; anything contradictory was labeled as false or impossible. Arrogance ruled: "I'm the king. Please bow." Pure self-interest governed: "As king, I must possess this island for its great bounty." Poor communication continued: "Don't tell me things that I don't want to believe or that are refuted anyway by our exquisite maps." All these things conspired to keep the myth of California as an island quite alive within European courts for over two hundred years; those who profited from the order of which this myth was a part could not believe in anything new until they had experienced it.

Just as resistance to learning has shaped much of history—and resulted in thousands of inaccurate maps—it can also undermine the effectiveness of global leaders in our New World. For example, IKEA, a global powerhouse in retail furniture, expanded in the 1980s from its Scandinavian roots to continental Europe, and then moved across the Atlantic to North America. A key component of IKEA's competitive strategy is sourcing extremely large volumes of moderate-quality goods at an incredibly low cost. As a result, it can sell its items to customers for prices lower than its rivals'—a perfect competitive position. This strategy works well around the world for most of the products that IKEA offers, such as curtains or dinnerware, but it failed miserably in the United States for some items, like beds and sheets.

When IKEA began its operations in North America, it shipped low-priced, moderate-quality, *metric-sized* beds and bedding to all of its North American stores. As one might expect, these items were not exactly hot sellers in the United States. In fact, they quickly became category failures, filling up entire warehouses. Local store and regional managers tried to communicate to corporate head-quarters in Sweden that metric-sized beds and bedding were not selling in the United States—in spite of the fact that they were priced lower than the king, queen, full, and twin-size bedding found in competitors' furniture stores. How did IKEA's senior managers, who were seven time zones away at corporate head-quarters, respond to this local dilemma? "Be more creative. *Pull* the customers into your store. Any good retailer *can* sell metric sized bedding; that's the solution to your inventory problems." Despite local and regional U.S. managers' constant attempts to convince headquarters otherwise, their bosses in Sweden held to this position for more than two years. Finally, the bursting warehouses won, and metric-sized bedding was reluctantly discontinued in the U.S. market.

Any global leader or leading global company can easily make the same kind of mistake IKEA made by getting sucked into the comfort zone of their own unexamined cultural heritage. For example, executives at Kmart were slow to challenge the decades-old assumption that big retail stores belong only in big cities, leaving many vital markets in smaller cities for years to Walmart.

Inquisitiveness keeps global leaders above water

As we stressed at the beginning of this chapter, without inquisitiveness, all the complexities of global business are draining. With it, they are invigorating.

We saw a great example of this during one of our recent trips to Asia. While in Shanghai, we interviewed the Dutch president of a European–Canadian joint venture. His factory employed 450 people, all Chinese except for himself and two other expatriates. His office was sparsely furnished and looked like it had last been redecorated in the 1950s. On the summer day we met, his air conditioning wasn't working properly. The elevator was broken. The linoleum tiles on the floor were gritty with dirt and dust. We were inclined to wonder, "Who in their right mind would want to be here when they could stay in a plush high-rise office tower in Toronto or Frankfurt?" We asked the Dutchman what kept him going in the face of adversity. His comments are revealing:

> Working in China can be tough. A contract here is like the minutes of the last meeting. It is viewed by the Chinese as the start, not the end, of negotiations. Also, in China, so long as your customer acknowledges that he owes you money, you can't take him to court. I have seen disagreements drag on for years. It can be frustrating and exhausting. I see a lot of people give up. You have to want to be here. In the mid-1980s, we made a decision to become

a major TV manufacturer in China. The government encouraged us and before long, there were 113 assembly lines for TVs owned by 88 manufacturers in China. The government knew that the market needed consolidation but didn't have the courage to do it themselves. So they decided to simply open the doors to imports and, essentially, we went out of business overnight. We ended up with nothing for our investment, but I didn't leave. The thought of going back to a job at headquarters in Europe was depressing. China is a real adventure—the wild west. So, I found another Western partner. The parent's ownership dropped to less than 40 percent, so I don't really work for them anymore. We changed our strategy and began focusing on making semiconductors for export. We are now making money while the rest all left and went back home. The country is changing so fast that my job is always new. There is something new to learn every day. I must be crazy, but I love the job.

Earlier we quoted former Motorola executive, Pat Canavan, and here again we highlight a key insight from him:

> To be fascinated with the world around you is central to psychological patience, stamina, acuity, and attention. I think the fascination of traveling the world, doing business, making deals results in renewal. It is not only more complex work—it is an opportunity to learn and enlighten. When you hear a lot of whining and moaning like, "Isn't it awful?," "I expected an airport!," or "You just can't trust these people," you know that the renewal process has stopped and the fascination is gone. As a result, people get worse and worse at what they do. They gnaw at themselves, feeling like they have to do what they have to do. This results in either a terrible product or no product at all. In contrast, renewal through constant learning snaps this downward cycle and keeps your personal edge in the global marketplace.

What is the bottom line for inquisitiveness? Global leaders don't go a day without learning. They are much more likely to pay attention to "to learn" lists rather than "to do" lists. Indeed, exemplar global leaders are no different in their daily quest for understanding and insight.

Inquisitiveness and perspective

As we mentioned in Chapter 3, in addition to inquisitiveness, our research uncovered what we label "perspective" as another critical capability. Fundamentally, perspective involves the ability to embrace ambiguity and manage the simultaneous tensions of global integration and local responsiveness. Although we address this capability in Chapter 5, here we want to illustrate how inquisitiveness plays a driving role in global leaders with effective perspective.

Without inquisitiveness, a common trap is to do business the same way in all countries, especially if it has been successful at home. After his successful development of the Disney Store concept globally, Steve Burke was asked to help turn around EuroDisney, a theme park near Paris then on its way to losing over U.S. $1 billion in a single year. The park was under fire from the local media and from shareholders understandably nervous about a possible park shutdown. Not only was Disney's reputation on the line, but so was Eisner's—EuroDisney was *his* first theme park as a CEO.

In his new job as EuroDisney's vice president of operations and marketing, Steve balanced a myriad of tensions. On the one hand, Disney was one of the most iconic brands in the world and, for the sake of consistency, some thought nothing could or should change for fear of hurting or diluting the brand. On the other hand, Europe in general and France in particular were not the United States. The park's billion-dollar loss was undeniable evidence that keeping things completely consistent was not the path to success. But it was not at all clear what could or should be kept consistent and what should be adapted. For some, such ambiguity and tensions might be debilitating; for Steve, his high level of inquisitiveness made them invigorating.

While all the specific decisions to keep things the same as well as to change things are beyond the scope of this section, we offer one example to illustrate how Steve's inquisitiveness won the day. Walt Disney set up the first theme park in California in part as a response to the seedy traveling carnivals common back in the 1950s. Walt wanted a safe, clean environment for family fun. As a consequence, there was a strict rule that no alcohol would be served. Walt didn't want drink-influenced bad behavior to ruin family fun. And so it was for decades, and with great success. Disneyland in California and later DisneyWorld and Epcot Center in Florida were astounding successes. How could you possibly go against the man himself, Walt Disney, and against such success?

Steve asked questions, listened carefully, and came to understand that in France wine and beer were simply an essential part of meals and not drunk in isolation. Because "no alcohol" in Disney parks had been a means to an end (clean, safe, family fun) for so long, it had become an end in and of itself. Steve's inquisitiveness helped many doubting executives back at headquarters see that in Europe serving wine or beer with food would not get in the way of maintaining a clean, safe, and fun Disney park in Europe. In the end, Steve's inquisitiveness helped him make a number of decisions about what to keep consistent (e.g., pricing) and what to adapt (e.g., changing the name from EuroDisney to Disneyland Paris) in order to achieve the right balance and configuration, and helped move the business from the red to the black.

Inquisitiveness and character

Like perspective, character, or the ability to emotionally connect with others and maintain integrity, is a critical element of our leadership framework and will be explored in depth in Chapter 6. As with perspective, inquisitiveness plays an important role in global leaders' character. Without inquisitiveness, you cannot maintain an emotional connection with people and consistently demonstrate the highest integrity. Neither the people you work with nor the ethical challenges you face stay constant. As one senior executive heading up new business development outside the United States maintained, "To connect with you when you are from a very different place than me, I must be curious or I am dead. If I don't pay attention to how you do things, why you do them, what the social and historical underpinnings are to your actions, what makes you tick, then forget it." Thus global leadership requires a huge, ongoing commitment to learn. For example, how can you connect with others on an emotional level if you don't seek an understanding of their world? If you are responsible for working with employees from 23 countries, how can you connect with them without knowing the subtle, but significant, nuances of each person?

Consider a mid-sized company that sent its marketing director to Asia. The marketing director did not want to go from the beginning and was essentially dragged overseas. As illustrated in the following situation, he was completely oblivious to any need for cultural sensitivity. During one visit to Korea he was socializing with a key client in front of a group of people. During the conversation, the client remarked, "No, this is the way it is." Immediately the marketing director shot back, "No, it is not!" Then, right in front of everyone, he took the Korean client to an exhibit area to prove (in public) that he was right and the client was wrong. The Korean client was thoroughly embarrassed in front of his peers. This marketing director's oblivious action devastated his company's relationship with the client's company for years. Afterwards, one senior executive inside the U.S. firm lamented, "There are people who are just oblivious and, no matter what you do, they are not going to pick up important cues during cross-cultural encounters." In this case, the result of not being inquisitive is self-evident; business with a key foreign client was lost for years.

Inquisitiveness is essential for global leaders to build the emotional connections required in high-performance, cross-cultural teams, as exemplified by one of our clients, a multinational petroleum exploration and production company. The company's major operations are in the rich offshore oil and gas fields of Southeast Asia. Each of its offshore platforms has 100 employees working 12-hour shifts in 28-day cycles. The crews include Chinese, Malaysian, British, American, Indonesian, and Indian workers. Conditions on the rigs are crowded and noisy. Temperatures often hit 120°F or nearly 49°C with high humidity. The situation is potentially explosive given the differences in language and culture. As this client knows, however, global leaders pick up subtle cues from employees and the company relies on very inquisitive team leaders who ask open-ended questions and use strong listening skills to learn about their crew members. These leaders engage employees in personal conversation: Where are you from? What is your family like? What kind of car do you want to buy? Simple but powerful questions, because through them people become more real to each another. Such banter between leader and crew gives everyone a much greater chance of working together as a cohesive team. Not a bad idea when offshore platforms cost well over $100,000 per day to operate. Whether in Asia or Africa, global leaders connect with others in every part of the world because they "always have their antennas out" for fresh information. As a senior executive at Merck suggested, "Wide eyes and closed mouth is probably one of the best prescriptions you could have going into a new culture."

How does inquisitiveness enhance your ability to demonstrate integrity? Curious global leaders carry a heightened awareness of potentially unethical contexts around them. They pay attention to the subtle cues that indicate that something is askew, something is out of place, something is *wrong*. In contrast, managers with limited inquisitiveness who work in multiple countries often act as if everything is just fine—and fail to notice when their own actions are unethical or illegal. For example, one manager at a European multinational wanted to see pictures of candidates for an engineering job in the United States and to know details about candidates' personal lives before hiring them for a U.S.-based research and development facility. This manager's actions were clearly against U.S. law, but he was oblivious to the fact. In this case, he found out about the law only after a lawsuit had been filed against his company for illegal hiring procedures.

Inquisitiveness and savvy

Finally, as with perspective and character, inquisitiveness helps global leaders see international and local business opportunities *and* take advantage of them through operations that span the world. For example, how can a worldwide president for a product line that is produced in 23 countries and distributed in 148 others learn all she needs to know without having a high level of inquisitiveness? How can someone in this situation keep from being overwhelmed without an inquisitive nature, a constant hunger for new information? They can't.

Global business and organizational savvy directly link to your methods for gathering knowledge of markets, competitors, best practices, internal organization, cultures, people, and technologies. Inquisitiveness helps you constantly retool in these areas. Technology, customer preferences, competitive products, and government regulations change constantly. Product and process innovations close in fast and furious. Volatile dynamics turn the global marketplace into a marathon in which the best global leaders know when to accelerate their pace as well as when to hold their position just long enough to see what the competition is going to do. Whether it is Gillette cutting production costs on the next generation of razors, Marriott International establishing new hotels around the world, or Sony introducing a stunning array of advanced digital sound devices, global leaders must constantly stay abreast of innovations and opportunities on a worldwide basis, or risk getting blindsided by more agile competitors. Levi Strauss faces this reality as the continued profitability of Dockers pants and 501 jeans is now threatened by dozens of upstart designer-brand and generic-brand denim pants producers in every part of the world, all scratching away at Levi's global market share.

Without an insatiable desire to learn, you can easily miss key facts, important relationships, and critical connections that can help you improve your specific approach to a local market, or, conversely, systematize your overall business approach to obtain global market efficiencies. In either situation, the key to creating new sources of global competitive advantage comes from your constant inquisitiveness about unique market and organizational contexts. What you gain from these frequent learning adventures becomes the foundation for writing and rewriting the maps that guide your exploration into the ever-changing global marketplace.

Conclusions

Inquisitiveness helps global leaders maintain their edge in a world that moves faster and grows *larger,* not *smaller,* a world constantly shifting, changing both at home and abroad. They know that doing business in today's global markets requires personal mapmaking skills, and they know not to rely on anyone else's chart to guide them across terrain that is always altering, always transforming. Inquisitiveness is the foundation from which you, as a global leader, can maintain a sharp personal edge and develop an enduring reservoir of knowledge and skills. It is a reservoir that is filled by your capacity to see things that others miss, to sense patterns where others find only confusion. It is a reservoir that gives you the desire and strength you need to handle an overwhelming amount of work and information. Although making time to learn presents a real challenge for any global leader, your commitment to learning constitutes the solid core, the essence of your ability to build business savvy, exhibit character, keep perspective, and create value in a hypercompetitive marketplace.

Notes

1 http://www.gilletteguard.com (accessed 23 September 2013).
2 Heidegger, M. (1966). *Discourse on Thinking.* New York: Harper Torchbooks, p. 45.

5   Global leaders have perspective

Do you remember when you last spent some time in a foreign country? Did you observe how the business practices, social norms, values, regulations, marketing channels, languages, and opportunities all changed? Global leaders can't help but notice these differences as they move from place to place. They know that while their world is in many ways "borderless," in many ways it is far from it. When crossing national, cultural, and language boundaries, they confront a fundamental challenge, as a Walmart executive we interviewed pointed out: "One of the biggest obstacles we face when traversing country markets is learning to get the right mix at the right time, learning and relearning what each area really wants."

Getting the right mix is never easy. Global leaders—whether at Walmart or any other multinational company—face enormous challenges as they strive to combine the upside of globalization with the harsh realities of a world full of differences. While success in global markets requires the right mix of products and prices, the key to unlocking the organization is the mindset of the leader. Global leaders need the mental skills—what we call "perspective"—to pull it all off.

Putting the challenge in context

So what does having the "right" perspective actually mean? And why is perspective important? From our research, we have uncovered two related but distinct components of perspective: uncertainty and balancing tensions. Both are essential if global leaders are to effectively navigate the dual imperatives of global business.

The first component of perspective is the capacity to manage *uncertainty*. While all businesses deal with uncertainty, the complexity and uncertainty of global business put it in a different league. In an interconnected world, complexity grows exponentially and, with this, uncertainty. In a global company, understanding and predicting market movements is anything but child's play. You can either bury your head in the sand or take on the challenge. And the best way to take on the challenge is to cut uncertainty down to size through study and research. Knowledge is a powerful antibiotic. Effective global leaders know how to balance the need to grow knowledge through research with the need to act.

The second component of perspective is associated with the challenge of *balancing tensions*. Global leaders understand what needs to change and what needs to stay the same from country to country, region to region. The ability to constantly balance tensions rests at the core of the concept of duality. Duality suggests the simultaneous existence of two contradictory or competing conditions. And in the case of global business, competition between local and global is intense.

We discussed this duality challenge with one of the senior executives in our research. He used an example from his past to describe the mental challenge he faces in getting globalization right.

> I remember a high school physics class where we studied the nature of light. We spent weeks learning that light was a particle. I became pretty good at understanding and predicting how light would react given that it was a particle. Then one day the teacher came into class and told us to forget everything that we learned. He told us that light wasn't a particle, but a wave. I was stunned to learn this. How could light be a wave, when it was a particle? How could two very different theories be true at the same time? I was confused and overwhelmed and I didn't know what to believe. It took me a while until I became comfortable accepting two competing ways of thinking.

Mastering global business is in many ways like mastering the principles of light. Global business is fast-moving, complex, and unforgiving. Unchangeable laws of nature govern it—everyone wants more, and the more you make, the lower the unit costs. At the same time, global business is anything but uniform. It involves waves of conflicting and offsetting pressures and demands. It is full of idiosyncratic customers, incomprehensible languages, and strange cultural norms that even locals might not fully understand.

While they are independent, managing uncertainty and balancing tensions are at the heart of perspective. In the following sections we'll lower the microscope on each of these dimensions.

Embracing uncertainty

Uncertainty is at the heart of every business. Every day, leaders face a dearth of quality data and a staggering number of questions. Where are today's competitors located? Where can we find tomorrow's competitors? What are their competitive advantages? What is the market potential of each country in which you operate and each country in which you don't operate? Which countries could make good platforms for global operations? How stable is the local currency? How strong and predictable are local and national institutions? What products, pricing, and distribution are best suited for particular markets? Do you know where your talent is located globally? Are you using the most appropriate tools to motivate key employees? Have you properly assessed the risks your business faces?

Uncertainty in global business

While executives operating in only one country certainly confront some of these questions, the degree of uncertainty faced by global leaders increases exponentially. The uncertainty stems from several problems.

1. *The sheer volume of data.* Leaders with responsibilities spanning dozens of countries are confronted with incredible volumes of data. Everything a smart manager needs to know to stay abreast of what is happening in one country or in one market now needs to be multiplied by the number of countries in which the company conducts business. But wait. There's more. Smart leaders shouldn't just collect data on what are today's realities, but also on tomorrow's competitors and customers. So the flood of data is indeed limitless.

2. *Inconsistent definitions and variable quality of data.* Within one country, managers develop an appreciation of certain key data sources. They understand that, on the second Tuesday of the month, the government releases national employment statistics or that, on February 1st of every year, the national industry association can be counted on to report sales data for key competitors. Also, within a country, definitions of key terms and data points are often standardized. Patterns of business can be studied, patterns identified and tracked. But, add multiple countries to the mix and the comparisons become more difficult. Definitions are not consistent. Not a huge problem if you are tracking automobile sales, but a potential roadblock if you are studying apparel sales and you realize that the definition for a "jumper" (sweater in the U.S.) varies enormously between Canada, the UK, and Australia. Also, the quality of the data can also be suspect or difficult to compare. For example, how do you compare quarterly data from one country with biannual data from another? And what about data from emerging markets—data that might be suspect in terms of quality?

3. *Lack of base comparisons.* When hanging a picture, a level will come in handy. Carpenters use them all the time to ensure wood components or fasteners are aligned. The same thinking is common in business, where leaders create base measures with which everything is compared. How are sales this year compared with last year? How does our quality stack up against our competitors? How many days' inventory do we have versus norms in the industry? But when global markets are added to the equation, which base measures are important? Should you compare the performance of an affiliate in Country X with that of Country Y? Or should you compare it with Country Z? Should you compare quality in one part of the world with the best in class— anywhere in the world—or with the best in class in the foreign market, or should you downgrade the importance of quality in certain markets because customers there don't put quality high on their priority list? These are all tough, often beguiling, questions that domestic managers typically don't confront.

4. *Growing interconnections.* If the world were full of walled-off countries, it would be enough to study each market in isolation. An image of a giant

database comes to mind. Each row would represent a different market. Columns would include relevant data points: sales, growth rates, profits, and the like. Take a picture and you have the world figured out. But if you were to develop the picture you would discover two problems: first, the rows and columns are all connected in a global world, and second, the numbers are constantly changing. The reality of global business is that floods in China impact the prices of silicon in Korea. The key is not only figuring out what is happening locally but understanding how the *system* works. And this isn't possible unless you figure out the interconnections. Unfortunately, none of this is visible to the naked eye of the global leader.

5. *Uncertainty over beliefs.* In a national market, managers become accustomed to paying attention to trusted institutions or respected members of society. In some parts of the world this may include government officials, religious leaders, academics, and so on. Within society there is a shared sense of who should be listened to. But beyond this, there is a shared belief not only in the messenger but also the message. Rightly or wrongly, patterns of belief are typically widespread in large swaths of society. In the Nordic countries, for example, some would say that the green movement has taken on religious overtones. Want to get thrown out of a meeting in Oslo? The fastest way is to deny global warming and argue that companies don't have a particular responsibility for the environment. And because Norwegians care a lot about the environment, the underlying belief that the world is self-imploding becomes self-perpetuating. Media tend to report on it more often, opinion leaders discuss it more regularly, companies start introducing more "green" products, and soon it has taken on a life of its own. To a degree, uncertainty has been replaced with a shared sense of reality.

    We see the patterns all the time. They cover a huge range of issues at the heart of any belief system—beliefs about health, economic prosperity, relationships between ethnic groups, the role of religion in society, and so on. A leader may recognize some of his or her beliefs, but because they may be so engrained, it is impossible for anyone to be completely self-aware. But even if it were possible, self-awareness of powerful beliefs *raises* uncertainty levels; it doesn't lower them. After all, a xenophobe knows no uncertainty. When you start asking fundamental questions about what you believe, then you also start asking questions about whom you believe. Asking too many of these questions can quickly overwhelm the best leader. Belief is the enemy of uncertainty.

While a reality, uncertainty is not per se a bad thing. Research has shown that uncertainty can provide a variety of benefits including facilitating organizational change and strengthening the position of leaders.[1] Other research has shown that employees who work in organizations that embrace uncertainty are more satisfied in their jobs. They are also more committed to their companies.[2] Rather, the problem with uncertainty is that to benefit from it requires excellent leadership. And managing it in a global organization requires some truly unique leadership skills.

Keeping the balance

In an increasingly complex international business environment, global leaders require an exceptionally high capacity for managing uncertainty. In some ways, they have to act like a juggler as they take on this challenge. Someone once defined juggling as having more objects than hands. It takes a combination of focus, balance, and timing to be a good juggler.[3] And, in a similar way, global leaders also need focus, balance, and timing. They have to be comfortable moving sequentially from topic to topic, shifting their attention ever more rapidly as their responsibilities increase.

If only it could be so simple. As difficult as juggling is, dealing with the complexity of global business is even more challenging. Why? Because the key to juggling is rhythm: each ball has to get precisely the same attention. Unlike juggling balls, global leaders can't rely on rhythm. Rhythm is the enemy of global leaders. They understand that some markets must get more attention than others. Knowing this doesn't stop the balls from moving around in a circle. But it does place a premium on knowing and anticipating the kinds of things that require special attention.

Whereas rhythm is the friend of jugglers, balance is the companion of global leaders. Global leaders who are effective dealing with the enormous complexity and uncertainty around them balance their attention between internal sources of information and external data sources.[4] Instead of thinking of the world as a series of markets, they think more about where and how they can get data. Good data. Timely data. And this includes external sources of information such as competitive intelligence, industry reports, and the like. It also includes internal information such as sales data, costing information, the tacit knowledge of employees, and so on. Keeping internal and external data sources in balance—not relying too much on one versus the other—will go a long way to helping leaders close their uncertainty gaps.

Overcoming organizational barriers

Many global leaders confront high levels of uncertainty that are actually built into their multinational organization's structure. Global businesses have seen a proliferation of complex organizational structures over the past 20 years. Few big companies don't have some form of matrix structure. Some are well designed, but others leave employees confused and burdened with bureaucracy.

Some leaders are fighting back. Take the example of the Swiss company, Sika. The Sfr 5 billion company is a leader in chemicals in the construction industry, including waterproofing, sealing and bonding, as well as concrete. Many of its customers are small construction or refurbishment companies. In some countries, the company has 8,000 customers, some large, others tiny in size. Not surprisingly, over time the company experienced a proliferation of products and customer solutions. In an effort to reduce redundancies and streamline operations, the head office added layer after layer of controls, structures, and systems. The result was stifling bureaucracy. When Jan Jenisch was appointed CEO in early 2012, one of the first things he did was to take a careful look at how the company organized itself. While his ambition was to drive profitable sales, he realized that the company's structures and systems were acting as barriers to innovation and customer-centric solutions. He described his approach:

> We had factories in most every country. Our adhesives enjoy large economies of scale. We also have scale in purchasing. But not everything is scalable. In fact, a lot of the things we do have very low potentials for scale. We made the mistake in the past of moving too many things to central control. We needed to stop this. We didn't want a lot of bureaucracy. We needed to focus on customers, not on our internal problems.
>
> We have always gotten a lot of fresh ideas by responding to customers. In the past we have built too much R&D in HQ. We need to push this out to countries. Products we developed in Switzerland sometimes didn't work well in other countries because materials are different, the weather is different, and so on.
>
> Clearly there is not a perfect organizational solution. But, for us, we decided to simplify and push decision making back to the local markets. Globally, we decided to organize ourselves around 7 key markets. But how these are applied and approached is up to each country general manager. The balance and emphasis placed on these markets is going to be different in Germany than it is in Peru. We now have a flat, decentralized organization. We are much faster than in the past. We can now customize very quickly.

Jenisch's experience has been that well-meaning managers can often introduce organizational solutions—like matrix structures—that unintentionally add complexity, sow the seeds of confusion, and reduce organizational responsiveness. The solution for Sika was to upend the matrix, simplify reporting lines, and shift authority back to the markets. While other companies may find different solutions, global leaders are constantly reassessing company structures and systems with the objective of reducing clutter and confusion for all employees.

Doing your homework

We find it amazing that many executives approach business uncertainty by copying others, like teenagers following fashion fads. If they don't know what to do, they impulsively watch what others do. They follow the leader. Yet benchmarking or following without thinking can be incredibly dangerous in the global marketplace. It's not much different than dancing blindfolded near the edge of a cliff.

In overseas markets, multinational firms blunder around most often when they fail to acquire the contacts, relationships, and connections—the essential conduits of information—that are held by local companies. When this happens, executives tend to do what they have always done *at home*, or they simply start imitating what others do overseas. Inevitably, problems result. For example, when UPS first entered the European market and established operations in Germany, it tried to attract quality drivers with the same pay and policies that had worked in the United States. However, the wages offered were too low to attract experienced drivers in Germany, and the traditional brown UPS uniforms put many potential employees off. The uniforms were too similar in color to those worn by the Nazi youth groups during World War II. By focusing on what made a job attractive to an experienced German truck driver, UPS finally came to understand that it had to offer higher wages and clarify in its recruiting advertisements that brown uniforms were required UPS dress in all parts of the world.

The world of business is full of companies who messed up badly in international markets because they didn't do their homework. The list of well-publicized[5] examples includes:

- In Taiwan the translation of the Pepsi slogan "Come alive with the Pepsi Generation" came out as "Pepsi will bring your ancestors back from the dead."
- In Chinese, KFC's slogan "finger lickin' good" first came out as "eat your fingers off."
- The Chevy Nova didn't do well in South America because "no va" means "no go" in Spanish. Chevy renamed it to "Caribe."
- In 2006, hair care company Clairol introduced a curling iron called the Mist Stick, which did very well in U.S. markets. When the company marketed the product in Germany, however, they failed to realize that "mist" means "manure" in German. Oddly enough, the "Manure Stick" didn't sell so well in Germany.
- Honda introduced their new car "Fitta" into Nordic countries in 2001 but changed the name to "Honda Jazz" when they realized "fitta" was an old word used in vulgar language to refer to a woman's private parts in Swedish, Norwegian, and Danish.
- The Swedish furniture giant IKEA somehow agreed upon the name "Fartfull" for one of its new desks. It later dropped the name.
- In 2002, Umbro, the UK sports manufacturer, had to withdraw its new trainers (sneakers) called the Zyklon because it was the name of the gas used by the Nazi regime to murder millions of Jews in concentration camps.

In sum, doing effective homework helps global leaders understand their target constituency, be they customers or potential employees.

Following the "80/20" rule

Notwithstanding the need for homework, companies can get too carried away and take it too far. High-profile blunders aside, most managers actually fall on the other extreme of the continuum and fail because they do *too much* research. They do this to avoid the risk of making a poor decision. After all, research is a comfortable tool to use in overcoming uncertainty. Another reason for a "more is better" perspective of research: corporate headquarters often demands hard data, particularly from far-flung foreign affiliates. Why? Because they either don't know the foreign decision makers or don't trust their judgment.

One problem with all this research: it is often completely useless and even counterproductive. Listen to the experience of a Thailand-based general manager of a large transportation equipment company from the United States:

> My head office keeps asking for reports that I have no ability to generate. The data they want do not exist here nor do my people have the skills to generate what they want. We might spend a month preparing a report that gets done in three days in the States. Headquarters thinks it is just a matter of hiring more people with better skills. But, after being here a while, I realized headquarters has got it mostly wrong. While we can always use more good people, I have come to believe that the American way of running the business just doesn't work here. The reports are not only a waste of time; they actually lead us in the wrong direction.

In today's hypercompetitive business environment, engaging in too much research and waiting for complete clarity might be an invitation for trouble. The competition simply does not stand still waiting for executives to figure out what to do. IBM provides a classic case in point.

Before Lou Gerstner became CEO of IBM in April 1993, managers in the company had a history of avoiding uncertainty. While the company produced some of the best technologies in the world, IBM's corporate culture in the early 1990s emphasized getting the product "right" before going to market. Every line of code was checked and rechecked; every piece of hardware had to perform perfectly before it was approved for sale. This policy minimized risk for employees and conformed with IBM's "product out" strategy at the time. Unfortunately, as technological change accelerated and customer choices increased, IBM's risk-averse approach became a huge problem.

Delayed by the need to "get things right," IBM's newest products often arrived on the market months late and over budget. When the products finally arrived, IBM's technology was no longer cutting-edge. According to Tom Bouchard, senior vice president for human resources at IBM at the time, "We no longer had the luxury of getting everything 'just right.' Once we embraced a 'customer in' strategy, the qualities for effective leadership changed."

Executives at IBM began actively promoting a new 80/20 rule. The idea was that IBM would strive to go to market when the product was 80 percent "right" and 20 percent still unproven. The features they focused on getting right were those customers cared most about. The result? Sales increased, enormous amounts of money were saved, and, most importantly, customers were much happier. Today, IBM leaders continue to emphasize the importance of not waiting too long for the entire picture to come into focus before moving ahead. They know that speed to market is the key to their competitive success.

Global leaders embrace uncertainty

In the global marketplace, creative leadership in the midst of uncertainty is not an option. It is a requirement. Effective global leaders do not shy away from uncertainty. Instead, they embrace uncertainty. They appreciate that, when managed correctly, uncertainty can bring important advantages to the organization. Global leaders understand that their skills managing and coping with uncertainty provide a competitive advantage. They ask smart questions, they sift through a myriad of unknowns, and, ultimately, they work the organization, and they act.

Without strong leadership, uncertainty can be a cruel enemy. For example, corporate executives at one major consumer products firm were given an edict from head office in the United States to ramp up sales of bubble bath products in Hong Kong. The only trouble was that few people in Hong Kong have bathtubs. What to do? Rather than feeling paralyzed with uncertainty, the local leaders had no choice but to rethink their challenge differently. They felt "liberated" by the challenge, realizing that the only way to win was to break traditional company norms. Realizing the mistake of their superiors in the United States, local leaders began to closely examine the personal hygiene needs and habits of Hong Kong consumers. This resulted in a number of innovative ideas, and the company ultimately relaunched the bubble bath as body soap packaged with a washcloth. The results were highly successful.

Embracing uncertainty means that global leaders not only accept but also partner with locals. To offset local surprises when entering new markets, global leaders exploit local understanding and global capabilities to achieve lower costs and superior product and service offerings.

Global leaders can rarely predict where new product development and process improvements will come from. As Kazutami Komada, general manager of the Visual and Audio Products Division of the Toshiba Corporation recognized:

> In our industry, product differences remain significant between Europe and North America. We do the basic design work for consumer electronics in Japan, but the models change in each region. In fact, we encourage local and in some cases regional production and want our local managers to take initiative.

Being comfortable in your skin

At the end of the day, no one can be prepared for every new situation. Sometimes, particularly in doing business globally, leaders are confronted with situations that are bewildering and for which there are significant consequences if they get a decision wrong. How you act in these situations will have a great impact on how you and your company are perceived. Managing uncertainty means being comfortable making decisions based not on data or thoughtful deliberation but on your innermost thoughts and beliefs. When you are 10,000 miles from home, it often comes down to you and your gut judgment. Global leaders who are comfortable enough in their skin, when unfamiliar situations arise, can move forward, make decisions, and avoid paralysis.

Carlos Ghosn, Chairman and CEO of both Renault and Nissan, addressed the difficulty of leading under certainty at the personal level.

> It is a paradox: on the one hand, you have to be more confident and secure, but on the other, you have to be a lot more open and empathetic. You need to listen, but then when you make a decision, that's it—you must be a very hard driver. Usually, these are not attributes you find in the same person. Once you have done the analysis and made the decision, then you have to learn to simplify the decision in communicating it to others. Everything's complex, but once you have decided, sometimes you need to simplify so much it's almost a caricature. You must say, "Nothing matters beyond this." You must reduce everything to zeros or ones, black or white, go or no-go. You can't have too much nuance. In a crisis, you have to be able to do all of these things—listening, deciding, and then simplifying—very quickly. That is what makes leading in a crisis so interesting. And because you have to move so fast, you have to empower people to make decisions themselves. That's the best way to restore calm.[6]

Archie Dunham, former CEO of Conoco and Chairman of ConocoPhillips, is the kind of leader who understands the truth of this statement. Earlier in his career, the chief of the Nenets, a reindeer-herding people in Russia, asked Dunham to meet face to face on the Arctic tundra to finalize negotiations on an oil and gas lease. Dunham began an encounter atypical of the normal life of an American CEO. He started by sitting cross-legged in a tent pitched on the snow. Then he offered a number of gifts to the Nenet chief. These were not letter openers or paperweights, but hatchets, matches, and ropes. In return, the chief of the Nenets respectfully rose, chopped a piece of reindeer meat from a carcass hanging in the tent, dipped the meat in a bowl of fresh reindeer blood, and held it out for Mr. Dunham to eat. What to do? Test the meat for food poisoning? Visit a library to investigate the health benefits of eating fresh reindeer blood? Call a culture consultant to consider the possible responses when offered such a gift by the chief of the Nenets? Dunham chose none of these options. Instead, he took the meat graciously and swallowed it whole.[7] The results for Conoco were positive; for Dunham, they were an experience of a lifetime.

Embracing uncertainty: like white-water rafting

Earlier in the chapter we discussed the similarities between juggling and global leadership. We learned that while they share certain common elements, global leadership is much more difficult than juggling. A better analogy for global leadership is white-water rafting. Like juggling, white-water rafting demands intense concentration. But, unlike juggling, white-water rafting also requires enormous preparation and skilled improvization.

Experienced white-water rafters first scout the river from the shoreline. They study maps, survey routes, and plan their attack. Yet no matter how valuable this preparation is, white-water rafters understand that once on the water, they must often make decisions in a split second. Even though they may be following a particular planned route, rafters make constant adjustments in real time and without the need to stop and think it through. In this fluid decision-making context, studying every detail of a river beforehand provides little direction in the swirling moments of decision that are forced by a river's unpredictable currents. Even more importantly, rafters know that if they approach large rapids timidly or with the slightest degree of hesitation, the water's powerful force will easily flip and sink their boat.

Just as rafters are constantly adjusting their game plans in the face of an ever-changing river, so too do global leaders weave and bob along the way. Even with the best market intelligence and the most up-to-date, comprehensive data-bases, global leaders can never know all the answers beforehand, because they simply cannot anticipate every question and because the scenery changes so rapidly. There are always new and unexpected elements along the way. One European global marketing executive disclosed: "Global leaders exhibit the ability to accept whatever comes at them in their jobs. They do away with what-ever they thought was fixed to traverse the unpredictable terrain of international business."

Balancing tensions

Perhaps the biggest single source of uncertainty for global leaders is how to balance the dueling demands for globalization and localization. We saw an example of this at play in the case of Sika. Global leaders demonstrate the ability to constantly balance ever-shifting global/local tensions and, by so doing, find ways to consistently grow profits and revenues.

A senior finance executive at Procter & Gamble who we interviewed reinforced this point:

> The secret is the balance. Global leaders know how to keep one eye on bottom-line business results and the other eye open to the local customer. To the degree to which global leaders do that well, I believe that a firm will succeed globally.

Another leader of a US-based technology company we interviewed extended this thinking:

> Global leaders who make the largest difference at any level of our corpora-tion are able to think and act on a scale that is different from acting only at a country or regional level. They have a way of thinking about the planet that they are on, a way of understanding where customers are coming from. It's built into their understanding of any situation.

Pressures for globalization

Companies around the world are facing huge pressures to globalize their operations. The potential to lower costs through economies of scale encourages companies to build ever-larger production facilities, often at capacity levels that exceed the demands of the home country. Companies are also facing rising product development and R&D costs and feel compelled to amortize these expenses quickly by broadening their definitions of markets and by simultaneously targeting multiple national markets.

Companies are also facing consumers who are more wired, better connected and who increasingly want the best or the latest products everywhere around the world at the same time. In other cases, companies find themselves immersed in global supply chains involving vast buyer–supplier networks that traverse the globe. Makoto Yamaguchi, Managing Executive Officer of Tokyo-based Mitsui OSK Lines, commented on this reality: "It is a traditional function of the shipping industry to look for global opportunities. Customers want global service. The biggest responsibility for shippers is to provide a service where there is a need. So we have no choice but to be global."

Pressures for globalization are also impacting how companies organize and deliver value for customers. Consider the experience of Colgate-Palmolive as described by Brian Smith, former director of global HR Strategy:

> The country manager used to be king of the hill in our company. They would come up with a nifty project and get approval to launch it. You'd get a German brand and a French brand and maybe it would translate across borders. It would take a great deal of time and create enormous redundancy. That approach is now over. Today, we have global bundles. While the big, red, standard, anti-cavity Colgate used to look 60 different ways around the world, now you can walk into any store in any market in any part of the world and Colgate is Colgate. It's a truly global brand.

Other historically locally focused companies like Nestlé and Unilever are finding great new opportunities with global brands. Nestlé brands such as Kit Kat, Gerber, Nespresso, Milo, and Nesquik represent major multibillion-dollar product lines with global appeal. Likewise at Unilever, where the company estimates that over 2 billion people per day use one of its products including Dove, Knorr, Timotei, and Bertolli.

Some of the fastest-growing companies in the world are essentially built on global products and services. Apple's iPhone, iTunes, and iPad are examples. Rio Tinto, Research in Motion, Boeing, ExxonMobil, Intel, and Swatch are examples of companies whose survival is dependent on providing standardized products for global customers. And titans like Amazon and Facebook, which have developed many country-specific applications, thrive because of the power of their global brands and global systems.

There are plenty of examples of global success stories to go around. A few other examples go a long way to illustrating this point. At the end of 2012, KFC had 4,260 restaurants in China alone. It was opening more than one new store per day in that country.[8] By the end of 2012, Sony's PlayStation 3 had sold nearly 600 million units around the world and operated the PlayStation Network in 59 countries and regions.[9] And recent data from the Motion Picture Association of America indicated that almost 70 percent of the studios' annual box office revenues comes from international (non-American) sales.[10] The audience for American movies is more non-American than American! There are countless other examples like this in the press almost every day.

Pressures for localization

Despite the imperatives to globalize—and the growing list of companies that are responding—localization has not disappeared. In some cases, companies face a growing backlash against what some would call soulless globalization. Antiglobalization feeds on reports of the abusive labor practices of some multinationals, environmental degradation, the loss of national culture, and the like. Others blame globalization for the stagnant and declining wages amongst the middle class in many developed countries. Politicians argue that something must be done to stop the hollowing out of manufacturing industries that provided generations of employees with stable, well-paying jobs. In Japan, some have argued that the upside of globalization that the country witnessed in the 1960s and 1970s has now flipped to become a giant negative. Today, Japan's manufacturing base is at risk and real incomes have stagnated.

Beyond the politics of globalization, real and tangible barriers to globalization have not gone away. Customers continue to want localized products and services. The expansion of Domino's Pizza into Japan provides a fun example of localization pressures. To meet the unique taste preferences of Japanese customers, Domino's has added chicken teriyaki, corn, squid, tuna, and sautéed burdock root as pizza toppings. While you might think that pizzas are a globally standardized product, what goes on top of the pizza is definitely not the same in Tokyo and Chicago. In Greece, McDonald's serves a burger on pita bread (the Greek Mac); in Israel they have McKebab, and in Mexico you can order McMolletes—refried beans and salsa on an English muffin.[11]

Not only can tastes differ, but so too can even basic customer needs. Walmart learned this lesson the hard way when it entered several countries in Asia and stocked its stores with thick flannel shirts. While these shirts sold well in Wisconsin, they weren't going to find many customers in hot, humid Asian climates. Walmart also realized that the size of packages that appealed to Americans often repelled customers in Europe and Asia, who generally have smaller homes and less storage space.

Pressure for speedy delivery is another barrier to globalization. In many industries, suppliers are required by contract to have a local presence in order to guarantee speedy delivery of their products and services. While companies seem to be able to move fish and flowers around the world at the blink of an eye, just-in-time manufacturing has put enormous pressure on suppliers to locate component manufacturing and warehousing close to their customers. Effective global leaders understand this dynamic and often forgo the potential for economies of scale that come through globalization. For example, as Japanese auto manufacturers set up operations in the United States and Europe, parts suppliers follow close behind with production operations located next to the auto factories to ensure speedy and reliable delivery.

Sometimes global manufacturing just isn't worth the hassle. In other cases, the promised cost savings disappear when lower productivity, duties, lower quality, and delivery costs are factored in. These were all factors in General Electric's decision in 2012 to move manufacturing of several of its white goods products including washing machines, fridges, and heaters back from China to a factory in Kentucky.[12] Speed of delivery, reliability, and product control influenced Google's decision to assemble its MotoX phone in the United States. One of the key features of the phone is the ability to customize the colors of the phone through interchangeable panels. By locally assembling the phones, Google can promise delivery of the customized phones within 4 days.[13]

It isn't that companies with strong local operations haven't done well. While not getting as much press as many global giants, many highly localized companies have prospered over the past two decades. Take the example of Singapore-based CapitaLand. With profits in 2011 of S$ 2.09 billion, Southeast Asia's largest property developer had expanded aggressively over the past decade to the UK, Japan, China, Vietnam, Austria, and India. Commenting on the company's strategy for growth, the company's President and Group CEO Liew Mun Leong asserted that:

> Decentralization is the cornerstone of our operational success. The key strategy supporting decentralization is empowerment through proper delegation of authority to SBUs [strategic business units] and country offices. Leadership and management in these entities have been given the authority to act independently and quickly, to allow for fast decision-making and execution.[14]

> How do we make decentralization and delegation work? The answer lies in full empowerment and independence given to business CEOs to lead their business units. Each of the 20 CEOs is delegated the power to hire and fire, power to reward and power on financial authorities. CapitaLand believes that such empowerment is key to leadership development. "Grow by letting go" is one of the philosophies of our leadership development program.[15]

Getting the mix right

Clearly, the tensions between local and global have not disappeared. While every company is different, few can escape the reality of globalization and localization. Just as light takes on characteristics of both particles and waves, markets are in some ways global and in other ways local. Figuring out how to deal with this is the $64,000 dollar question.

In deciding how to approach the myriad of global and local opportunities they face, leaders have three core options. They can:

1. treat their markets as if they were *all* global; or
2. treat their markets as if they were *all* highly localized; or
3. adopt a "dual" perspective approach, which will allow them to master a myriad of local differences instead of being overwhelmed by them.

While option three—embracing a dual perspective—sounds like the obvious solution, it is the toughest by far of the three and challenges even the best minds and talents. To be successful balancing tensions, global leaders have to find ways not only to accept but also to exploit competing ways of looking at the world and of doing things.

As they embrace duality, global leaders are better able to define their problems and opportunities. They are also better able to make sense of an international marketplace laden with complex and often conflicting data. And by doing this they are better able to act decisively and, in doing so, to buffer the organization from much of the confusion they must be feeling. Elliott Nelson, former vice president of Learning and Development at Pfizer, commented on this:

> When looking for talent, the ability to make tradeoffs between global vision and local application is a critical characteristic. In my experience, there are few leaders who can balance this properly. Balancing local and global tensions is one of the defining characteristics of successful global leaders.

It isn't just about products

Many think global–local tradeoffs are built only around products or customer services. They would be mistaken. Because employee practices, government policies, technology usage, national cultures, and the like differ so widely, the pressures associated with the concept of duality mean that policies, procedures, and processes that your company establishes in one country may need significant revisions for other countries. As an example, while a company may establish a code of conduct with global application, it may also allow for global interpretation. Or a company may establish global policies over how it pays its employees, but the benchmarks it uses and the comparison sets with which it compares itself may be quite different in one country or one part of the world than another.

A company like Frito-Lay provides a good example of the challenges of getting the global–local balance right. Frito-Lay, which operates in over 200 countries, has approximately 85,000 sales representatives around the world. To be successful, each must develop close personal relationships with everyone on their routes. Sales at Frito-Lay is a highly personal, high-touch activity. At the same time, the company has built, from the ground up, an elaborate customer relationship management system. Now integrated with an extensive system at parent PepsiCo, the Frito system allows sales reps worldwide to enter sales data though a company portal, check credit, track manufacturing and shipping information, connect with product development teams, and the like. The system also allows for sales reps—and the entire Frito-Lay community—to access a wealth of company data globally, and in real time. It also allows for the collection and analysis of reams of highly local information all the way down to the personal information of local customers.

What is happening at Frito-Lay is typical of what happens at many other companies. Systems are developed and rolled out throughout the global organization. The costs of developing and maintaining the systems are supported by the global "whole." And the system is chock-full of data, best practices, and tools that can be rolled out anywhere and anytime just for the asking. At the same time, the system is designed to support and enable certain activities that are both local and high touch.

Balancing tensions requires sensitivities not only to what customers want and will support, but also to what employees need for their jobs. Frito-Lay's customer relationship management (CRM) system is never in perfect balance. At times there is too much local input, which leads to redundancies and duplication; at other times, the system is bent too far in favor of global centralization and head office rigidity. Managing these global–local tensions in *real time* is at the heart of global leadership.

We found a case of these complex dynamics at play at Pfizer in Europe, where the discovery, development, and registration of products are globally managed. In contrast, pricing and work with physicians are the responsibility of local subsidiaries. Generally, subsidiary leaders are not allowed to take initiatives in the discovery of new products because regulations are different from country to country throughout the world. For example, the U.S. Food and Drug Administration does not accept clinical tests from Japan, and Japan does not accept clinical tests from the United States. In contrast, Malaysia and the Philippines accept both U.S. and European testing. Frank Hickson, former senior vice president for pharmaceutical marketing and development at Pfizer Pharmaceuticals Japan, explained his response to these challenges: "We can and do take initiatives here in Japan in areas of distribution and marketing. We can also decide how aggressively we will push clinical trials. What we really control in Japan is the speed and competence of bringing products through clinical trials and marketing."

Getting balance in systems is never easy. One of the biggest problems for leaders is the tendency to generalize for the entire organization. Several years ago, one of the largest banks in the United States attempted to motivate its employees worldwide by handing out a small number of company stock certificates to each employee. While this incentive worked well for financially savvy employees, employees in many countries perceived the stock certificates as relatively worthless. As a result, they simply gave the certificates to other employees in the bank who saw their worth. The savvy employees actually accumulated more significant financial gains from the gifts of fellow employees' stock than from the increase in market value of their own stock. The initiative, well intentioned as it was, created more problems than it solved.

Beyond getting systems in balance, global–local tensions can be found in company norms of behaviors and values. One of the biggest hurdles is in the definitions of concepts. Take for example a company that we worked with based in Japan. One of the company's values was teamwork. OK, so far. A lot of companies espouse teamwork. But in Japan, people associated teamwork with harmonious interpersonal relationships, lots of socialization in the evenings before returning home, and shared decision making. In the Middle East, the company's affiliate in Dubai also espoused teamwork. But there, teamwork didn't mean socialization and harmony. They defined it in terms of sharing the workload and holding non-confrontational meetings. You weren't a team player if you were slacking off on your job while others were burning the midnight oil. And you weren't a team player if you publicly challenged others in meetings. Still this didn't stop people from confronting other team members privately or behind their backs. And it didn't extend to team decision making. And, certainly not to socializing after work.

Getting the balance right is not just about espousing global values. This is the easy part. After all, who could disagree with the values of honest customer centricity, teamwork, and respect? The tough part is determining to what extent the definition of these values should be globally standardized. And, who should determine the definition? Should Japanese leaders impose Japanese definitions of teamwork on their worldwide operations? Or should Japanese leaders define a principle only and let each country or local office decide? These are tough, gut-wrenching decisions and getting the right balance is nearly impossible.

Unfortunately, managers who don't like balancing tensions typically cling to overly rigid company policies. They want a security blanket, and being told what to do, when and how to do it, no matter the circumstances, can be that blanket. Global leaders, on the other hand, understand that company policies should be considered something like a great bridge—stable enough to cross, but flexible enough to sway when the wind blows or the load increases. They know that a bridge built too unyielding will quickly collapse under stress.

One of the keys to balancing tensions is recognizing that not everything needs to be either universal or local. At the end of the day, relatively few policies can or should be implemented uniformly throughout the world. As Figure 5.1 shows, certain core elements, such as superior customer service, should be globally standardized. Other elements, such as leadership style, may vary from region to region. Finally, some elements, such as specific recruiting tactics, may vary widely from local operation to local operation.

A key to effectively balancing global–local tensions is focusing your unit of analysis to the lowest unit of analysis possible. For example, it makes no sense to ask if Coca-Cola should globalize marketing. It does, however, make sense to split marketing into component activities—branding, advertising, sponsorships, etc.—and ask to what degree these activities should be globalized or localized. Doing so allows for far greater precision in determining the optimal level of globalization for the company. Clearly, globalization does not produce scale or scope advantages for all activities. In the final analysis, you may optimize

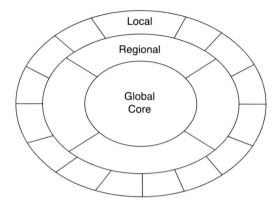

Global Core:	Examples may include purchasing, financial controls, definition of brands
Regional:	Examples may include management style, approach to customer relationship management
Local:	Examples may include recruiting, working norms, job titles

Figure 5.1 Managing globalization–localization tensions

some activities at the global level—with resulting global scale and scope advantages—and optimize others at the local level.

A key to balancing tensions is determining what activities, values, and the like should be globally integrated and what should be locally adapted in your company. As one senior finance executive from a major consumer products firm reasoned:

> Global leaders must have the capability to see an idea, a process, a technology, an approach to business, and be willing to not only reapply it, but to modify it to the degree and only to the degree that it is absolutely necessary for its success.

In reality, global leaders know that hard-and-fast corporate goals and policies must be supported and circumvented at the same time. Many managers are driven crazy by the personal risk and uncertainty associated with dynamic situations; they feel as if they're bumping their heads against the wall every day, all day long. Global leaders, on the other hand, emulate tightrope walkers who maintain their balance by constantly adjusting the angle of their poles. Freeze the angle of the pole by grasping for certainty in uncertain situations and you fall. Those who do not understand this, who are unwilling or unable to balance the necessary tensions of international business—they fail.

Indeed, American writer F. Scott Fitzgerald once observed that "the test of a first-rate intelligence is the ability to hold two opposed ideas in the mind at the same time, and still retain the ability to function." Global leaders do just that, while global followers either freeze up in these decision situations, or simply give in to one set of pressures while ignoring others.

Conclusions

Whether they are aware of it or not, superb global leaders have the perspective and experience to see what the designers of the F-16 fighter plane knew years ago: high performance requires the creation and support of dynamic tension, not its elimination. While the F-16 is one of the world's most agile fighter jets, it is an inherently unstable plane. To maximize maneuverability in sharp turns, the plane is designed to create opposing yaw and pitch forces. Without proper management of these aerodynamic forces, the plane would crash and burn. To handle the incredibly complex set of tensions, an onboard computer makes nearly a hundred complex calculations and adjustments per second. It is the continued existence of these contradictory forces and their effective management that contributes directly to the F-16 fighter jet's stellar maneuvering capabilities. At the time, they also increase the need for extraordinarily skilled pilots. Attempting to eliminate tensions would destroy exactly what makes the F-16 so effective.

Like those who design and fly the world's most sophisticated fighter planes, effective global leaders know that the dynamic tensions they encounter in international markets must be carefully managed. They live the advice of fighter pilot Chuck Yeager: "If you want to grow old as a pilot, you've got to know when to push and when to back off." Global leaders know when to push and when to back off. They recognize that tensions are absolutely necessary for high performance and that their focus on constant management and real-time adjustment are the keys to outmaneuvering the competition in global market dogfights. They embrace dualities by looking at a situation, suspending prior beliefs about it, creating a fresh perspective on the issue at hand, and—most importantly—acting on their insights. They embrace the duality of situations to arrive at better definitions of problems and opportunities; then they make choices based on these insights and act in spite of significant uncertainties. Gaining the perspective to master dualities is fundamental to your development as a global leader.

Notes

1 Eisenbert, E. (2009). "Ambiguity as Strategy in Organizational Communications." *Communications Monographs*, 51(3), 227–42.
2 Clampitt, P. G., Williams, M. L., and DeKoch, R. J. (2001). "Embracing Uncertainty: The Executive's Challenge." *Journal of Change Management*, 2(3), 212–28.
3 The foundations for good juggling can be found on the Juggling Information Service website, www.juggling.org (accessed 17 August 2013).
4 For more on the topic of global attention, see Birkinshaw, J., Bouquet, C., and Ambos, T. (2007). "Managing Attention in the Global Company." *Sloan Management Review*, Summer, 39–45.
5 These examples come from a variety of sources, including David Ricks, *Big Business Blunders: Mistakes in Multinational Marketing*. Homewood, IL: Dow Jones-Irwin,

1983, as well as Michael White, *A Short Course in International Marketing Blunders* (3rd Edition), Petaluma, CA: International Trade Press, 2009. Also, on the Internet, check out "10 Funniest Badly-Translated Ads" at: http://www.huffingtonpost.com/2011/05/12/funniest-badly-translated-ads_n_861030.html (accessed 3 July 2013). Other examples taken from the website: http://www.oddee.com/item_97732.aspx (accessed 28 August 2013).

6　Source: http://www.mckinsey.com/insights/leading_in_the_21st_century/ leading_in_the_21st_century

7　"Conoco's Dunham Makes Bold Moves to Hit Goal." *Wall Street Journal*, June 3, 1997, p. B4.

8　Source: http://yum.com/brands/china.asp

9　Source: http://techcrunch.com/2012/11/16

10　As reported by the BBC: http://www.bbc.com/culture/story/20130620-is-china-hollywoods-future.

11　Source: "Fast-food chains adapt to local tastes." *CNN Living*, April 8, 2010, http://www.cnn.com/2010/LIVING/homestyle/04/08/fast.food/index.html

12　Source: "Reshoring Manufacturing: Coming Home." *The Economist*, January 19, 2013.

13　Souce: "MotoX Has Promise, but Needs Polish." *International Herald Tribune*, August 7, 2013, p. 18.

14　Liew Mun Leong. (2011). *Building People—Sunday Emails from a CEO* (Volume 3). Singapore: Wiley, p. 180.

15　Liew Mun Leong. (2011). *Building People—Sunday Emails from a CEO* (Volume 2). Singapore: Wiley, pp. 287–8.

6 Global leaders exhibit character

Personal character forges the second critical dimension of global leadership. As we discussed in Chapter 3, the world is too big and diverse to command and control. Getting 100,000 employees in 100 different countries all marching in the strategic direction is no easy feat. Yet, as Sun Tzu, the Chinese military leader and philosopher concluded, "he whose ranks are united in purpose will be victorious."[1] How do global leaders get hordes of employees scattered across the globe united in purpose and direction? They achieve this not because they shout out orders from the top floor of corporate headquarters but because they have people's goodwill and trust.

Goodwill and trust cannot be ordered by superiors; they can only be given to them. Sometimes they are given in excess and sometimes in deficit of what is earned. Still, at the end of the day, people are free to give or withhold goodwill and trust. Our research found that it is a global leader's character that engenders the needed good will and trust. The most powerful elements of that character are manifest in emotional connections and integrity.

Emotional connections

To understand the powerful role of emotional connection, we need to appreciate that because trust is given, we should think of it as a gift—a personal gift. If you think about your own everyday life, to whom do you give your most personal gifts? Strangers? People with whom you have no emotional connection? Not likely. Most of us do not typically give gifts, especially personal ones, randomly to strangers. Typically, we give personal gifts to people whom we know and with whom we have a personal and to some degree emotional connection. Therefore, if people half a world away are going to follow out of goodwill and trust a leader's request, suggestion, plea, advice, policy, or decision, they are much more likely to do so if they feel an emotional connection *to* that leader and *from* that leader.

In support of this conclusion, we have held over 50 informal focus groups with employees and asked them about their willingness to follow the decisions of leaders who often live on the other side of the planet from them and whom they seldom see. Consistently they commented that they willingly followed those leaders in whom they had the greatest trust. When we asked them to describe how a particular leader engendered this trust, we received back some very consistent responses. At the top of this list was the notion of *empathy*. While many employees did not use this word, the words they did use got directly at the essence of empathy, as the following typical quotes indicate:

- She gets us.
- He understands our situation and at least takes it into consideration in making decisions.
- I have the feeling that she can relate to my situation.
- I feel she understands us.
- I don't always agree with his decisions that affect us, but at least he doesn't just view us as cogs in the gears.

Interestingly, we heard similar comments from other stakeholders (customers, suppliers, strategic partners, government officials, regulators, and so on) about the leaders in these companies whom they trusted the most. In every case, employees and other stakeholders expressed in one way or another that they felt the leader could understand and relate to them, and not just on an intellectual level but at an emotional level, which is at the heart of virtually any definition of empathy. Employees, especially, reciprocated this emotional connection and empathy with greater trust.

So how do effective global leaders convey that they understand and can relate to others? How do they create the needed emotional connections that engender trust? In our interviews both with executives and with those who work with and for them, three key actions emerged. Effective global leaders create emotional connections by (1) demonstrating a sincere concern for others; (2) listening effectively to people; and (3) understanding and respecting different viewpoints.

Demonstrating a sincere interest

Without a doubt trust is earned by being consistent, reliable, and having credibility. However, all the consistency, reliability, and credibility in the world does not generate much trust from others if they think that the leader is excessively self-centered, focused on his or her own interests, and takes little interest in the needs, feelings, situations, values, and so on of the people from whom the leader needs trust. You can almost think of trust as the outcome of consistency plus reliability plus credibility divided by the level of perceived self-interest. The higher one's self-interest and the lower one's interest in others, the lower the level of trust others are typically willing to give. The reason is quite simple. It is fundamentally not in someone's own self-interest to give a leader his or her trust and follow that leader when the leader's decisions and actions will be guided largely by what serves their own self-interest and is not guided by what serves the interests of whoever is giving the trust.

As subtle as it might seem, simply having sincere interest in others is necessary but not sufficient. Others need to perceive you have their interests at heart and can relate to their situation. While trust and relationships are important in every country, our research and that of others[2] suggest that the importance of relationships can range across countries and cultures from significant to critical. As a consequence, if you don't have the ability to project a sincere interest in others, you simply will not be able to do business in many countries.

When we spoke with Ravi Agarwal, a general manager at Intel Japan, he explained his company's challenge: "We need very close relationships with our customers here in Japan. It needs to be almost like a family." It is not enough for suppliers to be merely reliable; they must look after their customers' interests. "They need to feel that their problem is your problem," Agarwal continued. "How does an American company supply global Japanese consumer electronics and computer companies?" he asked. "It all comes down to relationships."

Such sentiments were the norm amongst the companies and leaders we studied. And it should come as no surprise that companies—and their leaders— that connect well with customers end up on top. In an interview with Wallace McCain, co-founder of McCain Foods (maker of one out of every three French fries sold in the world), and Chairman of Canada's largest food company until his death in 2011, we asked what was the key to his great success. His response, both simple and profound, was: "It isn't that complicated. At the end of the day, people do business with people they like." And a key element in any plan to get people to like you is to show a sincere interest in *them*.

The same central role relationships play in winning over customers applies to leading employees. If employees don't think their leader cares about them, they will not be happy or even willing followers. While a leader can order an employee to follow, unless they win over the hearts of employees, their ability to gain the discretionary efforts and attention of employees will be compromised.

Despite the importance of relationships, some managers have a difficult time appreciating emotional connections. Because relationships take time and provide benefits that are often difficult to quantify, managers who are fixated on short-term results often minimize the value in establishing lasting relationships.

This can be particularly problematic in cultures that place a high emphasis on relationships. Americans are often accused of being fast to call people friends, but weak on developing long-term, deep relationships. As one French manager we interviewed explained:

> It took some time for me to get used to American approaches to relationships. They are quick to pull out pictures of their kids and invite you to visit them whenever you are in their hometown. But then you never see them again and you are left to wonder if they were only being friendly to get you to buy something from them. We French have a different approach to relationships. We are slower at letting you in, but once we do we are friends for life.

No doubt culture plays a critical role in how leaders approach relationships. However, one thing became crystal clear in our research and it was something that transcended culture: effective global leaders actually *like* people. They successfully form business relationships because they actually enjoy talking with people and spending time with them. They seek out rich personal relationships. They care about people and want to make their lives better. Their interest is sincere; it is not an act, and it goes much deeper than Rolodex management.

We see the impact of sincerity in our coaching experiences. One Swedish manager we worked with was having a difficult time connecting with his team of 11 peers in his group. We asked him what he thought of them. His response: "They are mostly bright. But they stick together and won't let me in. I attend the meetings but I am not invited to the real discussions which take place in the corridors." We then asked him to provide one word that described how *they* thought of him. He thought for a moment, and then replied: "misanthropic" (definition: disliking humankind). And then he added a second adjective, "bitter." Whether his feelings were cause or effect is uncertain, but what is certain is that his ability to lead, or even be accepted, was being damaged by the perception that he simply didn't like people. Almost like a break in an electrical cable or wire, the greater the distance between the two ends, the more likely it is that electricity will fail to bridge the gap and a connection will fail to be made and the intended outcome will fail to be achieved.

As logical as this may seem, we have encountered companies that have advocated to their expatriate managers not to establish too close relationships with local people (employees, customers, regulators, and so on). They were told to stay a bit removed from and "above the fray." They advocated this on the basis of the belief that relationships actually hinder a global leader's ability to exert control and the fear that if leaders get too close to those they lead, they will "go native," lose their objectivity, and be less capable of making tough but needed decisions. While it is possible to allow feelings of empathy to crowd out good judgment, in our experience, rarely were those expatriates who followed the path of "staying above the fray" and not getting close to locals among the most effective leaders. Certainly they were not among the most trusted by the local employees on whom they depended for work to get done, nor were they among those who customers most wanted to do business with.

In many companies, a gulf—a sort of "us" versus "them" mentality—separated not only expatriate managers from local employees but separated head office from its international employees. Where this existed, it was often based on a mistaken reliance on command and control and a belief that developing relationships with locals would weaken or break the command and control system through which power is maintained.

Such a narrow-minded perspective, although not uncommon, can be disastrous. A Japanese deputy general manager of a multinational U.S. chemical company we interviewed was dealing with this exact problem. The subsidiary's general manager was an American from the company's international division. The deputy general manager was frustrated because his superior seemed interested only in maintaining the corporate perspective and discouraged any subsidiary initiatives. "There seems to be little room to maneuver because of the American general manager," the Japanese deputy GM lamented. "He speaks little Japanese and puts out very little effort to learn. He just seems eager to finish his assignment as soon as possible and go home." The Japanese manager had been with the company for 20 years and had witnessed this pattern of remoteness in every general manager he had worked under. "They don't understand us," he said with a shake of his head. "They act like they don't want to be here." No wonder there were problems!

This difficulty in communication and lack of mutual respect is not an uncommon problem for expatriate managers and it can be tremendously destructive. Without close personal relationships with expatriate managers, good local people lose commitment to or leave the organization entirely. Even with the best products, global companies cannot succeed overseas without strong local support. Establishing sincere relationships is essential in developing local leaders and in getting the most out of the global organization. To the degree that local leaders can empathize with global leaders as people, they are more likely to want and be able to emulate global leader behaviors.

As we mentioned earlier, having sincere interest is necessary but not sufficient. Effective global leaders have to demonstrate their interest so that it can be perceived. However, demonstrating a sincere interest takes effort. It requires that a leader spend quality time with people and have frequent and positive interactions. And for these interactions to produce emotional connections with people they cannot be limited to business content. Personal contact is essential. Vincent Lo, founder and chairman of Shui On Group, a Hong Kong-based property developer and construction giant, has made countless trips to China since the company's start in 1971. His objective was to show his sincerity and to build relationships. He spent so much time building relationships with business and government officials that he earned the nickname "King of *Guangxi*." His relationship building over a long period of time helped to turn his firm into one of the most successful foreign investors in China.[3] George Cohen, president of McDonald's Canada, estimated that he made over 100 trips to Russia before opening McDonald's first fast-food restaurant in Moscow in 1990. Although a great deal of business was done, particularly during latter trips, time after time he returned to Russia solely to build relationships. His commitment to establishing sincere relationships was at the core of the venture's success.

While Vincent Lo and George Cohen demonstrated their interest through face-to-face interactions, others rely on email messages or social media to provide a more personal touch. Liew Mun Leong, founder and CEO of CapitaLand Group, one of the world's largest property developers, is famous for his "Sunday emails" to all employees. In our interview with him, he discussed the importance of these personal emails in connecting with his employees:

> In my Sunday emails I talk about our company's values and our business experiences. I also talk about what I have been doing and seeing during the past week. These are long emails and are often quite personal. I take a lot of care and put a lot of attention into them. I learned long ago of the need to stay away from politics and religion, and to be sure to use the right language in

these emails for fear of offending anyone or miscommunicating. I send the email to 12,000 employees. And they have been a powerful tool for me.

Many of Leong's emails have now been captured and reprinted in three volumes entitled *Building People—Sunday Emails from a CEO*.[4]

In establishing emotional connections, the leader must overcome the temptation to succumb to pride. Some executives are simply too proud to go through the relationship-building process, particularly when it comes to interactions with low-ranking employees in the company. We have seen CEOs who stand in line with their employees at the company lunch canteen and we have seen CEOs who would not be caught dead eating with their employees; we can attest to the palpable difference in attitudes which the employees have for their CEOs. There is no substitute for rubbing shoulders with employees when it comes to connecting with them. Mass communication technology, especially when it is personalized, can be effective at reaching thousands of employees scattered across scores of countries. However, in our experience, the stories told about top executives' personal encounters with regular employees often have as big an impact as if employees had had the encounter themselves.

In interacting with employees, effective global leaders understand the need to project confidence and calm, particularly in the face of stress. Aggressivity and anger can be a leader's greatest enemies when it comes to emotional connections. Richard Branson provides a ready example of a global leader who projects warmth and caring even when times get tough. In a recent interview, Branson reflected on his approach to leadership:

> What leadership boils down to is people. Whatever your style, whatever your method, you need to believe in yourself, your ideas and your staff. Nobody can be successful alone—and you cannot be a great leader without great people to lead. You have to walk the walk as well as talk the talk. Nobody respects a leader who doesn't know how to get his hands dirty.[5]

A key to emotional connections is treating people with respect. This does not have to be costly. But it does require creativity that often translates to simple, basic gestures. Successful global leaders think of things like flying the flag of a foreign customer's home country when they arrive for a business meeting after a long flight or arranging for special meals or site visits. Simple things like avoiding the use of jargon and speaking slowly also show respect. One of the American companies we worked with was hosting a delegation from an Israeli client. Even though all of the visitors spoke good English, the company's director of business development arranged for presentations to be done in Hebrew. The visitors were impressed that so much effort was made to make them feel at ease. It was a simple gesture that generated valuable goodwill.

Learning, or attempting to learn, a foreign language is a highly effective way to demonstrate interest in other people. People appreciate the gesture because they know that learning a foreign language is difficult and represents the leader's personal commitment to the country and customer. One senior international human resource executive at Merck believed that language was the most critical determinant of demonstrating a sincere interest:

> At some point you have to have some visible signs that you respect the people, the culture, the history which you are going into. And it could be anything from sincere, honest, ongoing efforts to learn and speak their language, to understand their cultures, their customers, and their foods. What I've found is even if you stumble through the language, the fact that you're making some real, honest, sincere efforts, that in and of itself really broke down some barriers. Initially, you may be met with a lot of laughter, but taking the time to learn the language is important to connecting with the people.

Genuinely listening to people

Being interested in people is not the same as genuinely listening to people. For others to feel understood, you must not only have a genuine interest but also excel at picking up verbal and nonverbal communication. It is an active rather than a passive process.

Bhavesh Shah, global head of procurement for Swiss-based Fermenich, commented on the importance of listening:

> Active listening is critical. It can be too easy when you are in a leadership position to do all the talking. This is consistent with a Western approach to leadership. But this is not what I want to do. I have a natural appreciation for listening. I got this because I grew up having to learn other peoples' cultures. I have had to do a lot of listening in my life. And I appreciate how important this is in global business.

In an international setting, especially, it can be exceedingly difficult to listen effectively. We found three common barriers to effective listening: (1) managers falsely assume that everyone *already* thinks the way they do; (2) managers mistakenly believe that everyone *should* think the way they do; and (3) managers let language and cultural differences impede communication.

The "everyone thinks the same" assumption

Naive international managers often make the mistake of believing that everyone within the company thinks in a similar way. In most cases, this could not be further from the truth. Cultural differences, background, position in the hierarchy, training, proximity to the market, and perceived self-interest are all reasons why people view things differently.

Unfortunately, many managers leave their common sense at home when they travel overseas. When we asked a British executive of a U.S. multinational about her perception of executives from headquarters, she related the following:

> I too often watch our senior managers come to England from the head office in the U.S. They make a big speech to a group in London and assume the audience has the same background, beliefs, and sense of humor as he or she does. They try to ingratiate themselves, and yet they end up alienating themselves even further.

Believing that people think the same way around the world is a problem rooted in low inquisitiveness and is a key barrier to emotionally connecting with people. It suggests a superficial understanding of the aspirations, interests, and feelings of people. Faulty assumptions about the way people think is one of the major reasons companies fail in their efforts to penetrate international markets. For decades, for example, U.S. automobile companies sold left-hand drive cars in Japan, a country where people drive on the opposite side of the road. The large U.S. cars were too big for Japanese parking spaces and impossible to maneuver through Japanese toll booths, where money is collected on the right-hand side of the car. Other high-profile companies that have botched their globalization efforts include UK-based Tesco's expansion in the United States and Walmart's disastrous efforts to move into Germany.

The "everyone should think the same way" mistake

An even more difficult problem arises when managers believe that everyone—both inside and outside the company—*should* think the same way. Americans in particular have been accused of this sort of cultural arrogance in international business. Around the world, many believe that Americans think they have all the answers and know how to solve every problem. Others are often offended when Americans try to impose their management systems and values on them. This view was expressed by a vice president at Cargill, one of the largest private companies in the world. This vice president commented on what he had observed in the course of making a number of trips to Brazil to negotiate two separate joint ventures:

> The Brazilians are generally a very friendly people. They ask how my children are doing. They want to see pictures. They want you to meet their families. If you don't genuinely like these people, it will come through. Sometimes they feel that Americans believe that the U.S. is the only place where things are done right. Many think we are culturally arrogant. Too many Americans come to Brazil hoping to change the way Brazilians do business. If we want to be successful in Brazil, I've learned we need to do business the way the Brazilians do business.

While this example involves American ethnocentrism, countless other examples can be found involving managers from other countries.

Within companies, another type of arrogance is often observed: the assumption that the head office knows best and need never change its beliefs. A senior human resource executive at a large U.S. consumer products company shared with us an incident at a meeting in Amsterdam involving managers from the company's Northern European offices and American headquarters. A manager from the company's Amsterdam office asked the American vice president of human resources some tough, critical questions during a presentation. In the Netherlands, managers are expected to be "very forceful in making objections and so forth," he explained. "And this guy from Amsterdam took a very much 'in your face' type of approach. But it was done with respect." While the man from Amsterdam was asserting himself, an American sitting next to the executive we interviewed leaned over and whispered, "I hope that guy has a big bank account." The message was clear to the executive we interviewed: "The guy from Amsterdam was not doing it the American way, which is to bow humbly and say he's our leader so I won't ask these types of questions in a public forum—probably not even in a private forum." In this example, the American did not think overseas managers should have a significant role in decision making. Given this, there was no point in listening to what they had to say. In fact, global leaders know that it is the very rare idea or product that is perfect enough to sweep the world without undergoing some adaptation for foreign markets. Global leaders understand that good ideas can come from every corner of the world.

Genuine cultural barriers

Despite the best intentions, cultural and language barriers can severely restrict a leader's ability to listen effectively. It takes great effort and patience to understand the heart and soul of people. Working out the cultural nuances of communication can be a painstaking process. In Japan, for example, the word *kekko* can mean both "yes" and "no." Determining when "yes" means "yes" and "no" means "no" requires a deep understanding of context and nonverbal communication. This becomes a huge problem in such activities as negotiating contracts, working with government regulators, and establishing employee work expectations.

Overcoming genuine cultural barriers is a real problem for anyone working in a foreign culture. We met a senior partner in a major management consulting firm who shared an example of the difficulty of overcoming cultural barriers:

> I have been to the Middle East countless times. I have worked in nearly every Arabic country and I must say I enjoy my visits. On a recent trip to the Gulf I was invited to meet the senior HR executive for a major company in the Emirates. She was a local Emirati woman and she was also the most senior woman in her company. I was ushered into her office. She stood up from her desk and moved towards me in a welcoming gesture. I extended my hand

expecting her to reach out and shake my hand. Instead she froze. Then in a stern voice she said, "I don't shake hands." I was stunned. In all my life I have never experienced someone who wouldn't shake my hand. And for an instant I thought, "Who is this woman that she won't even shake my hand?" I was offended. I was insulted. And then I smiled to myself. I realized that in this part of the world many traditional women would never shake the hand of a man they had never met. While I knew this intellectually, my initial reaction surprised me. I had not internalized a proper approach to greeting women in these kinds of settings. So my instincts took over and this led to a very awkward situation. I learned that our behaviors are so ingrained that they often get ahead of our intellect.

Similar cases of cultural misunderstanding can have a severe adverse effect on your company's business interests.

In the absence of cultural sensitivity, mistakes frequently occur. One example arose in our interviews with a seasoned American manager based in Singapore. This manager, who had over ten years' experience in Asia, described an insensitive American superior, who was placed in charge of the entire Asian region, as "an American cowboy, acting just like a bull in a china shop when he'd go into a meeting with Asians." Because he had never lived in Asia, the American superior had no understanding of the subtle cultural nuances that exist there. "He was just kind of a Wild West American, six gun on the side, and away he went. He offended quite a few, and in the end he was terminated."

Understanding different viewpoints

Emotionally connecting with people requires more than sincere interest and skillful listening. It requires that you be able to understand many different sorts of people. To understand people, you need to be familiar with local conditions. Local conditions establish the context from which people develop and express their viewpoints. To understand different viewpoints, global leaders must relate personally to the lives of employees, customers, and others who are relevant to the business.

Sam Tan, Chief Operating Officer of MGF Sourcing, a multibillion-dollar sourcing company in the apparel industry, commented on his approach to understanding people of different cultures:

Part of the way you connect with people is by adapting yourself to them. When I am in Malaysia, I speak Malaysian English. When I am in India, I try to take on Indian habits. I don't do it deliberately. I find myself doing it naturally. You have to have a mindset that is very open. You cannot think there is a right way or a wrong way of doing things. I am non-judgmental.

I think the key is to be curious. You have to ask a lot of questions. And this becomes automatic. It is very difficult to cheat on this. You have to be genuine. You cannot be an actor, unless you are very good. And few people are. People are very perceptive and will easily understand when you are faking.

Effective global leaders put significant effort into understanding the context so that they can better determine how to interact with people in general and, more specifically, how to provide appropriate leadership. For example, how a 40-year-old American expatriate manager delegates to a 35-year-old Japanese subordinate with a U.S. MBA needs to differ significantly from the way in which she delegates to a 55-year-old Japanese subordinate with no U.S. experience. To delegate successfully, the American manager should pay much greater deference to the 55-year-old Japanese subordinate. For the young subordinate, she might be more direct about the assignment and comment on how confident she is in the subordinate's ability to take on the new task. To the older subordinate, she might be wise to first ask his general views regarding the problems and challenges relative to the assignment she might have in mind. She might even have more than one conversation with the subordinate about the issue. In the end, she might delegate the assignment to the older subordinate by asking for his help on the issue rather than saying she is delegating it to him.

We worked closely with a U.S.-based petroleum exploration company that had set up offices in southern China. To entice American managers to leave their comfortable homes in the United States, the company moved its expatriates into a gated housing compound not far from its Chinese headquarters. Expatriates were given subsidized housing comparable to U.S. standards—3,000 to 4,000 square feet in size, Western-style washing machines, dishwashers, etc.—plus a car and driver. Many expatriates expected these "perks" to soften the challenges of what they perceived as a hardship posting. Many local Chinese had a much different response. They had a clear view of the American compound from the top floors of the subsidiary's offices. The Chinese lived in much smaller and far less appealing apartments. As was the norm for China, the U.S. company did not provide the Chinese with washing machines, dishwashers, or cars and drivers. Even though the Americans listened to the concerns of the Chinese managers, they could not fully relate to their local counterparts' experience. In an attempt to improve relations, American managers sometimes invited the Chinese to their homes for social functions. Embarrassed by their poor living conditions, the Chinese felt they could not reciprocate, which left them in an awkward position and even more aware of the inequities that existed. This situation provides a classic example of listening without really understanding.

Not surprisingly, neither side fully understood the other. Many of the Chinese employees felt that although the Americans lived in China, their hearts were still back home in the United States. In contrast, many expatriate Americans blamed the Chinese for being lazy, unappreciative, and difficult to train. What the Americans failed to appreciate was the concern of the Chinese employees that no matter how well they performed, they could never receive the benefits Americans had come to expect. They simply lacked a comparable incentive for self-improvement. The Americans listened, but were too absorbed in their own difficulties to fully understand; similarly, the Chinese listened but also failed to fully understand the business performance stresses the Americans were under. The result was friction in the relationship that compromised the ability of the Americans to lead as effectively as they wanted in the Chinese venture.

Understanding differing viewpoints can be a painstaking process. Global leaders go out of their way to connect with individuals in far-flung locations. They shake hands, eat with employees, and pay attention with all of their senses. They visit customers in their offices and homes. They work hard at "being with" people—all kinds of people.

How far should you go in working to understand different viewpoints? Is it possible to go so far that you lose your own distinctiveness? Steve Holliday, CEO of the National Grid, one of the world's largest power transmission companies, offered some interesting insights into how global leaders approach very real cultural gaps:

> Over the years, I have worked with some great global leaders. What I see in these leaders is the ability to become like the people they are with. Teenagers are good at this. They can pick out the subtleties of fitting in. They can move from group to group and know what shoes to wear, what brand of jeans to wear, and so on. In some ways global leaders have the same basic skills that teenagers display. Instead of clothes, they seem to be very good at picking out a couple of key things that let them fit in. Global leaders are experts at figuring out the few things they need to say or do that will enable them to communicate effectively with people from different cultures. These tricks help them establish close personal relationships with people.

Emotional connections improve decision making

By emotionally connecting with people, leaders can significantly improve the quality of their decision making. Global leaders cannot fully understand current and evolving customer needs, competitors, and local conditions when they are acting in isolation. They must tap the eyes, ears, and best insights of their employees. And they must have the goodwill of external stakeholders to get them to open up and share their insights and interests. Connecting with people—both inside the company and out—provides quality information that is essential in keeping a company vibrant in a highly competitive global marketplace.

Emotionally connecting with people improves the quality of decisions in two ways. First, when leaders have close relationships with people in the field, they are far more likely to be fully accepted by them when they are overseas. Employees and customers open up more readily when they feel at ease with a visiting executive. They are much more prone to make honest and forthright comments when they feel understood by an outsider. Second, when leaders have close relationships with people in the field, they will receive more unsolicited information from them. Subordinates open up when they feel they are being listened to and understood, when they know that what they say matters.

But key to making this work is actually spending time around people. There are no short cuts in establishing strong personal connections with people. An international marketing executive in a Fortune 500 company underscored this point. "I just love being around people and talking to people," he began. He told us that he typically spends about 80 percent of his time out in the field with the sales force versus 20 percent of his time in administrative duties at home office. He continued:

> This approach gives me a clearer understanding of the sales force's needs. Then, when I spend that 20 percent of my time with [internal] staff, I can actually talk to them based on a real understanding of the field, rather than trying to learn details through emails across the water. Global leaders must know the people who make their business work. They are more important to you than anything else, because if you don't connect with them, you should just write off the deal.

Connecting with people promotes trust and goodwill

In today's complex and far-reaching organizations, solutions to problems and customers' needs come more from cooperation than from command-and-control processes. As a consequence, effective global leaders need webs of influence rather than "solid line" authority and reporting relationships. To be successful, leaders need to establish mutual trust with a host of other people. Our observation is that the best global leaders recognize that they have to build up their relationship bank accounts before, and in some cases long before, the leader needs to draw on that bank account.

Emotionally connecting with people also promotes goodwill. Goodwill goes a long way in facilitating strategy implementation. It encourages employees to give their leader the benefit of the doubt in trying times and on difficult matters. It also helps secure the best efforts of employees. In many cases employees will make huge sacrifices to help out their leader when they are motivated by goodwill. We saw examples of this throughout the world.

While in Japan, we were told an interesting story that illustrates the benefits of emotional connections. Shinichi Suzuki, the father of the Talent Education Movement that has swept the music world, was drafted by the Japanese military during World War II and assigned to manage a plant that prepared cypress wood for airplane manufacture. He knew nothing about managing a manufacturing plant nor about assembling airplanes. But he understood people and decided early on to treat the workers at his plant as if they were members of his own family. He started every workday at the plant by playing the violin to the assembled workers. After playing, Suzuki would often provide some gentle advice: Be kind to your spouse, teach your children, save money, and so on. He concluded early on that the employees knew far more than he ever would about cypress or airplanes and that his role was to help them "want" to do their jobs better.

Suzuki seemed genuinely interested in the needs of his employees. Most were terribly poor and many of their homes were in disrepair. He authorized the use of excess cypress from the plant's operations to keep all the workers' homes in condition. Full-time carpenters were sent out from the plant to work on employees' homes. Suzuki also knew that most of his employees had no financial reserves and worried greatly about their security. He promised the workers that if they devoted themselves to raising the plant's output, he would share the dividends with them. When the plant's output did go up, he gave each worker 500 yen, an amount that would give them security in the event of an emergency. The plant's efficiency rose even higher. Newspapers took notice, printing articles about the air force plant managed by a musician.

Suzuki's secret was simple: he cared about his employees and built warm personal relations with them. Concerning this he said, "During our short lifetime, being devoted to the same task with everyone helping each other creates a deep refreshing feeling, and both the employee and the employer care about each other."[6] After the war, these same principles of caring and empathy became the heart of Suzuki's world-famous music education methods.

Establishing goodwill in relationships outside the company also gives many tangible benefits. Goodwill facilitates sensitive negotiations and reduces the need for costly oversight. In the spring of 1997, Volkswagen relied on the goodwill of its executives at its Czech subsidiary, Skoda, to win approval to assemble cars from kits in Russia. In a similar case, managers at the Swire Group in Hong Kong used their goodwill relationships in the Peoples' Republic of China to establish numerous joint ventures in that country. Global leaders at virtually every company use goodwill to promote their companies' self-interests. What separates effective global leaders from the rest of the pack is their creativity and strategic foresight in doing so. The manager of materials purchasing and transportation for the U.S. petroleum company we worked with in China shared some interesting insights into establishing and leveraging connections in China:

> Relationships are everything. China has laws to stop you from doing anything it wants to stop. You need the relationships to help you figure out how to get things done. Initially, we hit the shore ready to work, as opposed to ready to get the relationship going. This means that you end up first contacting the government when you have a problem. This starts things off on a bad note. . . . Another problem is that when most experts have something go wrong, they send Chinese nationals to solve it. So the government people never see or interact with you. So take the time to go down there and say, "We are going to be starting an operation here and we are not anticipating any problems, but our operations are so big that I know that they are going to come; and what I am here to do is to introduce myself to you and say first of all that if anyone working for us does anything wrong, here is my card for me to help you work that out." The relationship here is always something you have to work on. The primary objective should be to meet the government agencies, the police department, the customs, the social security bureau, and

so on. . . . For example, I probably go out to dinner or have drinks with the local head of Chinese customs once every two weeks. We have a relationship where we can say, "Hey, what are you doing tonight?"

Goodwill can go a long way in determining the stability of joint ventures, in promoting dialogue with customers and governments, and in facilitating strategy implementation. In the example above, goodwill came only after personal relationships were established with the appropriate local officials. It would be naive to suggest that the local Chinese initiated these relationships; it would also be naive to suggest that they came naturally and easily to the American manager. He had to work at them. But over time, friendships emerged. There was a bonding of sorts. Emotional connections were made. And these connections have served the manager and the American subsidiary well by producing goodwill.

How do you know you are connecting with people? This is a tough question to answer, in part because employees won't usually tell their boss what they actually think. Sam Tan, Chief Operating Officer of MGF Sourcing, offers a personal experience that taught him a powerful lesson in the power of goodwill:

I think back to an experience I had in 2004. At the time, I had been working for the company for less than a year. Out of the blue, I got a call from a headhunter. He wanted to talk to me about a very significant new job in a large MNC [multinational company]. To me the job was a perfect fit. And it even included a substantial pay raise. I decided to go ahead with the interview and was offered the job shortly thereafter. On a Friday, I decided that I would accept the job and I determined that I would tell my boss the following Monday that I would be leaving. I spent the entire weekend trying to figure out how to tell my boss. In the end, I decided not to take the job. Even though it made complete sense to make the move, I could not bring myself to tell my boss I was leaving. I felt that there would be a sense of betrayal. And why did I feel this way? I respected my boss. But there is more to it than just respect. My boss had created an environment more like a family. It felt like I belonged here and leaving would be like abandoning my family.

I look back on this, and, in retrospect, it was a good decision for me to stay. But, the leadership lesson has stuck with me. When I ask myself if I am doing a good job connecting with people, I wonder: "Am I building a similar sense of belonging with people who are my followers?"

Connecting with people is emotional, not rational. It is not always about being right. Human beings are more often than not emotionally driven.

Emotional connections and business: some concluding comments

Establishing emotional connections is essential for leaders to maximize their effectiveness as a global leader. However, developing emotional bonds with people is not the same as "going native" and taking on the personas of your employees. Leaders who are interested in people, who are excellent listeners, and who are familiar with local conditions do not have to become like the people they are with. While leaders may need to change the parts of themselves that interfere with communication and are obstacles to empathy, they cannot lose sight of their position as a leader. Rather than passively accept local input, leaders must consider it carefully and weigh it against the greater needs of the global corporation. While effective global leaders keep an open mind, they never forget who they are or what they represent.

Integrity

Integrity forms the bedrock of excellent character and is essential in establishing genuine emotional connections with people. We define integrity as having and demonstrating a strong commitment to personal and company standards. This includes ethical behavior as well as loyalty to the company's agreed-upon values and strategies.

Both personal and company standards are substantially more prone to compromise when managers are overseas. When far removed from corporate oversight, managers face increased pressure to modify their personal ethics and alter their unit's standards to appeal to local values and demands. In many cases, such "flexibility" can bring short-term gains. Yet despite the opportunities for short-term advantage, the global leaders we studied were most effective when they consistently maintained the highest ethical standards in personal and company matters.

Ethical according to personal and company standards

Ethics is a tricky subject for most people. It involves moral decisions about right and wrong. Some kinds of behavior are black and white, judged similarly in all cultures—murder, blackmail, cheating, sabotage, and the like. However, there are plenty of gray areas that dot the international landscape. And how leaders maneuver through these gray areas will have a big impact on their ability to generate trust and goodwill.

While all managers inevitably confront ethical issues, global leaders face them regularly. Global leaders deal with ethical questions on two broad levels. The first involves those external activities by which a company is evaluated by the outside world. In these cases, the leader—as a representative of their company—can contribute positively or negatively to their company's ethical image. Second, ethical behavior includes internal activities involving the company's own units and employees. In these internal activities, the leader's appearance of ethical or unethical behavior is reviewed by employees, who—like it or not—will judge behaviors. Employees are constantly looking for inconsistencies and examples of hypocrisy and self-serving or indulgent practices demonstrated by their boss. Without appropriate ethical behavior inside and outside the company, neither the boss nor your company can lead over the long run.

External relationships

Ethical behaviors in relationships outside the firm pose particularly difficult challenges in a global context. One thing to consider is the difference between dominant behaviors within the national culture (i.e., descriptive ethics) and the judgments of what behaviors should be, irrespective of culture (i.e., normative ethics). Clearly, a global leader needs to understand the ethical norms in the country and markets where their company operates; not surprisingly, these norms can differ significantly. For example, in what was dubbed the Cowgate scandal, a Malaysian cabinet minister redirected almost RM 250 million (US\$82 million) in agriculture sector development funds to her own family. As was reported, the funds were intended to "'help transform Malaysia's cattle and beef industry' and reduce Malaysia's dependence on beef imports." Despite the enormous public outrage, "the politician still holds a senior position within the dominant party of the ruling coalition, the United Malays National Organization (UMNO)."[7] In this incident, what outsiders viewed as unacceptable was more accepted within the country and context.

When leaders act unethically, the negative consequence for the company can be profound and long-lasting. We only need to think of Enron to be reminded of the impact on not only the company's employees and shareholders, but its auditor Arthur Andersen. Beyond the headline-grabbing examples, academic research has shown that when unethical behavior is discovered and made public, companies inevitably suffer significant negative effects on their stock price and that unethical behaviour decreases a firm's wealth over an extended period of time.[8]

Internationally, problems occur when the leader encounters ethical norms in a particular part of the world that differ from company policies. This can happen in two ways. The first is relatively easy to deal with. It involves working in countries that lack strong legal systems and which permit behaviors that would not be tolerated at home, such as they ignore or leave unregulated pollution or abusive employment practices. Companies are not penalized nor are they censured for following a higher "law" or code of conduct. The second ethical challenge is more difficult to manage. It involves *requirements* that the company or its leaders act in ethically troubling ways as the price for doing business. Bribes and kickbacks are two common examples of these provisions. When your ethical standards are different from the norms of behavior in a particular country, you and your company have three basic choices: (1) you can avoid doing business in that particular country—this is what Levi Strauss has done in China;[9] (2) you can maintain your standards and risk being placed at a competitive disadvantage versus firms that follow the prevailing norms; or (3) you can change your standards and play the game the way the locals do. Our experience suggests that this last option, maintaining a checkerboard approach to ethical standards, is not sustainable in global companies.

One incident reported to us by an international vice president at a large U.S.-based bank underscores the importance of establishing and adhering to strict global ethical standards. The bank, although relatively inexperienced in international business, had seen huge opportunities to expand its business portfolio in Southeast Asia. Within a short time, it had negotiated a position as lead lender in a major power plant being built in the region. Over time it provided more than $800 million in financing for the project. Delay followed delay, and after some years, the power plant was still not operational.

Rather than write down the loan, the U.S.-based vice president instructed the bank's country manager—an American—to become actively involved in moving the project along. The manager pressed the lead contractor, who explained that a huge stumbling block was the refusal of the district water commissioner to finish the final water hookups to the plant. The banker decided to meet with the water commissioner himself. Feeling unsure how to proceed in the upcoming meeting, the banker asked an American friend for advice. The friend advised his banker friend that all local government officials were corrupt and that "grease" money would open the right doors.

The banker took matters into his own hands and arranged a meeting with the water commissioner at the best restaurant in the city. In preparation for the dinner meeting, the banker purchased a fancy wallet and placed in it fifty crisp $100 bills. A limousine was sent for the water commissioner to take him to the restaurant, where the banker met him at the front door. The water commissioner was seated first. As the banker sat down, he popped out of his back pocket the previously prepared wallet. It hit the floor with a thud, and the banker then picked it up. He looked inside, and finding no identification, turned to the water commissioner and said, "This is not my wallet. It must be yours." He then slid the wallet across the table. The water commissioner looked inside, paused, and then slid it back saying, "This must not be my wallet either. Mine had $25,000 in it." The story would be incomplete without mentioning that, unbeknownst to the banker, the water commissioner had hired a photographer to record the entire episode for future use. (As a postscript, the banker was saved by good fortune. At the time there was considerable unrest in the country in question. Within a week of the incident in the restaurant, the government fell and the water commissioner was out of a job. But the banker learned an important lesson on crossing ethical boundaries.)

Once ethical boundaries have been crossed, others will almost certainly exploit the breach. Global leaders and large multinational companies are high-profile targets and must develop global standards of conduct. When matters of ethical misconduct come to light—even in remote locations of the world—their impact inevitably surfaces in the company's home country as well. Questionable behavior in one country can rarely be contained. Eventually the entire world finds out. Global leaders understand that global companies have global reputations.

When moving into ethical backwaters, leaders often mistakenly assume that their home governments will provide guidance on issues of right and wrong. They are typically disappointed. The 29 countries of the OECD agreed in 1996 to make it illegal for corporations to claim bribes as tax deductions.[10] The U.S. government tends to be stricter than most in regulating conduct. U.S. corporations are bound by the provisions of the Foreign Corrupt Practices Act (FCPA), which prohibits U.S. companies from bribing foreign government officials or officers of political parties. While the FCPA does not technically affect foreign subsidiaries, in practice it applies to the degree that policies or money can be traced back to the U.S. parent company. Interestingly, since 2008, the U.S. Justice Department and Securities and Exchange Commission have extracted billions of dollars in criminal and civil penalties over alleged violations of the 1977 law.[11] In November 1997, the OECD extended its regulation of corporate "gifts" by approving a complete ban on bribery. The rules, while in many ways similar to those covered by the FCPA, were extended to cover executives at state-owned enterprises as well as members of parliament.

Despite the direction provided by some governments, most managers know that there are abundant gray areas not formally covered by the act. For example, where does one draw the line between a gift and a bribe? In countries like China and Saudi Arabia, where does the government end and the private sector begin? Further, how should activities of joint-venture partners be interpreted?

To get around the ambiguity and to minimize corporate exposure, an increasing number of global leaders are pushing to adopt strict, company-specific codes of conduct. Because the tremors of ethical misconduct are often felt around the world, stringent global policies on gifts and gratuities have become more common. In some cases, most notably Walmart and General Motors (GM), policies forbid all gifts beyond the most nominal of trinkets. Disney limits receiving gifts up to $75 dollars, but will approve gifts up to $500 under certain conditions. To encourage compliance, many companies publicize their policies on their websites.

Many companies are now pressuring suppliers to support their codes of conduct. This is common in the apparel industry, in electronics, and in the extractive industries. Typical is way Apple has extended its code of conduct to the company's suppliers:

> [Apple's Supplier Code of Conduct] requires suppliers to provide safe and healthy working conditions, to use fair hiring practices, to treat their workers with dignity and respect, and to adhere to environmentally responsible practices in manufacturing. But our Code goes beyond industry standards in a number of areas, including ending involuntary labor practices and eliminating underage labor.[12]

While it is always difficult to assess the economic payback of such initiatives, they no doubt bring costs and benefits to companies operating overseas. But if not carefully managed, they can severely restrict global competitiveness and in some cases may go too far. No doubt, U.S. companies are losing the business war in many parts of the world because of unnecessarily restrictive policies. In international contexts, for example, a manager's inability to pay for a customer's dinner or a round of golf is viewed with disdain.[13]

Finding a balance between what is ethically unacceptable—stealing, for example—and what should be negotiable is a critical and challenging task for global leaders. As a global leader, you must continually raise questions about what is appropriate and what is not. Tough cases must be championed and aired in the open within your company. In-house education and training programs must be promoted to inform employees of nonnegotiable policies.

Ethical decisions are not just limited to reacting to local laws and contractors. They include proactive moves that companies can make to benefit the local environment or society at large. More and more companies are searching for creative ways to push ethics beyond codes of conduct to include social responsibility. This requires proactive thinking and a broader vision that pushes the company beyond a fixation on short-term profits. One example of a forward-thinking company is French foods giant Group Danone, which has formed a joint venture with Grameen Bank to create a social business that sells a nutritious yogurt at a dramatically reduced price in poor villages of Bangladesh. Dell has worked with supplier Unisource to develop new packaging made from Forest Stewardship Council (FSC) compostable bamboo, now used to ship 70 percent of Dell notebooks. And IKEA is working with NGO partners to train cotton suppliers in India in integrated pest management, water conservation techniques, low-contamination harvesting techniques, and to promote decent working conditions for farmers. Patagonia, in partnership with the Nature Conservancy, has announced plans to restore 15 million acres of grassland in Argentina. They are committed to working with ranchers and farmers to ensure sustainable sheep-grazing to supply woolen products. Interestingly, research has shown that leaders who strongly support social responsibility are also rated higher on ethical leadership than their peers.[14]

Internal relationships

High ethical standards are also required for behavior within the company. Matters such as worker safety, fairness in hiring and promotions, and freedom of expression are all part of the environment leaders create for their employees. Figuring out what standards to embrace in the leader's personal conduct and what standards to hold employees to is a huge challenge. Clearly abusive, unethical leaders have a difficult time finding willing followers or creating high-performing teams. Indeed studies have shown that abusive leaders cause innovations and creativity to drop among team members.[15] Other research has shown that leadership integrity is directly correlated with employee engagement levels and overall performance.[16]

Unfortunately, many companies are facing an integrity gap at the top. In a 2011 survey of 1,857 individuals, only 14 percent of Americans believed their company's leaders were ethical and honest. The same poll found that only 12 percent of employees believed their employer genuinely listened to and cared about its employees. Only 7 percent of employees said that they believed senior management's actions were completely consistent with their words.[17] Such integrity gaps are not restricted to U.S. companies. Open a copy of any *Financial Times*, *International Herald Tribune*, or *South China Morning Post* newspapers and you are bound to find at least one article on ethical "lapses" among leaders around the world.

National culture has an enormous impact on how local managers interact with their employees. One study, for example, showed that men in Hong Kong and Taiwan were more likely than men in Canada and Japan to discriminate against women. The same study found that Canadians were less likely to show concern for the employment security of their employees than were managers in Hong Kong and Taiwan.[18] A different study found no cultural differences in the ethical standards of British versus Chinese managers working in Hong Kong.[19] In yet another study, older managers in the United States, Japan, Korea, India, and Australia were shown to place more value on trust than did their younger counterparts.[20] Each one of these studies shows what global leaders have long known: ethical norms governing relationships between managers and employees differ significantly from country to country.

To avoid conflicts and the giving of offense, as a global leader you must be committed to high personal standards in all your internal interactions in the corporation. Your standards of personal conduct cannot vary from country to country. You cannot get away with sexual harassment standards that are lower in Thailand than in Canada. All of your employees around the world must be treated with the same degree of respect.

In many companies we work with, a significant credibility gap exists between what top leaders say and what their employees actually believe. Sometimes the problem is the result of out-and-out unethical behavior on the part of the leader. However, more often than not, we have found that perceptions of unethical behavior or policies stem from communication problems. These come through verbal miscues or misinterpreted behaviors. Communication problems are almost always exacerbated by cultural differences.

As a leader assumes responsibilities in a growing number of countries, the potential for them to misunderstand or to be misunderstood increases exponentially. Their personal conduct in matters that involve employees is particularly open to scrutiny. Just as companies develop global reputations for ethical conduct, the reputation for how leaders treat other employees follows them throughout the world. Other people's perceptions can either enhance a person's ability to lead or essentially shut down their leadership capability.

Champion the company's core strategies around the world

At the same time as they adhere to a high standard of personal ethics, the most effective global leaders in our study firmly and unequivocally embraced their company's core strategies and policies around the world. They understand that strategies built on such core elements as product quality, total customer service, or leading edge technology should not be changed from country to country. They viewed their role as one of articulating what the company does and does not do, and acting as both a preacher and a teacher in getting the message out.

The more companies push into global markets, the greater the pressure on their leaders to alter the companies' core strategies. As companies enter developing countries in particular, short-term profits can often be increased by cutting quality or services. In setting up KFC's first restaurant in China in the late 1980s, Tony Wang quickly realized that Chinese customers generally did not place a high value on corporate standards for quality, service, and cleanliness. Customers didn't seem to care if the washrooms were cleaned every hour or every day. Whether cooked chicken sat under a heat lamp for 20 minutes or two hours did not appear to concern Chinese customers. Yet Wang also understood that KFC's ability to attract new franchisees around the world depended on its ability to ensure globally consistent standards. If Wang lowered standards, profits in China would rise, enhancing his own image on financial statements. Yet Wang refused to pursue this option. He unequivocally supported corporate policies. His commitment to the company not only gave him enormous credibility at corporate headquarters but also among subordinates. Because his employees in China knew he would not compromise the company's interests, their respect for and commitment to both Wang and KFC increased.

Even if you are not in a position to dismantle your company's core strategies, you may be tempted to criticize your company's strategies and your leaders. The farther a leader is from home, the greater the temptation to pander to local appetites for scandal or dissension. We witnessed on numerous occasions managers who fell victim to this temptation. At one meeting we attended in Brazil, a visiting executive vice president of a Fortune 50 company told local managers about a litany of problems she perceived with the corporation's CEO. She went on to criticize the company's strategy and suggest several new alternatives. Why did she do this? She no doubt believed she was right. And maybe she was. But beyond this, she also felt a need to be accepted by an unfamiliar group of senior employees. She wanted to be admired and treated with respect; critiquing the CEO and the company's strategy might well have seemed a way to demonstrate superior intelligence and insight. She also believed it highly unlikely that her words would ever make their way back to headquarters. In her mind, she had a license to sound off.

After the meeting we privately asked the participants what they thought. While some agreed with her observations, there was universal condemnation of the visiting executive. While she thought local managers would be impressed with her insights, instead they viewed her as disloyal, self-serving, and arrogant. They had expected a leader who would give them direction and get them fired up. Instead, the meeting was a major disappointment. Some even wondered if perhaps they were working for the wrong company.

With few exceptions, leaders are also followers and must support company policies and management. In a *Harvard Business Review* article, Robert Kelley described the fine line between leading and following:

> Many effective followers see leaders merely as co-adventurers on a worthy crusade, and if they suspect their leader of flagging commitment or conflicting

motives they may just withdraw their support, either by changing jobs or by contriving to change leaders.[21]

In a survey of 705 employees at 70 U.S. companies, 64 percent of respondents said that they were regularly skeptical of what management said.[22] We are convinced that this widespread problem is due largely to the fact that too many managers spend too much time attacking the organizations they work for. Global leaders know that undermining your company or colleagues brings your own character into question.

Integrity is good for business

A leader who lacks integrity can do serious damage to a company much faster than a leader who does not have a good strategy. Short-term compromises— whether in matters of environmental degradation, cheating, bribery, shoddy product quality, or abusive labor practices—may bring temporary benefits for the misguided decision maker and his or her business unit, but invariably cost dearly in the long run. Such compromises can undermine relationships with customers and government agencies, and tarnish the company's and leader's reputation for years to come.

While a lack of integrity brings about a litany of negative consequences, an abundance of integrity produces much good for the leader and company. Employee engagement and productivity improve. Absenteeism drops. Retention problems diminish. And because integrity strengthens the atmosphere of trust, leaders can delegate more and free themselves up to pursue higher-order strategic challenges.

Maintaining high ethical standards is clearly good for business, as well as one's career. In our earlier study of Fortune 500 companies, the ability to consistently display high ethical standards was rated the strongest leadership determinant by high-potential managers. The message is clear: the highest integrity is demanded of all global leaders. Warren Buffett echoed this sentiment in a speech:

> When looking for managers, I basically look for three things: integrity, intelligence, and energy. The problem is that if they don't have the first, the other two will kill you. Why? Because if someone doesn't have integrity, you really want them to be dumb and lazy. It is only if they have the first, that the second two really count.[23]

Conclusions

Character plays an important part in global leadership. The two main elements of character are emotionally connecting with people and demonstrating a high degree of integrity. Combining these two dimensions of character produces global leaders who are superbly skilled at building trust and goodwill—both inside their companies and outside, in the communities in which they live and work.

Notes

1 Sun Tzu. (1971). *The Art of War*, trans. Samuel B. Griffith. Oxford: Oxford University Press, p. 87.
2 Hofstede, G. (2001). *Culture's Consequences*. London: Sage Publications; Trompenaars, F. (2012). *Riding the Waves of Culture*. New York: McGraw-Hill.
3 Source: http://www.economist.com/node/3219902 (accessed 15 July 2010).
4 Liew Mun Leong. (2011). *Building People—Sunday Emails from a CEO* (3 vols.). Singapore: Wiley.
5 Source: http://www.virgin.com/entrepreneur/blog/richard-branson-how-to-be-a-real-leader (accessed 21 April 2004).
6 Suzuki, S. (1981). *Ability Development from Age Zero,* trans. Mary Louise Nagata. Secaucus, NJ: Warner Brothers Publications, p. 69.
7 Source: http://blog.chron.com/bakerblog/2013/05/whats-the-problem-malaysia/ (accessed 22 June 2013).
8 DuBrin, A. (2008). *Essentials of Management*. Boston, MA: Cengage Learning, Inc.
9 Source: Grace, D. and Cohen, S. (2005). *Business Ethics* (3rd edition). Oxford: Oxford University Press.
10 For an excellent review of the OECD's efforts, see "Who's Bribing Now?" *Christian Science Monitor*, April 16, 1996.
11 Source: *Wall Street Journal* (2013). "Is It a Bribe. . . . or Not?" July 21. http://online.wsj.com/article/SB10001424127887324021104578551251640574378.html?mod=WSJ_JRLeadership_3_3_RIGHT (accessed 29 July 2013).
12 Source: http://www.apple.com/supplierresponsibility/accountability.html (accessed 3 August 2013).
13 GM's policy allows for workers outside the United States to accept meals and outings to comply with local business norms. For more information on GM's "Revised Policy on Gifts, Entertainment and Other Gratuities" see "New GM Rules Curb Wining and Dining." (1996). *Wall Street Journal*, June 5.
14 De Hoogh, A. H. B. and Den Hartog, D. N. (2008). "Ethical and Despotic Leadership, Relationships with Leader's Social Responsibility, Top Management Team Effectiveness and Subordinates' Optimism: A Multi-Method Study." *Leadership Quarterly*, 19(3), 297–311.
15 Liu, D., Liao, H., and Loi, R. (2012). "The Dark Side of Leadership: A Three-Level Investigation of the Cascading Effect of Abusive Supervision on Employee Creativity." *Academy of Management Journal,* 55(5), 1187–1212.
16 Vogelgesang, G., Hannes, L., and Avolio, B. (2013). "The Mediating Effects of Leader Integrity with Transparency in Communication and Work Engagement/Performance." *Leadership Quarterly*, 24(3), 405–13.
17 Maritz survey, "Americans Still Lack Trust in Company Management Post-Recession." http://www.maritz.com/Press-Releases/2011/Americans-Still-Lack-Trust-In-Company-Management-Post-Recession.aspx. (accessed 19 June 2012).
18 See Mee-Kau Nyaw and Ignace Ng (1994). "A Comparative Analysis of Ethical Beliefs: A Four Country Study." *Journal of Business Ethics*, 13, 543–55.
19 Kain-Hon Lee (1982). "Ethical Beliefs in Marketing Management: A Cross-Cultural Study." *European Journal of Marketing*, 15(1), 58–67.
20 England, G. (1978). "Managers and Their Value Systems: A Five Country Comparative Study." *Columbia Journal of World Business*, 13(2), 35–44.
21 Kelley, R. (1988). "In Praise of Followers." *Harvard Business Review*, 66(6) November–December, p. 144.
22 *Business Week*, May 16, 1994.
23 As quoted from a speech given to students at the Marriott School of Management, Brigham Young University, Provo, UT, 1996.

7 Global leaders demonstrate savvy

Savvy is an essential characteristic of global leadership. Savvy traces its roots to the French expression, *savoir faire*, which literally translates as "know what to do." There is no escaping that successful global leaders know what to do, and know how to get things done. They possess unique knowledge and skills that set them apart from the rest. Again and again, we heard about the importance of savvy in our interviews. Whether in Frankfurt or Chicago or Singapore, employees described exemplar leaders with statements like "He just seems to know what to do," or "She has a golden touch—everything she does is a success."

We uncovered two critical dimensions of savvy through our research. First, leaders exhibit *global business savvy* when they recognize global market opportunities for their companies. Second, global leaders know how to capitalize on these market opportunities by accessing the full resources of the worldwide organization. We call this *global organizational savvy*. Quite simply, effective global leaders know how to both create and capture value.

Savvy is part of both the duality and dispersion dynamics. Business savvy requires a solid knowledge of the drivers of globalization and of the potential to maximize profits and growth through globalizing each activity and process along the company's value chain. As such, business savvy is tightly connected to the duality dynamic. In contrast, organizational savvy focuses on gathering information and influencing decisions beyond the limits of the global leader's lines of command and control. As a result, organizational savvy is tightly linked to the dispersion dynamic. In this chapter we explore both dimensions of savvy and discuss their impact on global leadership.

Global business savvy

Maximizing value

Global business savvy is essential for the simple reason that for-profit companies must make money for shareholders. The impact of a leader rests on their ability to maximize value creation for their company, to make money on a worldwide basis—ideally, lots of it. As Homi Patel, former vice president and general manager of Manufacturing at General Motors Powertrain and a member of the

Fiat General Motors joint-venture Board of Directors, put it: "Globalization is ultimately about growing the business and making money. A global leader has a vision of doing business worldwide with the ultimate goal of making money." This view is common in many leading companies. At these companies, as in many successful businesses, results are the sine qua non of leadership.

Why are business results so important to leadership? Two reasons: the first is practical; the second is psychological. From a practical perspective, managers who create the most value are generally rewarded with more rapid promotion to leadership positions.[1] In many companies, you simply cannot get into a global leadership position without a track record of making money. From a psychological perspective, business results generate credibility and respectability for the manager: when a division makes money, the division president gets the credit. When the company's stock is doing well, the CEO is lauded as a great leader. When market value falls, those same individuals are viewed as failures.

The power of global mindsets

Leaders with global mindsets view the world—not just the home country—as the arena for value creation.[2] Their world is a borderless marketplace. The global convergence of product preferences, increasingly intense international competition, and overall growth in international trade exert huge pressures to assess how international market opportunities benefit the corporation as a whole, rather than a particular home or host country.[3] Companies as diverse as Electrolux, Michelin, Shell, Unilever, Nestlé, and others have led the way by becoming essentially stateless competitors; they integrate operations tightly throughout the world, and over 75 percent of their sales are generated outside the home country. For global companies like these, the sun never sets on their operations.

This relatively new vision of stateless competition forces you to rethink the role of countries as you formulate business strategy. Global leaders continually pound away at the importance of global markets when meeting with employees. In virtually every stump speech by GE's Jeff Immelt, Unilever's Paul Polman, Shell's Ben van Beurden, P&G's Alan Lafley, and Daimler's Dieter Zetsche, the crucial importance of global markets is emphasized. Intense competition at home and rapidly growing demand in developing countries have compelled these leaders to look beyond traditional markets. Whether companies have worldwide operations or focus on single markets, thinking globally is essential for all business leaders.

Recognizing global market opportunities

To have global business savvy you must move beyond simply *thinking* about the world to actually recognizing global market opportunities for your company. Making money and growing sales are ultimately about winning in markets. Global leaders recognize three types of global market opportunities: (1) arbitrage opportunities involving cost and quality differences in production inputs; (2) new market opportunities for the company's goods and services; and (3) opportunities to maximize efficiencies by reducing redundancies.

Arbitrage opportunities

Global leaders who scour the world for the cheapest and highest quality inputs of production give their companies an enormous advantage in the marketplace. Cost differentials for land, energy, labor, and raw materials differ widely from country to country. For instance, a 2010 study showed that industrial labor averaged €27.37 per hour in Norway, €16.95 per hour in Germany, €16.27 per hour in France, and €7.71 per hour in Portugal.[4] At the same time U.S. labor rates were $22.01 per hour.[5] India's organized manufacturing sector compensated employees at an average rate of $0.91 an hour.[6] In some sub-sectors of manufacturing, hourly labor costs in India were less than 3 percent of levels in the United States.[7] In 2010, average hourly wages in southern China averaged $0.75.[8] But this was changing rapidly, as were the rates in India and other developing countries.

Global leaders are aware of the need to constantly track cost differentials, looking for ways to lower costs. Costs are never static and global leaders know that an ideal platform for manufacturing or sourcing should never be permanent. Indeed, a 2013 study by Deloitte found that depending on the industry, China may have permanently lost its position as the cheapest place for foreign companies to do business. Not only have labor costs sky-rocketed in China, but real-estate costs have also shot up, electricity rates have risen, and corporate income tax rates for most foreign companies have increased from 15 percent to 25 percent. In addition, government incentives are becoming increasingly difficult to obtain.[9] Li & Fung, a Hong Kong company that handles sourcing and apparel manufacturing for companies like Walmart and Liz Claiborne, reported that its production in Bangladesh jumped 20 percent in 2010, while China, its biggest supplier, slid 5 percent.[10] Other companies are reconsidering their commitment to overseas manufacturing. In what is often referred to as "reshoring," companies are quietly repositioning manufacturing closer to home. In 2012, General Electric moved manufacturing of refrigerators, washing machines, and heaters back to the United States. Google has also decided to make its Nexus Q media streamer not in China, but in San Jose, California.[11]

The same arbitrage opportunities that apply for labor can also apply for raw materials and components. Global leaders appreciate that a range of inputs can often be sourced from international markets at lower costs, even after factoring in quality. Combining First World process technologies with Third World costs can produce huge competitive advantages for companies.[12] Not surprisingly, statistics suggest that trade flows of intermediate goods are actually growing faster than the trade of final products. According to the World Trade Organization, during the 1990 to 2008 period, exports of final products increased an average of 7 percent per year, while exports of inputs rose by more than 10 percent per year.[13] The same pattern is evident in the trade of services. According to an OECD report, nearly 75 percent of services trade is in intermediate inputs.[14] In this sector, intra-firm trade accounted for 22 percent of U.S. services imports and 26 percent of its services exports.[15]

Determining sourcing locations involves complex calculations and difficult tradeoffs. Take automobile components, for example. If you are a manager at Honda, you may be interested in either making or buying bumpers for cars manufactured and sold in the United States. To determine the make or buy decision, you must know the cost of labor, cost of steel and plastics, U.S. import duties for finished bumpers, business tax rates, shipping costs, currency exchange rates, and so on for a wide range of countries. Global leaders know they need this type of data in order to weigh a range of input factors. Labor costs, for example, are far less important in the auto industry (at companies like Nissan and Toyota, labor represents less than 9 percent of total variable costs) than in the apparel industry (where labor may represent 35 percent or more of total variable costs). Global leaders proactively search for input costs and quality differences between countries to maximize arbitrage opportunities.

The ability to recognize global cost and quality differences increases when procurement activities are coordinated across geographies. In a major study of the advantages of global sourcing published in 2010, PwC identified four key sources of cost saving that can be achieved through global sourcing: labor arbitrage, which, if done properly, could result in 20–40 percent savings; process harmonization, 15–20 percent savings; IT standardization, another 10–20 percent savings; and improvements in service-level performance measurements, a further 5–10 percent savings.[16] While not all companies can achieve all of these cost savings, global leaders are constantly questioning where and how they can use global scale and scope to reduce their costs.

New market opportunities

Not only must global leaders be skilled at recognizing arbitrage opportunities, but they must also be skilled at identifying new markets for their company's goods and services. Much of the reason boils down to the fact that, for future growth, leaders have little choice but to reach out to and dive deeper into international markets, especially emerging markets. Over the past 40 years, the U.S. economy's share of world GDP (purchasing power parity—PPP—adjusted) has held surprisingly stable at about 22 percent; in contrast, the top 15 countries in the EU have seen a decline in their share of world GDP from about 36 percent of world output in 1969 to only 27 percent in 2009.[17] In general the share of world GDP from emerging markets has risen significantly and is projected to continue to rise, so that by 2020 emerging markets' share of world GDP will surpass that of developed markets (see Figure 7.1). No matter your home country, the message is clear: if you want to increase revenues, look to overseas markets.

From management consulting to telecommunications equipment to consumer products, market opportunities are rapidly globalizing. Companies as diverse as Microsoft, Facebook, Unilever, Exxon, Tesco, and the New York Stock Exchange have made global expansion central to their growth strategies. Japan-based

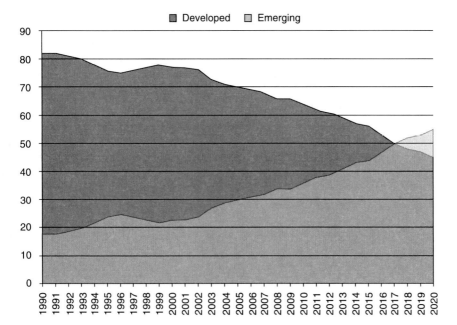

Figure 7.1 Economies' share of world GDP

Sources: World Bank; IMF; UNCTAD World Investment Report 2013

Komatsu is a case in point. Since the late 1980s, when Komatsu received 40 percent of its sales from Japan, the company has seen a steady decline in the relative importance of domestic sales. By the mid-2000s, Komatsu was receiving just over 18 percent of its revenues from Japanese customers.[18]

Even industries with strong legacies of country-focused competitors are fast becoming global today as executives come to realize that global sales are the route to sustained revenue growth. In airport management, for example, Fraport AG has long run one of the highest-rated airports in the world in Frankfurt. The airport is favored for its cleanliness, efficiency, and retail outlets. For years, Dr. Stefan Schulte, Fraport's CEO, has scoured the world for opportunities to sell his company's unique design and management skills. In 2013, the company was operating airports in four continents and a wide range of cities including Xi'an, China; Cairo, Egypt; New Delhi, India; and Lima, Peru. Assumptions that some industries have limited international growth potential are proving very shortsighted.

Global markets also provide the potential for companies to increase product features or underwrite the development of entirely new product offerings. Global leaders do this through the globalization of technology. An example of this leadership was shown when Gillette launched the Mach3 razor. Gillette spent six years and $750 million to bring the Mach3 to market. By comparison, only nine years earlier, it spent $200 million to launch the twin-blade Sensor razor.

During the first year of the launch, Gillette budgeted $300 million to market Mach3. Of this amount, two-thirds was targeted for international markets. The company estimated that within one year the Mach3 was sold in 100 countries. By comparison, it took five years for Sensor to reach this milestone. By 2013, Gillette operated 64 manufacturing facilities in 27 countries. Its products were sold in more than 200 countries and territories. Interestingly, less than 40 percent of its sales came from the United States. So great are its scale and scope advantages that one analyst estimated that Gillette enjoyed a whopping mark-up of almost 3,000 percent against its costs of manufacturing each cartridge.[19]

Accessing global markets helps companies amortize costs associated with new product development. From aircraft to semiconductors, the costs associated with developing a new generation of products can be huge. In civil aircraft, estimated costs of developing a plane like the Boeing 777 aircraft (launched in 1995) ran between $12 billion to $15 billion.[20] The company's "game-changing" Boeing 787 aircraft was much more expensive. A conservative estimate by the *Seattle Times* newspaper put Boeing's total investment in the program at more than $32 billion.[21] And this was just the cost of bringing its first plane to market. Airframe and battery problems have added to these costs. Unfortunately, no single national market is large enough for Boeing to fully recoup these costs while at the same time providing competitive prices for airline customers. For companies like Boeing, global markets serve as a means of amortizing these enormous capital and technological investments.

Efficiency opportunities

Global leaders understand that globalization provides opportunities to maximize value through increased operating efficiencies. These come through the elimination of redundancies, the use of company size as an advantage, and the capturing of economies of scale. The ability to shave off costs through cutting redundancies has been a major driving force behind plant consolidations at many companies. At Hershey, for example, in 2008 the company shut down production at its Smith Falls, Ontario, and Oakdale, California, candy plants and shifted these to a new mega-facility in Monterrey, Mexico. This saved money by eliminating costly duplications in system design and process engineering. There is nothing new or earth-shattering about such moves. Virtually every major company is following similar approaches. Henkel provides another example. The German company is one of the largest manufacturers of home care products, soaps, and adhesives in the world. In 2011, it consolidated manufacturing of adhesives throughout the Asia-Pacific region and China by opening a 150,000-square-meter adhesives factory in Shanghai. The facility, the largest of its kind in the world, has a capacity to produce 428,000 tons of adhesive products per year, providing cost-efficient glues not only for the region, but for the rest of the world as well.[22]

By searching for ways to eliminate redundancies, global leaders are better able to exploit company size. One advantage of size comes from the ability to consolidate demand and negotiate lower prices with outside vendors. It is not simply finding the cheapest inputs around the world, but being effective at pressuring vendors to offer volume discounts. Central purchasing also allows companies to better manage global inventories, reduce exposure to single-country suppliers, and develop specialized employee skills in support activities.

Beyond purchasing advantages, global leaders are able to maximize efficiencies through reaping the benefits of economies of scale. In disparate industries such as consumer electronics, medical diagnostic equipment, shipbuilding, commodity chemicals, and automobiles, firms reach maximum production efficiencies when volumes *exceed* the potential demand of virtually every national market. In the petroleum industry, for example, technical developments in refining shifted plant capacity from about 500 barrels per day in the early 1920s to well over 100,000 barrels per day by the mid-1950s. Since then, the optimal size of refineries has grown, albeit at a slower pace. Still, the largest refineries have a capacity in excess of 500,000 barrels per day. While these efficiencies help margins, the volumes drive the output far beyond the boundaries of most countries in which the product is produced.

In many cases, increasing production volumes moves companies significantly down learning curves. We all learn through repetition; in some industries, learning has a direct impact on efficiency. Civil aircraft are a good example. Airbus's first A300 aircraft took an estimated 340,000 person-hours to produce; its eighty-seventh plane took only 78,000 person-hours.[23] In the civil aircraft industry, global markets lead to better quality, introduction of advanced technologies, and ultimately lower prices for customers.

Recognizing efficiency advantages is often difficult for managers. In many cases, they have worked in and around the activities in question for decades and this effectively blinds them. They have become *too* familiar with how things are run and find it difficult to imagine any other organizational configuration. In contrast, savvy global leaders constantly search for new and better ways of organizing activities with the objective of maximizing efficiencies.

Critical knowledge areas

To recognize global market opportunities, global leaders must have a broad and deep knowledge base. This should include an understanding of external markets as well as their company's competitive positioning. Savvy global leaders master fundamental business principles in their quest to uncover global market opportunities. These include:

- *international finance*, including an understanding of foreign exchange management and global financial markets;
- *international accounting*, including an understanding of financial statement consolidation and differences in national accounting standards;
- *international marketing*, including an understanding of country differences in market size, segmentation, distribution, branding, and advertising norms;

- *international human resource management*, including an understanding of employment norms and expatriate selection and management;
- *international operations*, including an understanding of differences in production techniques and technologies;
- *international relations*, including an understanding of national and regional politics, business–government relations, and the role of nongovernmental organizations such as the World Bank and the International Monetary Fund;
- *international economics*, including an understanding of fiscal, monetary, investment, and employment policies of key countries;
- *international industry conditions*, including an understanding of the strategic capabilities and intent of key and emerging competitors, trends in customer demands and key technologies, and the relative advantages and disadvantages for globally integrated versus locally standardized competitors;
- *international strategy*, including an understanding of competitive positioning, alliances, exporting, and FDI options.

Your customers: a moving target

A vast body of knowledge and a large pool of subject-matter experts support each of these activities; entire university courses and small libraries are devoted to each topic. As we discussed in Chapter 4, developing business savvy requires an enormous commitment to learning. This commitment is not just to understanding compartmentalized business *subjects*, but also to developing a deeper understanding of subtle *interrelationships* between knowledge areas. Gaining a feel for how the pieces fit together is critical in identifying and weighing global market opportunities.

Beyond developing a breadth and depth of global business knowledge, leaders face another more daunting challenge. The pieces of the knowledge puzzle change continually. Frequent and substantial changes in customer needs and market conditions are unavoidable. Understanding market trajectories and the speed and magnitude of market changes across multiple markets is a daunting task and yet essential for global business leaders to maintain global business savvy.

Key to all of this is staying close to customers, and understanding non-customers. You cannot develop global business savvy without *being out there.* There is no substitute for pounding the pavement, knocking on doors, and connecting with the markets. Bhavesh Shah, chief of global procurement for Fermenich, explained the importance of "connecting" with key stakeholders.

> If you want to be a global leader, you need to be physically in the market. If you are in marketing, this means spending time at the consumer level. Nothing substitutes for firsthand experience. There is only so much you can delegate. If you are in marketing, you need to connect with clients personally. If you are in procurement, you have to go to their factories to see them, to get to know them. This is critical to develop fine-grained knowledge. But, it is also critical for the relationships.

By getting out in the field a senior leader can see the potential to grow key relationships that less experienced people might not see. Someone with less experience might be blinded by rules, procedures, and not see the potential for new business relationships.

It is interesting to note that Bhavesh Shah is based not at company headquarters in Geneva, but in Singapore, where he is closer to the action. Other companies are following similar patterns and are moving either entire divisional headquarters or functional headquarters overseas. A few examples help to illustrate this trend.

- In 2000, Bunge, a large Brazilian agribusiness company, moved its headquarters to White Plains, New York, before going public. It did this, not only to access larger talent pools, but to avoid being perceived as an emerging market company.[24]
- In 2004, Rupert Murdoch uprooted News Corporation from Australia and reincorporated it in the United States.
- In 2011, Merck announced the creation of a 470,000-square-meter regional R&D center in Beijing, China.
- In 2011, General Electric announced it was moving the headquarters of its X-ray business from Waukesha, Wisconsin, to Beijing, China.

Global organizational savvy

Beyond a mastery of global business markets, global leaders also need an intimate knowledge of their own company. *Global organizational savvy* is required to mobilize company resources necessary to capture global markets. Understanding and working with complex global organizations require a set of skills that many managers lack. One senior human resources manager at AT&T expressed a concern shared by many global leaders at other companies: "Here, we are heavily steeped in technological, engineering, and financial thinking. Most of our people are not so comfortable on the organizational side of the business. Yet you have to understand your organizational side as critically as your hard asset side."

Many managers we interviewed spent an inordinate amount of time familiarizing themselves with company policies and programs to the detriment of developing a sound understanding of the fundamental strengths and weaknesses of their companies' far-flung operations. They understood company rules and policies, but were far less certain about the location of critical knowledge and capabilities within the company. A good example of this lack of familiarity with the global organization was found in our meeting with the chief financial officer of a highly successful Swiss company. When asked if he could identify the types of products sold by the company's large Brazilian subsidiary, he could think of only four products. In fact, the subsidiary sold over 30 different products, and the four he mentioned represented less than 20 percent of sales. Many decision makers know a great deal about the global organization in an abstract sense, but often lack detailed knowledge of what is really going on in key markets.

Lack of organizational knowledge is an even bigger problem if you are posted outside head office. In many far-flung parts of the word, employees have only a limited sense of what the company is all about. Local managers are often not known by, nor do they know, key decision makers at head office. Not surprisingly, their effectiveness in anything but the most local tasks is severely limited.

While global leaders have a breadth of knowledge and global awareness of opportunities, they have no choice but to rely on local people for input. After all, in most cases local employees are much better at getting close to customers and markets than are expatriates. Local employees often have an instinctive sense of the markets, and an ability to establish strong long-term relationships with decision makers and knowledge generators. Many are also very smart about business. In a business world that is changing too rapidly for any one leader to keep up with, the know-how of local employees must be tapped. The challenge for global leaders is to *focus* these localized skills and insights in ways that maximize organizational learning while at the same time exploiting the company's existing strengths.

While tapping local skills is essential, expatriates risk getting cut out of the home office information loop once they take an overseas assignment. One U.S. country manager for an American auto-mobile company in Asia complained that although he had been gone from Detroit for only two years, he felt totally lost in terms of what was going on back home. The people who sponsored his overseas assignment had either been reassigned to other jobs, left the company, or had largely forgotten their promises to keep him informed. Not surprisingly, he felt isolated organizationally and uncertain when it came time to make decisions. While his subordinates turned to him for direction, he hesitated in making decisions in what for him was an organizational vacuum.

Keeping the local and global connections in place is a huge challenge for global leaders. If one set of stakeholders receives too much attention, the leader faces the risk of losing touch with the other. As a result, global leaders need to limit their focus to a few critical topic areas.

Critical knowledge areas

Familiarity with the global organization is critical to effective decision making. To lead effectively, global leaders need to focus their attention on a limited number of critical topics:

- The product and service lines offered by key subsidiaries, their strengths and weaknesses and potential for further globalization.
- The cost structures of key subsidiaries and how they compare to the organization as a whole.
- The location and quality of technological resources (both hard assets and people) within the global organization.
- The location and nature of any unique business models within affiliated companies.
- The location of managerial and employee talent within the global organization.

Knowing these dimensions of the organization gives a much better feel for what the organization can and cannot do.

Beyond a factual knowledge of what the organization *can do*, global leaders also need a clear understanding of what their company *wants to do*. Figuring this out is not a simple task. First and foremost, they need a familiarity with the backgrounds, interests, and personalities of the key decision makers in the company. In most cases, company objectives and personal interests are not in perfect synch.

In one U.S.-based medical products company we worked with, head office managers spent endless hours worrying about European integration. The company had six manufacturing subsidiaries spread across Europe. Many had been in operation for decades and functioned as autonomous, stand-alone subsidiaries. While each of the six subsidiaries manufactured and sold the same four product lines, significant differences existed in product specifications, pricing, and services provided. The company's U.S.-based head of international operations decided that the tradition of autonomy needed to change. A meeting with the six country managers was called, and they were charged with working out a rationalization plan within four months.

When four months passed and no action occurred, the head of international operations stepped in. Instead of manufacturing four product lines in six countries, he decided that manufacturing would be focused in four countries: France, Germany, Great Britain, and Italy. Each subsidiary in these countries was given full European responsibility for one of the four product lines. This approach created clear winners *and* losers. The two subsidiaries, one in Spain and one in Denmark, facing the ax fought hard to have the restructuring overruled. Furthermore, even the so-called winners were unhappy, because three-quarters of the divisions in the surviving subsidiaries were also dismantled. The reorganization struggled to get off the ground. Resistance to change was enormous, morale plummeted, and customers were too often overlooked. Performance tanked. Within a year, the head of international operations was fired.

The decision to reorganize was not itself the problem. In fact, the reorganization made perfect sense—at least on paper. When asked why the reorganization failed, the resisting country general managers cited two reasons. First, the U.S. head office had overestimated the benefits of rationalizing operations within Europe. In the minds of the country general managers, distribution, tax, and branding differences between countries continued; as a result, the reorganization's economic rationale was weak. Second, the subsidiary managers felt that the U.S. head of international operations had picked the wrong countries for the European product mandates. France was given responsibility for product line A because it was the strongest of the six countries in making product A. However, the French general manager thought that the subsidiary was comparatively stronger in product B than A. Furthermore, he viewed product B as more strategically important to the global aspirations of the company than product A. Germany, given responsibility for product line B, really wanted product line C, and so on. The end result? A global disaster for the company. Business savvy without a keen sense of organizational realities is a formula for failure.

Lack of familiarity with the global organization means that while managers may have administrative titles, they may not actually lead. People in the trenches almost always know more than the manager and become resentful when their input is not valued. In extreme cases, the failure of managers to seek input generates significant employee contempt. This is a particularly acute problem overseas when headquarter managers show up once a year as part of an around-the-world junket. Ernie Gundling, currently CEO of Aperian Global, calls this "typhoon management." The managers sweep in like a typhoon, mess things up, go away, and the locals rebuild all over again.

An understanding of different personal interests of internal stakeholders is essential in developing organizational savvy. These interests must be weighed against each individual's power base in the organization. The problem is that determining who is gaining and who is losing power is never easy. Factors to be considered include:

- The decision maker's external constituency (relationships with shareholders, customers, bankers, etc.).
- The decision maker's internal constituency (relationships with the Board of Directors, superiors, peers, subordinates).
- The decision maker's degree of dependency on others to implement change.
- The degree to which the decision maker has a reputation for asserting his or her interests. After all, power that is not asserted often leads to the diminution of power.

Understanding the different interests and powers that permeate global organizations is time-consuming and requires substantial interaction. The majority of the most effective global leaders we met spend at least half of their time visiting the troops in the field. They want to see and be seen. Mr. Liew Mun Leong, currently Chairman of Changi Airport Group, commented on the importance of personal contacts when he was formerly serving as CEO of CapitaLand, one of the world's largest property development companies:

> I made a lot of personal visits all over the world. I traveled at least 150 to 180 days per year. I would go to China two or three times every month . . . you need strong relationships with key people—both inside and outside the company. The CEO has to be personally involved.

Mobilizing resources

To mobilize a global organization's resources, global leaders not only have to understand how and why the organization works, but they must be known by key corporate decision makers. Getting the attention of the top decision makers in the company is a critical prerequisite for effective global leadership—without such recognition, global leaders will have a hard time securing control over key organizational resources.

Developing a high profile within the company necessitates that global leaders serve on key global committees, participate in task forces, and attend critical meetings. They must become an active participant in two-way communication networks involving head-office and subsidiary decision makers. It is a mistake to assume that position alone is sufficient to automatically secure these contacts. Substantial personal effort is required.

The importance of personally seizing the initiative is illustrated in the story of two senior managers we met in the course of our research. One gentleman was the European general manager of a Japanese consumer electronics giant. The manager was a British national who, by the time we first met him, had worked for the Japanese parent in Europe for eight years. He was the most senior non-Japanese manager in the company and the first non-Japanese to hold the title of regional vice president. During our meeting, we indicated that we were going to Japan the next week to meet with his boss, who was the worldwide head of consumer electronics for the company. Suddenly the man's face turned red. He seemed very worried. He then asked a favor. "When you see my boss," he said, "can you ask him how I am doing?" We were surprised that this senior manager didn't know himself how he was doing. So we decided to ask several more questions.

Q. How often do you travel to HQ in Japan?
A. Every three months.

Q. Do you speak Japanese?
A. Only enough to get by. I can maybe take a taxi and order a basic meal but that is about it.

Q. When you go to Japan, who do you meet with and what do you talk about?
A. I meet with my boss, the same man you will be visiting next week. He asks questions about our sales targets. But he already knows the numbers. I send them to him every week. And no matter whether we are on target or not, he says the same thing: "We need to accelerate sales." He never seems impatient. In fact, he is hard to read. I honestly don't know whether he is happy with my performance or not.

Q. Do you sit on any HQ committees?
A. Of course not. All of the meetings are in Japanese.

Q. Does your boss ever ask your opinion on strategic issues?
A. Not really. Headquarters controls product design. They send us the designs just before they introduce a new product in Japan. I can drag my feet on certain products I feel wouldn't go over well in Europe. But basically, I am here to do what they tell me to do.

Q. Do you have much contact with your peers running other regions?
A. We usually have some overlap during my visits to Tokyo. But that's all.

The European general manager felt as if he were working in the dark. He felt insecure as a non-Japanese and, even after eight years with the company, did not know how to read the global organization in general, or his boss more specifically. When we visited his boss in Tokyo the next week, we were surprised by his impressions of the European general manager. "He is doing a fine job," he told us. "I just wish he would take more initiative. He seems reluctant to come forward with ideas for new products. Europe should be playing a much bigger role in our overall global strategy."

Both the British general manager and his Japanese boss seemed disconnected from the global organization. While we could fault the Japanese boss in Tokyo for not really knowing his British subordinate, perhaps more of the fault rested with the British general manager. He took no initiative to assert himself in the global organization. He did not make himself or his ideas known. He waited to be invited in, but by hesitating made himself less attractive to superiors. Unfortunately, within six months of our interview, the British manager left the Japanese company.

Linking organizational and business savvy

Central to understanding how organizations work is figuring out the key drivers of the business model. How the company—or your division within the company— makes money will usually tell you who has power, or who likely will have power in the future. It will also tell you a lot about where the resources are flowing and help you identify the key gatekeepers in the organization.

Managers can only develop organizational *credibility* after they first demonstrate business savvy. Your employees, no matter where they are in the world, must have confidence that what you ask them to do makes good business sense. Too often this is not the case. Remember the subsidiary president of a large transportation equipment company in Thailand who shared his experience with us:

> Head office keeps asking for reports that I have no ability to generate. The data they want do not exist here nor do our people have the skills to generate what they want. We might spend a month preparing a report that gets done in three days in the States. Headquarters thinks it is just a matter of hiring more people with better skills. But, after being here a while, I realized headquarters has got it mostly wrong. While we can always use more good people, I have come to believe that the American way of running the business just doesn't work here. The reports are not only a waste of time; they actually lead us in the wrong direction.

To this manager, no one at head office was thinking globally. They did not understand his business or his organization. In his mind, they were anything but credible global leaders. But if he didn't stand up and push back, he would have lost the confidence of those who report to him directly. And his ability to lead them would have been compromised.

Without credibility, a leader will never be effective accessing and mobilizing organizational resources. And this is a contest that never ends. A case in point is the experience of the U.S. president of the Japanese subsidiary of a major European medical equipment company. The president talked about the challenges of running a subsidiary and building credibility inside and outside the subsidiary:

> If you are hired to run a subsidiary, you should not have to worry about head office. But in reality, you have to constantly fight for the subsidiary. In Japan, the staff is always watching. If you are not fighting for them and with them, you are out in their minds. There will always be negotiations with the parent. Headquarters will always want to get involved. . . . Headquarters wants to be the hub. I have had a lot of fights with HQ. The problem is that if we wait around for HQ to make decisions or come up with ideas, we would have been bankrupt long ago. But it takes time to effectively build a company. . . . As we have built our organization and proven that we know how to run our business, the parent has shifted from skepticism to support.

Contacts and credibility are precursors to actually mobilizing resources. Getting things done requires going out of one's way to call on people outside the normal organization chart who can make things happen. It involves sometimes going beyond reporting relationships. It means building a broad and deep network across geographies and product lines. It means knowing the right people and being known by them. And it means having a track record of performing.

Getting your way in complex global organizations means developing a repertoire of skills. They include:

1. *Listening to and understanding* the interests and needs of key internal stakeholders. Managers who are skilled at generating internal resources often create maps of key stakeholders, and include information on what they want, who they know, and where they stand on key issues. Some actually go so far as to create extensive files and databases; others are less explicit.
2. Using *motivational tools* above and beyond using pay or promotions to generate goodwill. Because mobilizing resources requires you to stretch your influence beyond your position in the organization chart, you need to become more skilled at non-traditional motivational tools. For key people you want to influence, this might include providing them with access to private sources of knowledge or key personal contacts. It might also include providing them with public recognition or other non-financial rewards.
3. Using a variety of *persuasion tools* in one-to-one interactions. In our experience, managers often rely on a limited number of tools in their efforts to win people over. For some, they come back again and again to the tool of exchanging support for support. Others appeal to past relationships. And others still rely on appealing to the other person's values. While each of these approaches can and often does work, they have their place and time. And, place and time don't usually always line up. This is particularly true internationally. While an "exchange of favors" approach might work well in say China, it might be a disaster if applied in Norway. As a result, leaders who are

good at mobilizing resources are those who have a broad set of "convincing" tools up their sleeves and know when, where, and how to use them.

4. Knowing when to *stop pushing*. Effective global leaders understand the difference between a good cause and a winnable fight. A good cause is something that the leader believes makes strategic sense for the firm. Maybe it is a belief that the subsidiary should change its role, or maybe it is a belief that a certain product or technology has great global potential. Good causes make logical sense and at the same time engender an emotional response on the part of the leaders. Together they create a formidable force that motivates leaders to fight for what they believe to be right, in fact what they know to be right. Unfortunately, just because the leader believes in good causes doesn't mean the rest of the organization agrees. Head office may see it differently. Rightly or wrongly, being an effective global leader means at times walking away from what you sometimes believe to be right. Some battles can be won; others cannot. Effective global leaders are not so arrogant or naive that they believe they can win at everything. Picking the right battles is important in earning the respect of those in power and securing the resources you need over the long haul.

Conclusions

Demonstrating savvy requires that you have a high level of global business and organizational skills. Savvy involves recognizing new markets and mobilizing organizational resources in a manner that significantly increases shareholder value. Unfortunately, many managers have limited skills actually making money for their companies. They lack the interest, experience, or motivation. They are weak on organizational skills. They limit their interests to employees and projects close to them, expressing little to no interest in what the company is doing in distant, unfamiliar markets. Furthermore, they dislike internal politics and disdain internal networking. These managers have a place in organizations, performing useful, if narrow, duties and helping sustain their companies' ongoing viability. However, they are not—and perhaps never will be—savvy global business leaders.

Demonstrating global savvy is no easy accomplishment. At one level, it involves factual knowledge of the world of business and of people and organizations. Yet it also demands a level of understanding that is much deeper. Savvy leaders often don't know what it is that they know. While savvy is built on foundations of factual knowledge, it includes a broader understanding of complex relationships and judgments about what is and isn't important.

Notes

1 While research has demonstrated cultural differences in the emphasis companies place on short-term versus long-term value creation, we found that, broadly defined, value creation is a significant objective in all cultures.

2 For more on global mindsets, see Bouquet, C. (2005). *Building Global Mindsets: An Attention-Based Perspective.* New York: Palgrave-Macmillan.

3 This point is strongly argued in S. Ghoshal (1987). "Global Strategy: An Organizing Framework." *Strategic Management Journal,* 8, 425–40, and Morrison, A. (1990). *Strategies in Global Industries: How U.S. Businesses Compete.* Westport, CT: Quorum Books.

4 Source: Eurostat (2010). http://epp.eurostat.ec.europa.eu/portal/page/portal/labour_market/earnings/database (accessed 15 June 2012).

5 Source: U.S. Department of Labor, Bureau of Labor Statistics (2010). http://www.bls.gov/oes/current/oes_nat.htm#00-0000 (accessed 1 June 2013).

6 Sincavage, J. R., Haub, C., and Sharma, O. P. (2010). "Labor Costs in India's Organized Manufacturing Sector." *Monthly Labor Review,* May, 3–22.

7 Ibid., p. 16.

8 "As China's Wages Rise, Export Prices Could Follow," *New York Times,* June 7, 2010.

9 Buelow, D., Gish, D., and Timberlake, J. "Manufacturing Beyond China," in *Business Trends 2013,* March 19, ed. by M. Canning and J. Kosmowski, Deloitte University Press, 2013.

10 "The End of Cheap Chinese Labour?" *The Economist,* July 18, 2010.

11 "Reshoring Manufacturing: Coming Home." *The Economist,* January 19, 2013.

12 See Doz, Y., Asakawa, K., Santos, J., and Williamson, P. (1996). "The Metanational Corporation." Paper presented at the Academy of International Business Annual Meeting, Banff, Canada, September 26–29.

13 Escaith, H., Lindenberg, N., and Miroudot, S. (2010). "International Supply Chains and Trade Elasticity in Times of Global Crisis." *World Trade Organization,* Economic Research and Statistics Division, February 1.

14 Miroudot, S., Sauvage, J., and Shepherd, B. (2010). "Measuring the Cost of International Trade in Services." OECD working paper, October 4.

15 Lanz, R. and Miroudot, S. (2011). "Intra-Firm Trade: Patterns, Determinants and Policy Implications." OECD Trade Policy Papers 114, OECD Publishing.

16 PwC (2010). "Why Global Sourcing? Why Now? Creating Competitive Advantage in Today's Volatile Marketplace." December. http://www.pwc.com/en_us/increasing-it-effectiveness/assets/global-sourcing.pdf (accessed 22 October 2013).

17 National Center for Policy Analysis (2009). "United States Share of World GDP Remarkably Constant." December 19. http://mjperry.blogspot.com/2009/11/us-share-of-world-gdp-remarkably.html (accessed 9 June 2013).

18 Yoshino, M. (2010). "Globalization at Komatsu." Harvard Business School case study, no. 9-910-415, April 8.

19 Ritson, M. (2009). "5 Reasons Gillette Is the Best a Brand Can Get." *Branding Strategy Insider,* June 23.

20 Woodward, R. "The Value of a Growing Airplane Family." From a speech given at the Farnborough International Air Show, September 2, 1996.

21 Gates, D. (2011). "Boeing Celebrates 787 Delivery as Program's Costs Top $32 Billion." *Seattle Times,* September 24.

22 "Henkel Builds New Adhesives Factory in China," Henkel press release, August 22, 2011.

23 Busch, M. L. (1999). *Trade Warriors: States, Firm, and Strategic-Trade Policy in High-Technology Competition.* New York: Cambridge University Press.

24 For more on the globalization of headquarters, see Desai, M. (2008). "The Decentering of the Global Firm." Harvard Business School, Working paper no. 09-054.

Part III

The path to global leadership

8 Global leaders: born or made? Buy or build?

Having read through the descriptions of the global leader competencies in the previous chapters, at this point you no doubt better appreciate why our research found that 80 percent of companies feel that they do not have enough global leaders for their ambitions. Not everyone has these capabilities and they cannot be created overnight. Nonetheless, we still encounter people who feel that the number we found is too high and believe that demand cannot outdistance supply that badly. However, our data are not the only ones to show that the supply of global leaders significantly lags demand. A 2011 study by DDI of over 2,600 organizations across 74 countries similarly found that roughly 80 percent of the HR professionals surveyed believed they had inadequate leader bench strength to meet their companies' future global business needs.[1] A 2012 survey of more than 800 business executives working in 35 markets found that nearly 70 percent did not have confidence in their top management's ability to build and execute a global talent strategy.[2]

All these data paint the same basic picture: the vast majority of companies do not have the global leaders they need. The importance of this leadership shortage is amplified by two other findings in our research. First, as we highlighted in Chapter 1, the greatest growth opportunities for companies lie outside their domestic borders. Put simply, if you are a moderate-size to large corporation and want to continue to grow, you have little choice but to go global. This is true even if your firm resides in a large developed country like the United States or Germany. This is why, as we presented in Chapter 1, we have seen a significant increase in both the percentage of international sales in the last decade and why we have seen a dramatic in foreign direct investment to help drive firms' international sales. Second, when we asked executives what factors had the biggest impact on capturing or missing global business opportunities, the highest-rated item was "capable global leaders." If you pull these three findings together, it paints a stark picture:

- To grow, you have to go global.
- To go global, you need capable global leaders.
- Unfortunately, most firms have far fewer global leaders than they need.
- Therefore, firms either have to scale back their growth plans, or
- Firms have to do whatever it takes to bridge their global leadership supply gap.

When we talked to CEOs and other senior executives about significantly scaling back their growth plans because of inadequate supply of global leaders, we heard a very common reply that is probably best illustrated by a quote from the CEO of a large U.K. multinational: "That is not what I get paid to do, especially if the barrier to growth (i.e., inadequate supply of global leaders) is something I can do something about." As a consequence, we found very few top executives who were willing to scale back or give up on global growth. Logically they then had little choice but to fix their leadership talent shortage. However, as one executive put it to us, "If fixing the gap were easy, we would have done it already." So how can a firm bridge this global leadership gap? This question naturally raises an even more fundamental question: "Are global leaders born or made?"

Born or made?

Our research is consistent with other studies that suggest the answer to this fundamental question is "Yes." Global leaders are both born and made. In fact, our research suggests not just two but three factors that produce global leaders. They are DNA, Drive, and Development, or what we label the 3Ds (see Figure 8.1).

Perhaps the easiest way to illustrate how the 3Ds interact to produce global leaders is by repeating an analogy given to us by one of the European managers we interviewed. This manager pointed out that to become a singing virtuoso, you need some level of an endowed gift (DNA) that enables you to hear a note in your head and then have it emerge from your mouth. Many people without this DNA gift can hear a given note in their head but unfortunately a different note comes out of their mouth. However, even if someone had this gift to the extent of having "perfect pitch" (i.e., they can perfectly reproduce with their voice any of the notes they hear in their head), if that person had no drive to practice and improve, the individual would not become a singing virtuoso. The person would be a naturally good singer but not a virtuoso. Finally, the manager concluded by stating that even with perfect pitch and practice, one's *full* potential would likely not be realized without opportunity and training from an experienced and wise teacher. "Even with drive and perfect pitch, you cannot hear or experience your singing

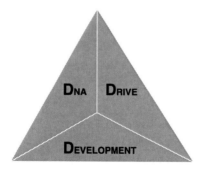

Figure 8.1 The 3Ds of bridging the global leader gap

as an audience does." Quite true. And therefore without performance opportunity, feedback, and coaching you could not **D**evelop your **D**NA and **D**rive to the point of becoming a singing virtuoso. A great singer is the result of superior endowed talent via **D**NA, **D**rive, and **D**evelopment. The same is true for a great global leader.

Global leaders need the right DNA, that is, they need to be born prewired with good aptitudes for all the capabilities we described previously in this book. For example, some people seem to have a natural aversion to ambiguity, while others innately embrace it. However, even though global leader aptitudes are necessary, they are not sufficient. Great global leaders also need immense drive—a passion to work hard, learn, and ultimately get things done. Finally, natural aptitude and motivation can take a global leader only so far. In addition, he or she also needs purposeful development. In this chapter we focus on the first two Ds—DNA and Drive—of global leadership and devote the entire next chapter to Development.

Meeting the DNA challenge

As we mentioned the "nature versus nurture" or "born versus made" debate regarding leaders in general has been with us for a long time. Those on the DNA side of the debate assert that great leaders are born, that they are imbued with God-given skills and proclivities that separate them from the rest of the pack.[3] Part of the reason that this school of thought still has ardent supporters is because there is research that finds consistent associations between certain aptitudes (i.e., inherent abilities) and leadership.

For example, a variety of studies have found that managers and senior leaders are disproportionately taller than the average.[4] For example, a 2005 survey of Fortune 500 CEOs found that the average CEO height was 6 foot (183 cm) while the average U.S. male was only 5 foot 9 inches (175 cm). In addition, fully 30 percent of CEOs were 6 foot 2 inches or taller (188 cm), while only 3.9 percent of the U.S. male population was that tall. Whether above-average height causes confidence that then leads to leadership opportunities or whether some ancient artifact of evolution causes us to view taller people as stronger and more capable leaders is not really a point we care to resolve or even believe can be definitely put to rest. Our point is that there is a long-observed relationship between physical attributes that are largely driven by DNA and leaders.

While it is easy for most people to understand the relationship between DNA and physical attributes such as height, it may not be as easy to see why there is a relationship between DNA and aptitudes, such as a naturally high level of inquisitiveness or tolerance for ambiguity. Yet, this relationship goes to the heart of the role of DNA in global leaders. As a consequence, we want to spend just a minute highlighting this dynamic.

Without getting at all technical, it is easy to appreciate how DNA impacts aptitudes by quickly reviewing some basics. DNA (DeoxyriboNucleic Acid) is the cellular-based genetic material that contains the instructions for the development and functioning of living organisms. It stores the information required for an organism to grow and thrive. It governs such basic characteristics as eye and hair color, stature, bone density, and propensity for certain diseases.

Almost every human cell contains a complete sample of DNA identical to the DNA of every other cell within that same person. DNA is a long, narrow string-like polymer that is packed into the nucleus of the cell. It is divided into nucleotides, the majority of which contain the encoded instructions that dictate to cells how to make up the body. These are called genes. Genes determine people's external features (e.g., pigments in hair and eyes, skin color, etc.) as well as how internal organs—including the brain—are formed and function.

The relationship between the brain and aptitudes such as tolerance for ambiguity is not hard to appreciate. Whether it is fair or not, some people are born with brains that process information much faster than others. Some people are born with brains that can categorize information and store and retrieve it more efficiently and accurately than others. On this general relationship between the nature of our brain and aptitudes, our understanding of how genetics impact our intelligence quotient or IQ has grown rapidly. For example, scientists have learned that the influence of an individual's genetic makeup on their IQ increases with age, irrespective of upbringing or environmental influence. One exhaustive study of 11,000 pairs of twins found that genetics determined 66 percent of the cognitive abilities of 17 year olds.[5] In other words, two-thirds of our cognitive ability is prewired.

Other research shows there is a link between DNA and an aptitude for learning a foreign language. American psychologist John Carroll is perhaps best known for his contribution to our understanding of human cognitive abilities with regard to language acquisition. He developed the Modern Language Aptitude Test, which has become a benchmark in assessing the innate skills of individuals for learning a foreign language.[6] Additional studies have linked genetics to memory,[7] the ability to concentrate,[8] innovative ability,[9] and so on.

The field of behavioral genetics focuses on how inheritance impacts the ability to express emotions, recognize the needs of others, demonstrate antisocial behavior, levels of anger, and so on. The challenge for neuroscientists is that of the 50,000-odd gene pairs that make up the human genome, most behaviors are linked to complex interactions involving multiple genes. This makes it extremely difficult to study and assess the direct impact of genetics on behavior.[10]

However, for our purposes, it important only to recognize that there is a powerful link between endowed aptitudes and global leader capabilities. Earlier we discussed the inevitable tensions and ambiguities that emerge as a consequence of the simultaneous pressures of global integration and local responsiveness. We also discussed why embracing ambiguity and balancing tensions emerged as one of the key capabilities of successful global leaders. While it is impossible to know the exact influence of DNA on tolerance for ambiguity, there are a variety of studies that show that DNA plays a role and as a consequence people have significantly different levels of tolerance for ambiguity even as young children.[11] The same is true for inquisitiveness, or emotional empathy and connections, etc.[12]

What this means is that in bridging the global leadership gap, firms need to think about the role of selection. For example, someone with very low inquisitiveness is unlikely to see the same benefits from development opportunities and training as someone with high inquisitiveness. Companies such as Nestlé, Colgate, GE, and others first look for evidence, signs, clues, cues, etc. that individuals have both interest in and capabilities for global leadership before they invest significant time and money in various development activities. For example, Colgate wants to see that young marketing candidates have already shown interest in the larger world by having previously done something on their own, such as a semester study abroad or a foreign student exchange, before they put them on their global marketing development track.

From DNA to inheritance

Whereas DNA focuses exclusively on the transfer of abilities from one generation to the next, inheritance is about the transfer of opportunities. Often it is impossible to separate DNA from inheritance in determining leadership success. It is easy to see the impact of genetics and inheritance in the lives of respected global leaders. Success and achievement often run in families. Take, for example, Winston Churchill, who was voted as the greatest person in the history of Great Britain.[13] Churchill was born at Blenheim Palace in 1874. Blenheim Palace was designed in 1705 for John Churchill, the 1st Duke of Marlborough, as a reward from Queen Anne for his victory over the French at the Battle of Blenheim in Bavaria the previous year. Winston, a man who would become Prime Minister of Great Britain twice and who was a recipient of the Nobel Prize, was the elder son of Lord Randolph Henry Spencer Churchill, a British statesman who rose to become Chancellor of the Exchequer and Leader of the House of Commons.

Other examples permeate business. About a third of Fortune 500 U.S. firms are family owned.[14] In the United States, the Ford, Vanderbilt, Du Pont, Morgan, Rockefeller, and Watson families stand tall for their generations of successful and influential leaders. In Canada, the McCain, Bata, Irving, and Bronfman families have produced generations of successful business leaders. In Europe, the Rothschild, Agnelli, Mohn, Moller, Peugeot, Albrecht, and Dassault families have all demonstrated strong leaders across the generations. Indeed, in virtually every country examples of multigenerational leaders can readily be found.

To be certain, being born rich or being closely related to a powerful leader provides a certain leg up in life. Money and influence open doors and provide opportunities and exposure to educational and other developmental opportunities that might be beyond the reach of others. In addition, they can also provide a "halo effect" that can help make even a mediocre manager look like a rock star. Nothing is fair in life, including genetics and inheritance.

Of course, it would be faulty to assume that being born into a successful family promises success. While inheritance and DNA help, they do not guarantee achievement. Often the same press that pays rapt attention to the success stories fails to chronicle the lives of the random siblings and offspring that end up as wastrels and deadbeats. Their numbers are often far greater than the numbers of great success stories. At the end of the day, DNA has to be catalyzed with drive.

The importance of drive

On the basis of our interviews, drive is as important as, if not more important than, DNA in producing global leaders. Drive reflects the hard work and ambition of the individual. Someone demonstrates drive when they strive to get things done, learn, and improve performance. Isaac Newton, the man who introduced the world to Newtonian physics, was once asked how he realized what would become known as the Universal Law of Gravitation. His reply, simple yet profound: "I thought about it all the time." It didn't just come to him by an apple falling on his head.

Multiple Olympic gold medal winner Michael Phelps was notorious for his work ethic. During peak training periods, he would swim "at least 80,000 meters a week, nearly 50 miles. That includes two practices a day, sometimes three when he's training at altitude."[15] Even when not preparing for special races, he would swim an average of 52 more days per year than most of his competitors. Other athletes with a famous passion for practice include Wayne Gretzky, Michael Jordan, and Tiger Woods, who is famously quoted as saying,

> People don't understand that when I grew up, I was never the most talented. I was never the biggest. I was never the fastest. I certainly was never the strongest. The only thing I had was my work ethic, and that's been what has gotten me this far.[16]

The importance of practice and hard work comes as no surprise to coaches and athletes everywhere. In his bestselling book *Outliers,* Malcolm Gladwell tries to answer the question: What makes high achievers different? His conclusion is that success in sports has much to do with practice, though there are clear relationships between inherited body type and success in sports like basketball, marathon running, and gymnastics. Beyond this, Gladwell introduced what has become widely referred to as the 10,000-hour rule, which stipulates that no athlete—no matter how naturally gifted—can achieve world-class levels of performance without accumulating at least 10,000 hours of "deliberate practice."[17]

Drive is a determinant of success in every facet of life. Star violinist Itzhak Perlman first picked up the instrument at the age of 4. His first teacher reportedly screamed at the horrible sounds produced by the young boy, but Perlman persisted. That same year he contracted polio, a condition that forced him to use crutches for mobility. Such a condition would have sidetracked almost anyone, but not Perlman. At age 5 he shifted his studies to the Music Academy of Tel Aviv and practiced with a work ethic that few could rival. He has since gone on to win four Emmy awards and entertain audiences around the world. During his prime years, he would routinely perform more than 100 concert performances per year, losing sometimes 3 pounds in weight during the 2-hour concert. With age, he has dropped to a mere 90 concerts per year. Now in his late sixties, he still packs concert halls and has guest-conducted for almost every major orchestra in the world. When asked about what creates greatness, Perlman is quick to point out the limits of innate talent or what we call DNA. In Perlman's experience, "for every child prodigy that you know about, at least 50 burned out before you even heard about them."[18] Talent is one thing. What you do with it is another.

Where drive is most important

The global leaders in our research all displayed enormous drive in their professional lives. Their drive was manifest in three key areas: the drive to learn, the drive to connect with key stakeholders, and the drive to get things done.

Learning is central to maintaining personal vitality and organizational relevance. It is key to responding quickly and effectively to changes in technologies, competitors, and new customers. And yet learning was typically not a passive activity for the leaders we studied. They regularly went out of their way to meet with customers and employees, often in remote locations. Sam Tan, COO of global sourcing giant MGF Sourcing, commented on the importance and difficulty of connecting with far-flung employees.

> The issue we have, because we are global, is that you cannot actually see the people you are leading. If the employees have their offices in Hong Kong, where I work, I can see the interpersonal dynamics personally. But, most of my employees don't work here. So, you have to find new ways to observe behavior without actually seeing them with your own eyes. One thing you have to pay more attention to is outcomes. For examples, we sometimes have country managers who don't get along with each other. Perhaps they are competing for sales in their respective countries. I may not be able to derive this competition directly, but if I study their behaviors I can often pick this up. For example, if a Korean country manager only supports Korean vendors, I can start to better understand the potential issues I have. But this takes extra effort to figure out.
>
> You also have to think a bit deeper about things you are reading and about things that you see because you are likely looking at them through a foreign lens. It takes more effort to put the pieces of the puzzle together.

In addition to the need for keen observation skills, effective global leaders demonstrate a commitment to building data gathering and processing capacities within their organizations. Not surprisingly, these capabilities are not cheap, nor do they typically provide a bounty of short-term benefits. Establishing a powerful learning infrastructure doesn't materialize without strong and driven leaders.

The key objective of global learning is to understand what is happening in the world, in as close to real time as possible. And it isn't easy. Tim Huxley,

CEO of Hong Kong-based shipping giant Wah Kwong, summarized the challenge:

> My world exists beyond Hong Kong. Very little of our actual business involves Hong Kong. So I need to be organized for this. Every day at 17h00, I talk to a select group of people in Europe. This has become a learning routine for me. The good news is Hong Kong is incredibly international. But, to stay globally connected, I frequently go to the Foreign Correspondents' Club. You have to work at it to understand what is going on in the world.

Beyond learning, *connecting* with stakeholders also requires huge effort and drive. Sam Tan commented on the need for a strong network of relationships:

> A strong global leader creates value to the organization when he is able to solve complicated, difficult problems. It is impossible in today's world to solve problems by what you know yourself and through those who report directly to you. The richer your network, the stronger your toolbox for solving problems.
>
> Today, I have someone I can contact in almost any imaginable area of problem. They could be inside the company or outside. To get to this point, you have to identify key people and then connect with [them] and establish close personal relationships. When these people are in far-flung locations, you need to spend time and energy investing in these relationships

Building layers of relationships is tough work, particularly when crossing a dozen time zones and numerous language and culture groups. It can be simply exhausting. Singapore-based Liew Mun Leong, former CEO and founder of Asian property development powerhouse CapitaLand and now Chairman of Changi Airport Group, commented on why connecting was so important as well as the personal challenges this posed:

> It takes a huge amount of energy to be an effective leader. In my job at CapitaLand, I made a lot of personal visits all over the world. . . .
>
> Part of the reason I traveled so much is because you need strong relationships with key people—both inside and outside the company. The CEO has to be personally involved. The Chinese will only trust the number one man in the organization. And that's me. You cannot send your number two person to see the governor or premier.

The number of 180 days on the road didn't appear out of the ordinary amongst the group of senior executives we met. We met with one CFO just off a long-haul flight who asked us several times over the course of our one-hour meeting what city we were in. He simply didn't know or couldn't remember where he was. He reported being home only 3 days during the past 5 weeks. Another vice-chairman of one of the Big Four accounting firms reported that he had traveled over 2 million kilometers in the past 2 years—about 1 million kilometers or 600,000 miles per year. Another vice-chairman of one of the world's largest chemical companies reported that for the past 10 or more years he been visiting his employees the entire month of December, returning home only on Christmas eve. The head of business–government relations for one of the world's largest mining companies reported that he had been to practically every country in the world for business. He estimated having been to Africa alone well over 100 times. When asked about the importance of drive, he explained that he preferred the term "resilience." He went on to explain: "Resilience is critical to us. A lot of our locations are difficult. It is too hot, too cold. Too humid. Too isolated, etc. It takes a lot of resilience to take on these jobs."

Drive is also important for the simple reason that it leads to action and action leads to results. Global leaders are people who like to get things done. They like results. And one thing global leaders appreciate, perhaps more than any other aspect of drive, is that when the bias for action starts and ends with the leader, not much can happen. The key to drive is not that the leader acts like a ping-pong ball bouncing from topic to topic, but that he energizes *others*. While global leaders are driven, the key is to turn personal drive into organizational drive with the end result being a highly energized organization.

Understanding what drives drive

We found it interesting that most of the global leaders we studied recognized that they were driven people but they could not fully explain why they worked so hard or what motivated them. It would be tempting to say that DNA is the key determinant of personal drive. And perhaps for some people it is true that they are wired for hard work. But this explanation is too simple. We believe that the forces that create employee drive are far more complex and difficult to understand and explain.

Previous research has shown that money by itself is not much of a motivator when it comes to getting people to pay attention to global issues. Adding global titles to job responsibilities has actually been shown to have a negligible effect on raising and sustaining global interest levels. [19] People tend to not be driven as much because of external pressures as they are by passion. And for the most part passion comes from within. It cannot be imposed.

For some of our global leaders, drive has roots in personal feelings of inadequacy and the need to prove themselves. Often these feelings go back to childhood, when they were bullied, ostracized, ignored, or picked on by siblings, wayward parents, or other children. Psychologists have long studied this phenomenon. One example often referenced is that of Winston Churchill. Some believe that the poor relationships Winston had with his parents and more particularly his father were huge driving forces in the young man's life. Lord Randolph Henry Spencer Churchill often denigrated young Winston and some speculate that this drove the boy to prove that he could accomplish more than his father.

Another determinant of drive is *passion* for the job, for the people, and for the company. These are the most noble and positive motivators. And passion was frequently sighted in our interviews. One global CEO told us, "I love this job. I cannot think of anything I love more, save my wife. And even here, some days I wonder." A mining executive, fresh off a red-eye flight from central Africa was quick to explain to us how he looked forward to these trips. When we opened the door for him to complain—even just a little—about what seemed to us a travel nightmare, he refused to take the bait. Instead, he responded that the ability to reconnect with employees and customers who had become his friends, the opportunity to take in the sights and sounds of the local food markets, and even the plane ride itself were invigorating. "If I don't make a trip like this every few weeks, I start to get bored," he responded.

Liew Mun Leong from CapitaLand was eloquent in capturing what drove him to work so hard:

> I get the energy because I love what I do. You must love the people. You must be happy to see your people. You have to say, "I have groomed this fellow . . ." and I am happy to see him grow. This is what has kept me going.

We found that love of the people was perhaps the most powerful motivator in determining the long-term drive of global leaders. While red-eye flights across the Pacific and conference calls in the middle of the night were in and of themselves painful, the reward of seeing colleagues, customers, and suppliers more than offset the downside. When friendships don't exist or begin to grow stale, personal levels of commitment to taking on global leadership roles suffer.

Global leaders: buy or build?

Even without yet getting to the next chapter in which we focus on what companies can do to develop global leaders, you can anticipate that it is not easy or quick. As a consequence, we often get asked, "Is it better to buy or build global leaders?" Clearly, the fastest way for a company to build up its bench strength of global leaders is to hire them from other companies. There are lots of executive search firms out there more than happy to help you with this task (for a non-trivial fee).

As every student of basic economics knows, when supply exceeds demand, price goes up. Our experience with both executives and with global executive search firms confirms this, and as a consequence "buying" global leadership is not cheap. Successful global leaders recognize that they can command a price premium and therefore they are often (though not always) open to opportunities to capture that value and to take the call from a headhunter. Over the years, some companies have become prime targets for poachers. Management consultancies such as McKinsey and companies such as PepsiCo, P&G, BMW, Disney, and Siemens are frequent targets for headhunters. And the headhunters don't just focus on big name companies from the United States and Europe. They are increasingly seen circling emerging market giants like HTC in Taiwan, Vale in Brazil, and FEMSA of Mexico.

Bangalore-based technology company, Infosys, has long been viewed as a recruiter's dream company and has over the years witnessed the departure of dozens of high-end executives who have been poached by the competition and beyond.[20]

In addition to the speed that this approach offers, bringing in new people with different experiences, backgrounds, and the like increases diversity. This diversity can in turn can enhance innovation, elevate decision quality, and so on.

While fast, poaching has its limitations. One always wonders about the loyalty of people who jump ship, particularly when they are motivated by money alone. Newcomers also often bring a different set of values and approaches that may make it difficult for them to fit into the new organization. Their experiences may be focused in parts of the world that are less interesting to their new company. They do not know their way around and may be unfamiliar with their new company's products, services, and brands. And because they are new and unfamiliar to others, they may face skeptical direct reports or lack the internal network to be of much use. So, while poaching may appear to be a quick solution, it often takes a lot longer to bring new people up to speed than anticipated.

A few final comments

Creating global leaders is certainly not an easy task. If it were, there would be a lot more global leaders moving their companies forward. In this chapter we explored the role of DNA and drive in creating global leaders. We learned that some things are controllable, while others are not. This means that, where possible, the process of building global leadership bench strength should always begin by picking the right people in the first place. Look for people who are born with certain skills. Find those who are predisposed to particular behaviors. Search for those with the passion and the drive to push forward when they are tired, to explore the world, and to motivate and lift the organization.

In our next chapter, we move beyond DNA and drive. Instead, we focus on what companies can do to *develop* global leaders. What we will find is that organizations can indeed take charge of building their global leadership pipelines. It is not something that can or should ever be left to chance.

Notes

1 Boatman, J. and Wellins, R. (2011). "Global Leadership Forecast 2011: Time for a Leadership Revolution." https://www.deloitte.com/assets/Dcom-SouthAfrica/Local%20Assets/Documents/DDI%20-%20Global%20Leadership%20Forecast%202011.pdf (accessed 7 October 2013).

2 Brook, B. (2012). "The Art of Developing Truly Global Leaders." *Harvard Business Review*, November.

3 See, Glaser, J. (2006). *The DNA of Leadership: Leverage Your Instincts to Communicate, Differentiate, Innovate.* Avon, MA: Platinum Press. See also, Okum, P. (2012). *Leadership DNA: Why the Accepted Premise that Anyone Can be a Leader is Utterly False and the Main Cause of Poor Leadership in America.* Bloomington, IN: iUniverse Press.

4 Lindqvist, E. (2012). "Height and Leadership." *Review of Economic and Statistics*, 94(4), 1191–6; Bass, B. and Bass, R. (2008). "Traits of Leadership." *The Bass Handbook of Leadership.* New York: Free Press, p. 82.

5 Haworth, C. M. A., *et al.*, (2010). "The Heritability of General Cognitive Ability Increases Linearly from Childhood to Young Adulthood." *Molecular Psychiatry*, 15, 1112–20.

6 Carroll, J. B. (1993). *Human Cognitive Abilities*. Cambridge, MA: Cambridge University Press.

7 Finkler, K. (2005). "Family, Kinship, Memory and Temporality in the Age of The New Genetics." *Social Science & Medicine*, 61(5), 1059–71. See also, DeZazzo, J. and Tully, T. (1995). "Dissection of Memory Formation: From Behavioral Pharmacology to Molecular Genetics." *Trends in Neurosciences*, 18(5), 212–18.

8 Faraone, S., Tsuang, M., and Tsuang, D. (1999). *Genetics of Mental Disorders: A Guide for Students, Clinicians and Researchers*. New York: Guilford Press.

9 Dyer, J., Gregersen, H., and Christensen, C. (2011). *The Innovator's DNA*. Boston, MA: Harvard Business School Press.

10 For more on this topic, see the peer-reviewed academic journal, *Behavior Genetics*.

11 Furnham, A. and Ribchester, T. (1995). "Tolerance for Ambiguity: Review of the Concept, Its Measurement and Application." *Current Psychology*, 14(3), 179–99.

12 Dyer, J., Gregersen, H., and Christensen, C. (2011). *The Innovator's DNA*, Boston, MA: Harvard Business Press.

13 "Ten Greatest Britons Chosen," BBC News article, October 20, 2002.

14 Landes, D. (2007). *Dynasties: Fortunes and Misfortunes of the World's Great Family Businesses*. New York: Penguin.

15 Michaelis, V. (2008). "Built to Swim, Phelps Found a Focus and Refuge in Water." *USA Today*, August 3.

16 Source: http://www.brainyquote.com (accessed 12 November 2013).

17 Gladwell, M. (2008). *Outliers: The Story of Success*. New York: Little, Brown and Company.

18 Tabachnick, S. (2012). "Falling in Love with Itzhak Perlman." *The Daily Page*. http://www.thedailypage.com/isthmus/article.php?article=36410 (accessed 7 December 2012).

19 Bouquet, C. (2005). *Building Global Mindsets*. London: Palgrave Macmillan.

20 Nandakumar, I. (2013). "Constant Changes Makes Infosys a Poaching Ground for Rival Companies." *The Economic Times (of India)*. September 23.

9 Developing global leaders

In the previous chapter we argued that in order to bridge the global leader gap, firms have to look for and select leaders with aptitudes for the capabilities we described and that they also need to ensure that the leaders have the drive to amplify and improve on those aptitudes. In this chapter, we want to focus specifically on the successful development steps we found companies can take in order to complete the bridge and fix their global leader gap.

In our research throughout Europe, North America, and Asia we found that four strategies, when properly used, are most effective in developing global leaders: Transfers, Training, Teams, and Travel or what we label the 4Ts (see Figure 9.1).

Although for simplicity sake, Figure 9.1 illustrates these 4Ts as equal in impact, as we will discuss, it came out very clearly in our research that some of the Ts are more powerful than others. In examining these development strategies, keep in mind that companies do *not* believe the 4Ts are a means of turning anyone and everyone into effective global leaders; instead, they believe that they are the primary way to maximize the capabilities of *high-potential* individuals.

Figure 9.1 The 4Ts of global leader development

Development strategy #1: transfers

When we talked with exemplar global leaders, we asked them a very simple question: "What has been the most powerful experience in your life for developing global leadership capabilities?" Keep in mind that these 200 interviewees came from more than 50 different nationalities, worked in over 30 different industries, from mining to mobile phones, had different educational backgrounds, from physics to philosophy, and operated in a variety of functions, from finance to marketing. Thus, the potential for very diverse answers to this simple question was huge, and so we expected variety. As a consequence, we were amazed at the consistency of response. *Some 80 percent of these individuals identified living and working in a foreign country as the single most influential developmental experience in their lives.* This is a remarkable and totally unexpected consensus.

The power of international transfers

From our research it is clear that international assignments are the most powerful means of developing global leaders. The question is "Why?" What is it about international assignments that can have such a powerful impact? To answer this question, we need to take just a small step back and highlight the basic process of globalizing one's mind. Fundamentally, a global leader needs to get himself or herself around the whole world—not just one or two countries. For most of us, it can take some pretty hard knocks before we are prepared to stretch our minds far enough to accommodate the entire world. Those hard knocks come most often—and most productively—from direct confrontations with new and different terrains. The contrast between the new terrain and the familiar landscape of the past is frequently the catalyst that forces us to redraw our mental maps.

This basic process of redrawing and stretching our mental maps was brought home to us during a trip to Japan for an international management conference. After a day's sessions, several colleagues decided to go out to dinner. Since Stewart Black had lived and worked in Japan before, he was asked to pick a traditional Japanese restaurant for dinner. He did and explained a couple of things in advance for the small group. He explained that most traditional Japanese restaurants have similar entries. The design consists of a thin wood-and-glass sliding door that opens onto a foyer on the other side. The runners at the bottom of the door, along which it slides, are typically not recessed; patrons must step carefully over them as they enter the restaurant.

Stewart warned his colleagues about the door runners and the need to step over them, so as not to trip. Stewart found what looked like a nice traditional restaurant. As the group approached the restaurant, Stewart opened the sliding door and carefully stepped inside. A second colleague, and co-author of this book, Allen Morrison, who is about the same height as Stewart, followed, also making sure to step over the door runner. The next thing anyone knew there was a thunderous crash in the entryway that reverberated throughout the entire restaurant. Everyone inside turned to see what had happened. A third colleague, Hal Gregersen, was staggering in the doorway, a gash on his forehead with blood trickling down. What happened? Hal, on seeing his two colleagues negotiate the entry so easily, had been looking down at the wood runners as instructed but being nearly 6 foot 6 inches (2 meters) had smashed his head on the *top* of the door frame. The impact had nearly knocked Hal out and caused patrons to wonder momentarily if an earthquake were starting.

The most interesting part of this story is that the next day, when the group went to another traditional Japanese restaurant, the exact same thing happened. Hal had a matching cut on the other side of his forehead. It wasn't until the third time that Hal remembered that he needed to duck as he entered. In a sense, it took getting smacked in the head hard and twice for Hal to rearrange his thinking about what he needed to do to successfully enter a traditional Japanese restaurant.

Most of us are like Hal in this sense. It takes getting smacked in the head, hard and probably more than once, before we are ready to rearrange our mental maps. Hard knocks to the head are not always pleasant, but they are necessary. They help us see the limits to our mental maps; they help us understand that to become effective global leaders, we must stretch and redraw those same maps. We need to be able to adjust our mindsets in order to embrace the constant dualities and tensions of global and local business demands. We need new maps to help us thrive in the turbulent environment of global business and take action when uncertainty reigns. We need a good shake-up in order to learn how to emotionally connect with people who are different from ourselves and engender their good will. We need broader mental maps to understand people of various ethical frameworks and demonstrate integrity in a way that inspires their trust. And, finally, we need new and expanded mental maps in order to hold all the business savvy required to recognize global opportunities and to marshal the worldwide organizational resources necessary to capture those opportunities.

One of the key reasons that inquisitiveness is such a differentiator between successful global leaders and those who struggle with worldwide responsibilities is that it ignites and fuels the motivation to go through this process. Inquisitiveness actually makes head-cracking experiences that rearrange and stretch our minds *fun.*

As we will discuss, it is not that the other 3Ts do not have impact but their impact is almost always less than international assignments because the head-cracking potential is less. Unlike training programs, international assignments do not provide the safety of a simulated environment. During an international assignment, you have to grapple with real people, real problems, real goals, and real consequences for success or failure. You cannot retreat into familiar territory when the workday is done, as you can in many global teams. During an international assignment, whether at home or at work, you are constantly surrounded by new, unfamiliar, and often unsettling terrain. An international trip might be three weeks long, but many international assignments are three years long. Unlike the short-term experiences of travel, you do not have the option of waiting things out and avoiding the real fabric and texture of the country and culture.

While these sometimes bruising, head-rattling experiences are inevitable during an international assignment, there is no guarantee that it will produce the desired result or the result that our sample experienced. In fact, in this project and other research, we have discovered that there are four basic reactions to smacking your head against the doorways of an unfamiliar restaurant or against the cultural differences that arise during international assignments, as Figure 9.2 illustrates. Each is quite telling in terms of an individual's global leadership potential.

Two dimensions underlie this simple matrix. The first is the level of awareness of individuals that their view is not necessarily the world's view and therefore they need to take a larger, global view. The second dimension is the level of willingness to change to a larger, global view. Although for simplicity of illustration we have drawn the four cells equal in size, in terms of our research, the frequency of each case was different, as we will explain in the description of each case.

The neanderthal

Individuals with zero latent global leadership potential are easy to spot during international assignments because they are so thick-headed that they don't even realize that they've smacked their head and made cultural blunders. They don't even know that they've run up against the new and unexpected. They smack their heads, roll around for a moment, and then plow forward, oblivious to what has happened. As a consequence, they learn nothing that might help them with future global leadership responsibilities. The good news is that these folks are usually easy enough to spot long before being sent on an international assignment and so they usually are not sent—usually but not always. When they are sent, their "thickheadedness" tends

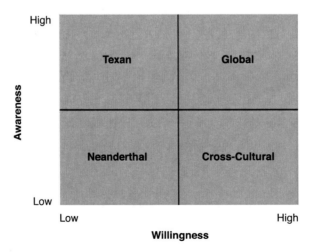

Figure 9.2 Reactions to head-cracking opportunities

not to come from being an unsophisticated cave dweller but from a thick set of credentials, experience, and expertise in a certain area. This area of thick expertise seems to dull their ability to see the various cultural, interpersonal, political, and other relational mistakes they make and therefore they are oblivious to the need for change and reject that need when others try to point it out to them.

The Texan

Clearly we give this label with a bit of "tongue in cheek" and mean no disrespect to people from the great state of Texas. People in Texas are known for their "dogged" determination. Taken to an exaggerated extreme, determination evolves into stubbornness. Extreme stubbornness can cause people who realize they've smacked their heads to remain unwilling to change. Putting the label aside, in our research we encountered people who realized that they had made mistakes in the foreign environment but the pain of change was greater for them than the pain of smacking their heads and so in the end they didn't change their worldviews much at all. In some cases, we found that some people in this category didn't change because they were not sure how. As a consequence, when these individuals were provided with a roadmap for change (perhaps through some training), their unwillingness to change softened and a few made rather dramatic transformations. However, there are some who simply like or feel so secure in their old maps of the world and their familiar home turf that after smacking their head they put the pieces back together just as they were before they were shaken up. As a consequence, these individuals often don't learn even the most basic cross-cultural or country-specific lessons, let alone any advanced global business lessons.

The good news is that there are not so many of these individuals out there representing their companies. While they are not as easy as Neanderthals to pick out in advance of the assignment, you can spot them. One of the signs to watch for is whether they resist change in general. If you spot this too many times in an individual, the odds that they will gain the developmental benefits of an international assignment are not high.

Cross-cultural managers

Individuals in this group recognize that they have smacked their head and are willing to change but tend to take a narrow view of the needed change. Taking the incident of Hal smacking his head on the door lintel, they would walk away with the lesson, "When in Japan, I need to duck." They learn what we would label country- or culture-specific lessons. But they have a hard time extrapolating to a higher level of learning such as, "When I move around the world I have to pay attention to the height of door lintels." One executive's description of a person who fell into this group captures much of the essence.

> José is a great guy. He is humble and willing to change, but he can't extrapolate. By that I mean he can really only see changes as they apply to Germany,

where he is on assignment. He thinks, "Germans don't like it when I am late; they are a bit hung up on time, so I will try not to be late." The adjustments he makes are helping him be more effective in Germany but peers and colleagues from other countries and cultures who have to interact with him don't find him all that easy to work with. He understands that he needs to do things differently in Germany compared to back in Spain, but has a hard time going to a higher level.

People in this category take what we call a "dos and dont's" approach to cross-cultural management. They can think, "When in Japan I need to always give my business card deliberately and receive their card with two hands." But they have a hard time extrapolating and realizing that it is not just about how to exchange cards in Japan but it is about how important titles, rank, and hierarchy in general are to different cultures and how much hierarchical differences do or don't influence behavior.

But we need to be clear here. There is a great need for people who can adjust to working in a new and different country and culture. Companies need good cross-culture managers. Obviously, this is far superior to the alternative of not adjusting either because one does not recognize the need or because one is unwilling to change. However, it is important not to assume that just because someone was successful moving from country A to country B that they will be good at global responsibilities. One executive put it this way:

> We all know that just because someone was a great sales person does not mean that they will be a great sales manager. Or just because they were a great engineer does not guarantee that they will be a great engineering manager. They are related but different. Similarly, just because someone could adjust to one foreign country does not mean that they have the mentality to lead a business unit or function across 50 countries.

As we quoted earlier, two-country culture managers are plentiful. While maybe not a "dime a dozen," as the executive we quoted said, there are many who fall into this category. Unlike the previous two categories, it is hard to know in advance if someone sent on an international assignment will take up the assignment and gain from it only country-specific lessons or whether they will be able to leverage the experience into a more global mindset. However, when they come out of it, you can usually spot the difference and for those who take global lessons away, additional assignments, training, teams, and travel as development opportunities will likely provide great returns to the individual and the company.

Global leaders

This is why people in this fourth category are so valuable and somewhat rare. Individuals with great global leadership, when smacked in the head, *do not* ignore the shake-up, *do not* merely reconstruct their original mental maps, and *do not* just create unique mental maps for each new country-specific situation. People with global leadership talent say, "Aha! I just smacked my head. This is good! This means there is something to learn." This reaction unfreezes their minds and disrupts their mental maps. When these individuals put things back together, they do so in a different way. Individuals with great global leadership talent create "modifiable" general maps. Instead of drawing a mental map that says, "When in Japan, duck upon entering a restaurant," they create mental maps that say, "When moving around the globe, I need to check the height of doorframes and duck when necessary."

In other words, high-potential global leaders identify variables that seem to change from country to country and that have important consequences. *They create a general map, but do not expect it to be accurate in all specific situations.* Rather, they know it is contingent and have identified those factors that are likely to change and whose change can have a significant impact.

As a consequence, individuals with high global leadership potential not only learn country-specific lessons while on assignment, but they move beyond them to broader perspectives. They learn that *what works in one country doesn't necessarily work in another* and that *what is a mistake and doesn't work in one country is not necessarily a mistake or won't work in another.* High-potential individuals learn this not only at an intellectual level but at a behavioral level. That is, they can do more than merely spout these phrases—they actually change their behavior and worldview.

Given this mental process, it is easier to see why international transfers are such a powerful developmental experience. As a senior manager in Sunkyong emphasized, "Nothing can compare to living and working in a foreign country in terms of what has shaped my global business perspective." The daily challenge of living and working in a foreign country virtually guarantees a few hard knocks, and therefore the opportunity to exhibit and develop this adaptive mental map-making process. This is the essence of the developmental power of international transfers.

Enhancing the effectiveness of international transfers

Given the power of international assignments in developing global leadership capabilities, we should encourage firms to send people on these assignments. The reality is that many firms are not that good at selecting, training, sending, and repatriating managers and therefore the full developmental power of international assignments is not harnessed. This is important, because the costs that firms and individuals bear because of poor international assignment policies and practices can be quite severe. For example, each failed assignment costs an average of $250,000 in direct expenses, such as moving, transfer, and travel.[1] Furthermore, this figure does not begin to take into account the indirect costs of damaged reputations, dissatisfied customers, demoralized employees, and missed business opportunities.

For most firms, these problems are only the tip of the iceberg. From our research, we know that 20 to 30 percent of those who stay the full term of their assignments are nevertheless considered unsatisfactory performers (or "brownouts") by their companies. Given the high costs of expatriates (an average of $400,000 a year for salary, housing allowances, cost-of-living adjustments, and other expenses), a firm with just 300 expatriates could be wasting $30–$40 million annually on unsatisfactory performers. Bringing these people home, however, may not solve the problem. In many cases, capable local managers have not been developed. Bringing brownouts home without capable local replacements can make a bad situation worse.

But the problems don't stop with failed assignments or brownouts. On average, one in four managers returning from a successful assignment leaves the firm within a year after repatriation. Not only must the firm spend time and money to replace the individual, but it receives no long-term return on the $1 million or more it has invested during the average three-year assignment.

All these problems can combine to set off a vicious circle that can erode or even destroy a firm's global competitive advantage.

- Failed international assignments, rumors of brownouts, and repatriation turn-over problems can lead the best and brightest throughout the organization's worldwide operations to view international assignments as the "kiss of death" for their careers.
- This "kiss of death" problem makes it difficult to recruit and send top-quality candidates, and this in turn increases the likelihood of more failures.
- This decreasing quality of candidates and declining performance can cause the firm to send fewer and fewer people outside their home countries on assignment, which in turn can lead to coordination and control problems as well as information exchange problems.
- Ultimately, this vicious circle can lead to a dearth of future global leaders with vital international understanding and experience.
- This in turn can in turn lead to even poorer strategic planning and implementation and to an ever-worsening global competitive position.

Many managers and executives no doubt feel that such a dire scenario is unlikely in their own firms. For those who are not vigilant, however, the price is high, because this type of vicious circle can easily start and is nearly impossible to stop. All things considered, we are left with several conclusions:

- There is no substitute for the development power of an international assignment. (In fact, in some firms, such as Shell and Samsung, an international assignment is now a requirement to get into top management positions.)
- Too many companies do a poor job of setting you up for success in an international assignment.
- You can do a variety of things to manage a successful international assignment and maximize its global leadership development potential.

Accepting

There are two keys to selecting and accepting the right international assignment. The first is to begin with the end in mind: ask yourself, "How will this person – or I – use and leverage this international experience down the road?" Without a good answer to this question, the individual may still successfully complete the assignment but lose most of the assignment's developmental potential. The second key is to ensure that the individual and the family are in a solid position to adjust successfully to living and working in the foreign country. Box 9.1 provides a list of questions addressing factors that research has linked to successful cross-cultural adjustment and performance. The more questions answered "yes," the greater the likelihood of success overseas. A predominance of "yes" answers is particularly important if the answer to the last question is "no," that is, if the person will be going to a country with a culture quite different from that of his/her home country. The greater the differences in culture, the more important are the personal, family, job, and organization factors of success. The assessment is worded for the individual candidate to answer but obviously you can simply plug the candidate's name in where it says "you" in the assessment to do an assessment of the candidate's probability of success.

Box 9.1 International assignment success factors

Personal factors

- *Technical skills.* Do you have knowledge of the tasks and technical information required by the assignment?
- *Managerial skills.* Do you have the general ability to work effectively with and through others?
- *Low ethnocentricity.* Do you have a strong tendency to tolerate other beliefs and behaviors and not insist that your way is by definition superior to that of all others?
- *Flexibility.* Do you tend to try new food, activities, forms of entertainment, etc., and can you easily replace old favorites with new ones when the old ones are not available?
- *Willingness to communicate.* Do you persist in efforts to understand and be understood independent of foreign language fluency?
- *Sociability.* Do you tend to be comfortable in new social situations and seek out mentors who can provide guidance and feedback?
- *Conflict Resolution.* Do you tend to keep both your own and others' true objectives in mind and seek out solutions to conflicts which can satisfy each party's objectives?

Family factors

- *Spouse.* Is your spouse willing and excited to go?

- *Children.* If you have any children, are they over the age of 13, and are they excited to go?

Job factors

- *Job discretion.* Will you have freedom to decide what goals to pursue and how to achieve them in the overseas job?
- *Job clarity.* Do you know what is expected in terms of task outcomes?
- *Low job conflict.* Are there few conflicting or competing expectations?

Organizational factors

- *Pre-departure training.* Will you receive at least two days of both general cross-cultural training and country-specific training before leaving for the international assignment?
- *Post-arrival training.* Will you receive at least three days of logistical, job-related, and culture training during the first six months after you arrive?

Environmental factors

- *Cultural distance.* Will you be going to a host country that has a culture quite similar to your home country culture?

Training

Many U.S. executives assume that business is business and good management is good management, so a candidate who has been successful in the United States will succeed in France, Hong Kong, Brazil, or anywhere else. As a consequence:

- Only 40 percent of American firms offer any pre-departure cross-cultural training for their global managers (a figure half that of Japanese, Korean, and European firms).
- Even at those firms that do offer cross-cultural training, the training is typically not very rigorous in nature—averaging only a half-day in length.
- Some 80 percent of U.S. firms do not provide training for spouses.
- Few U.S. firms offer any significant cross-cultural or country-specific training *after* arrival in the international post.[2]

However, business is *not* simply business, and what made you a success in New York will *not* necessarily lead to success in Hong Kong. Furthermore, well-designed cross-cultural training programs enhance your job performance, speed your adjustment to the new culture, and improve the development of cross-cultural managerial skills.

In general, training effectiveness requires matching the training approach to the candidate's specific situation. Three factors can call for more extensive pre-departure and post-arrival training. First, examine the difference in the underlying values and ways of doing business between the candidate's "home country" and "destination country" (often called *cultural toughness*). Second, examine the degree to which the candidate will be called upon to interact personally with members of the local populace such as employees, government officials, customers, and suppliers (often called *communication toughness*). Third, analyze the extent to which the new job is different from what the candidate has done in the past (often called *job toughness*).

In considering training needs, however, do not limit it to just pre-departure training. While important, on its own it is inadequate. Pre-departure training should focus mostly on basic, day-to-day, survival-level concerns, because the candidate and the family will encounter these issues as soon as they step off the plane. As time passes in the new country, both will need less training on day-to-day survival issues and will, instead, need an understanding of the deeper cultural aspects of the country. While they should get some cultural training before an international assignment, in-depth cross-cultural training is most effectively delivered *after* you are "in-country." Mastery of "culturally tough" concepts does not automatically come with time. Thus, post-arrival training is needed to help people master these elements. Post-arrival training is particularly effective because:

- Individuals will be more motivated to learn because they will have since bumped into the more subtle and important aspects of the culture.
- They will have direct experience of the local culture, which will provide them with a foundation for learning deeper cultural values, norms, and ideas.
- They will be in an environment where they can immediately apply in the workplace what they learn in the training seminar.
- They will be in an environment that itself lends a "reality" factor to the training content that does not exist when training is undertaken in the home country before the assignment.

In terms of timing, most pre-departure training should be completed a month before departure, and in-country training should not begin in earnest until you have spent two to four weeks in the country. This is because just before and immediately after arriving overseas, the candidate and the family will be overwhelmed by all the logistics of the move and have little energy or attention to focus on retaining knowledge from the training programs.

Adjusting

Support and contact with the home office during the international assignment is critical. Too many expatriates feel "out of sight and out of mind," and this usually results in repatriation turnover problems. We have several recommendations to help people adjust, gain support during the assignment, and ensure that they can leverage it into greater global leadership opportunities:

- *Stay connected.* Even though people may be tempted to take "home leave" and go off with their families to new and exciting countries for vacation, make sure that employees and their family have time periodically to remain connected to people back home. Repatriation adjustment at work and home will be difficult anyway, so taking time to reduce the "out-of-sight and out-of-mind" phenomenon is a wise move.
- *Find some anchors.* Throughout the assignment, it is important to maintain some anchors, such as writing in a journal, exercise, religious worship, or other familiar pursuit, to keep things on a somewhat even keel.
- *Get a cultural mentor.* Employees need someone—preferably a host-country national—who knows all the cultural road signs and traffic rules, and can both guide them and give them feedback as they form new mental maps and behavior patterns.

Repatriating

Repatriation may be the least talked about and for many the most difficult aspect of international transfers. Without effective repatriation, individuals will have difficulty taking full advantage of their overseas experience as a global leader. As we noted before, approximately 25 percent of managers completing successful international assignments leave their firm within a year after coming home. The following quotes reflect why the repatriation problems are so severe:

> Coming back home was more difficult than going abroad, because you expect changes when going overseas. It was real culture shock during repatriation. I was an alien in my home country. My own attitudes had changed, so that it was difficult to understand my own old customs. Old friends had moved, had had children, or had just vanished. Others were interested in our experiences, but only sort of. They couldn't understand our experiences overseas or they just envied our way of life.
>
> (Expatriate spouse returning from three-year assignment in Vietnam)

> If you look at repatriation as a "homecoming," you're setting yourself up for failure. My company left me dangling in the wind, so to speak. I think that is wrong. I took a real demotion when we came home. No one in the company volunteered anything. I had to initiate everything. I fell through the cracks in the system—if indeed there was a repatriation system in this company. Why can't companies deal more efficiently and compassionately with employees returning from overseas assignments?
>
> (American expatriate returning from a four-year assignment)

To some top executives and line managers (especially those without international experience), these comments may seem a bit overstated; however, 60 percent of expatriates experience "reverse culture shock" during repatriation more severe than the original culture shock they experienced when they went overseas.

Many expatriates and their families expect a "hero's welcome" after returning home from a successful international assignment. However, most are lucky to receive *any* welcome at all. In fact, one expatriate told us that he actually lost his "identity" during repatriation. Apparently he did not exist on his own company's records for three months after his return. He found out about the problem from a credit firm when he was denied two critical loans (house and car) because he was unemployed! While this might seem like an atypical case, it is not. In fact, too many expatriates returning home are functionally unemployed when their airplane lands. The individuals might be on the company's records, but don't really have a solid position in the firm because the return has been inadequately planned.

Monsanto has been often cited for the attention it pays to repatriation issues, and the company now has a one-day repatriation program that all employees must attend. Samsung, though it has not received the same kind of recognition, places an even greater emphasis on repatriation issues. All returning Samsung managers spend one *month* in a repatriation program designed to help them understand the dynamics of "reverse culture shock," and to capture the lessons learned while overseas. Samsung has created a giant database in which information about various countries, cultures, governments, competitors, and markets is extracted from each and every returning manager during the one-month repatriation program.

Returning expatriates at most U.S. firms are not lucky enough to have such programs available and so must rely more on their own resources. Individuals who succeed at repatriation and use international assignments to develop their global leadership capabilities do several things right that most do wrong. Box 9.2 is a list of what you should do; the manager quotes reflect how things usually go for most people.

Development strategy #2: training

Most of the executives we interviewed indicated that formal training seminars and programs play a central role in their global leadership development. This is because good training can provide an intense experience within the context of a structured learning environment. Real experiences provided by assignments are powerful, but their costs and real-time nature can frustrate all but the most determined attempts to reflect on and learn from them. By its very nature, training is based on reflection and learning.

From a company perspective, training is viewed as a powerful developmental tool for high-potential employees. A large majority of the firms in our research plan to increase the money spent on programs designed to "globalize"

Box 9.2   Keys to repatriation success

- *Look for a sponsor to help with placement and re-entry into the firm.*

    No one accepted responsibility for placing me back in the organiza-
    tion. I ended up without a job when I was expecting a promotion! My
    wife also gave up her job with the same company to go overseas
    (she had 12 years of experience). We were promised a job for her
    upon our return. Again, no one has helped us find one.

    (Expatriate with 15 years of experience in the parent company)

- *Plan your repatriation three to six months ahead.*

    After being home three months I am still waiting for a permanent
    office. All this after 30 years of experience in the company and three
    international assignments!

    (European expatriate)

- *Locate a suitable position.*

    When I was overseas, I felt I had an impact on the business. In the
    United States, I feel as though the impact—if any—is minimal.
    When I came home, I was assigned to a newly created, undefined
    staff job where I had no friends, no contacts, and no access to
    management. Firms need to realize that expatriates have developed
    independent decision-making skills, become accustomed to having
    final authority, and conditioned to having their business judgment
    given a lot of credibility by top management. In my new job, my
    business judgment is much less valued than when I was overseas.
    Until firms change, expatriates should expect the worst when coming
    home to avoid disappointment.

    (American expatriate with a large commercial bank)

- *Allow yourself some "downtime" upon repatriation.*

    I arrived home on Tuesday and started work on Wednesday. I haven't
    adjusted yet to much of anything and really feel depressed. I worked
    14-hour days, six days a week. There was little time to look for
    housing; yet the company still pressured me to move out of a hotel in
    order to get me off the "expense" status.

    (Japanese expatriate)

- *Request repatriation training.*

    We received absolutely no training or orientation concerning
    common repatriation adjustment problems. Just knowing about them
    and having a few ideas of how to effectively cope would have been
    of great value to us and to the company in terms of my performance.

    (Expatriate returning from Japan)

- *Set realistic return expectations.*

  I went on my foreign assignment to the UK as a favor for the department. In return I received nothing special for the 10 months I spent away from my family and the hardship I put them through. I really expected a promotion after coming back home and did not receive it.

  (French expatriate)

- *Consider family adjustment issues and the spillover effect on work.*

  My spouse has had a very difficult time coming home from Europe and living in the suburbs of America. She hates it. Her adjustment difficulty has made my life less than wonderful and my work performance less than excellent.

  (American expatriate)

- *Search out opportunities to utilize your international experience.*

  Firms must value international expertise—not only appreciate it but actually put it to good use. Don't let a corporate headquarters' environment destroy the lessons, "business savvy," negotiation skills, and foreign language proficiencies which expatriates learned from the real world—a global marketplace.

  (Japanese expatriate)

- *Seek out a return job with reasonable autonomy.*

  If you have been the orchestra conductor overseas, it is very difficult to accept a position as second fiddle when coming home.

  (American expatriate recently returned
  from the UK)

their management and executive ranks. Virtually no firms planned to reduce their investment in global leadership development programs.

Recently, Carrefour, the second-largest retailer in the world, relaunched its global leader program for its senior directors as a key vehicle for training its future global leaders. The program draws participants from all of Carrefour's worldwide business and includes both classroom and action-learning experiences. In the first module, participants embark on an expedition journey and visit companies and executives in Silicon Valley to get a firsthand feel for innovation and new ideas in retail. In addition, they work on global action-learning projects in teams and present their analysis and recommendations to the CEO and other top executives. Upon their return, participants presented their findings to senior management. Participants uniformly felt that the experience significantly altered their worldview and felt that exposure to various people through the company-provided training program enhanced their organizational savvy. As participants came to know peers and their capabilities throughout the company, they expressed confidence that they could draw on this understanding and the far-flung resources in the worldwide company to tackle future complex projects that exceeded the capabilities of their immediate set of subordinates.

In looking at the programs companies offer, there are three critical points of assessment: Participants, Content, and Process.

Participants

Executives consistently commented on the long-term benefit of programs they attended when those programs drew participants from outside their home country. Fortunately, companies increasingly bring managers and executives together from throughout their worldwide operations. While many firms still offer "regional programs" that draw participants primarily from within a region, the clear trend is toward offering global programs. For example, Exxon conducts its "Global Leadership Workshop" for high-potential managers twice a year and draws only half of the 30 participants in each program from the United States. The rest come from its affiliates throughout the world. In addition to drawing in participants from around the world, IBM has also conducted an eight-day program at its training sites outside the United States. A typical program involving 26 to 30 participants will have 13 to 16 different nationalities represented.

For managers at companies anywhere, the value of attending programs with international participants includes the following:

- International participants have different perspectives and practices, and this helps people open their minds and embrace new perspectives.
- Participants from different countries have knowledge about customers, competitors, governments, markets, and economies that can be of value to each other.
- The networking and relationship-building opportunity the program provides facilitates the sharing of valuable information long after people return home. This can greatly strengthen a firm's efforts to coordinate and integrate its worldwide activities.
- Participants develop a much broader perspective on their company's global challenges and opportunities.

We did, however, find regional differences in terms of the emphasis placed on training programs. European firms place more emphasis on executive education and training than do either U.S. or Asian firms. Interestingly, of all the major nations, Japanese firms place the least emphasis on executive training, while Korean firms spend a higher proportion of revenue on executive education and development than any other national group of companies. Korean managers spend an average of 14 days a year in education and training programs. European firms also place a much stronger emphasis on seminars and programs with in-company participants than do U.S. or Asian firms.

Content

In terms of content, the following were the topics most often covered in global leadership programs:

- formulating global vision and strategy
- designing and structuring organizations
- managing stakeholders
- leading change
- fostering innovation, and
- managing global and virtual teams.

First, programs that address how effective *global vision and strategy* are formulated and communicated enhance the global business savvy and global organizational savvy elements of the global leadership model (see Chapter 3). Participants increasingly see value in programs designed to enhance global analytical abilities, especially concerning competitive, economic, social, or political drivers.

Second, programs that examine *designing and structuring organizations* for global reach enhance participants' "perspective" capabilities (i.e., balancing tensions and embracing ambiguity). Successfully positioning a corporation in the international marketplace calls for a deep understanding of the tensions between global integration and local responsiveness. In most companies, both approaches are necessary. Global integration capitalizes on economies of scale, scope, and opportunities for reduced costs. Local responsiveness is also required, because customers in different countries and regions do not have identical preferences and tastes. In many industries, customer demand for customized features and services has, if anything, increased.

Third, even a decade ago *stakeholder management* was not a common topic in most global leadership programs. However, time and technology have shifted the management of stakeholders from the periphery to the center. Stakeholders are more interconnected today than ever before through technology and that technology allows them to get their messages and views out more quickly and to more people than ever before. As a consequence, all leaders, not just functional heads of "external relations," must be good at stakeholder relations.

Fourth, most programs examine the effective *management of change.* In today's business environment, the only constant is change. While you can lay out new directions, visions, or strategies with relative ease, none of these makes any difference unless they are well executed. Consequently, a key difference between winners and losers in the marketplace rests not so much on the content of particular strategies but on the ability to execute and implement change. This relates to the dimensions of embracing uncertainty and global organizational savvy in the global leadership model.

Fifth, given the changing nature of the world, *innovation* is critical to staying in the game. However, the best companies stress not just product innovation but process and even business model innovation as well. Sometimes the winner is not just who has the better product but who has a more efficient and effective process for creating and delivering the product. This also relates to the dimensions of embracing uncertainty and global organizational savvy in the global leadership model.

Sixth, increasingly programs are including *global and virtual team leadership and effectiveness.* The increasing complexity of the business environment dictates that one person cannot know all the requirements. Cross-functional, cross-cultural, and virtual teams are and will become an ever bigger part of organizational life. The ability to lead these teams effectively is becoming a critical differentiator between winners and losers in the marketplace. This theme relates most directly to the skill at emotional connection that global business leaders rely on.

Process

Our analysis of company training programs also revealed two important process trends. The first is the increased emphasis on learning partnerships. Many firms are decreasing the use of "canned" programs, whether provided by universities or consulting firms. Increasingly, companies want customized programs and are working with proven external providers who deliver the desired content and work effectively in partnership with clients.

Consortium programs are an interesting outcome of this tendency to customize programs developed with partners. For example, we are involved with several consortia. These consortia typically have six to eight member firms. Member firms share the following characteristics:

- They currently have international operations.
- They seek to expand their global presence.
- They highly value the development of future global leaders.
- They do not compete directly with each other.

Each firm has a representative on the consortium's advisory board. We work with the advisory board to design a program that meets the general and common global leader development needs of all participating firms. Typical participants have the following in common:

- They are nominated and selected internally by each member firm.
- They have high potential for significant leadership responsibilities.
- They occupy now or will occupy in the near future positions with international responsibilities.

- They demonstrate a strong commitment to learning and further personal development.
- They come from throughout the firm's divisional, functional, and geographic units.
- They are typically 30 to 50 years old.

The typical consortium has the following structural characteristics:

- Member firms send approximately five participants to each program.
- Each program is usually two weeks long.
- Member firms make an initial two-year commitment to the consortium.
- Programs are run between two and four times each year, so a given firm sends a total of 20 to 40 participants over two years.
- The advisory board meets two times a year to review program content and structure and provide input into upcoming programs.

Firms that do not have comprehensive systems for developing future global leaders and do not have scores of high-potential managers find the consortium approach highly effective at meeting their needs.

Companies in consortium programs cite several reasons for their participation in lieu of more traditional, "in-house" programs. First and foremost, companies cite cross-fertilization: the opportunity for their high-potential employees to be exposed to individuals from other industries. The fact that none of the firms involved competes with each other allows for in-depth discussion of challenges and best practices. In addition, participants are able to leverage the relationships developed during the program long after its formal conclusion. Companies also like the consortium approach, because it lowers the per-participant costs by leveraging the collective purchasing power of all the consortium firms.

Beyond the use of consortia, a second process trend is the increased emphasis on "action learning," the exact definition of which varies from firm to firm. In general, however, action learning involves some project, case, or exercise that relates to the real problems, challenges, or opportunities the firm and program participants face. For example, we worked with IFF to design its global leadership program, which has three distinct segments conducted over approximately six months, including a trip to an important emerging economy and an examination of a strategically impor-tant company challenge there. The projects were defined and sponsored by the company's executive committee and their CEO, Doug Tough.

Summary

In focusing on training and development, companies should consider several key points. First, training programs can be a powerful development approach. Companies should take advantage of and seek out partnering opportunities, whether that is with professional providers or with other firms via consortia.

Second, companies should look to enhance opportunities for participants to interact with others from throughout the firm's worldwide operations. Third, companies should emphasize international strategy and vision, organizational structure and design, stakeholder management, change management, fostering innovation, and global and virtual team leadership. Finally, firms should look to include action-learning components in programs.

Development strategy #3: teams

We found that 60 to 70 percent of European and American executives felt that global task forces or project teams composed of diverse members (e.g., functional background, nationality, culture, ethnicity) were an important developmental strategy. In contrast, only 20 percent of Japanese executives felt this way. This may reflect the history and practice of most Japanese firms, which use project teams composed almost exclusively of Japanese nationals even when the project's scope is global in nature.

When used properly, global teams work as a developmental opportunity, because the intense and prolonged interaction with individuals of different backgrounds in a team context presents each member with constant opportunities to face different or contrasting terrain in terms of values, business models, decision-making norms, and leadership paradigms. This mode of intense and prolonged contrast forces team members to examine their own values and business paradigms, a process that is easier to avoid on short international trips where one can easily seek a safe harbor from the strange smells, words, traditions, and perspectives by never leaving the familiar surroundings of the local Hilton Hotel or Hard Rock Cafe. When you are part of a task force, safe harbors are harder to come by.

A large mining firm illustrates the effective use of teams. Recently at one of the largest mines in the company's portfolio and one of the ten largest mines in the world the government asked to reopen negotiations so that it could take a large share of ownership of the mine and thereby get a larger share of the money coming from the mine's operations. This was after the company had spent billions on assessing the feasibility of the mine, studying environmental impacts, and constructing the mine. Changing the ownership structure could mean that the mine would go from having a positive to negative return on investment for the company. Therefore, it put together a cross-cultural, cross-functional, and cross-location team. In other words, they had people on the team located in the particular country and from elsewhere, people from cultures represented by the country as well as many others, and people across a variety of functions from supply chain to production to government affairs, and so on.

Someone from the supply chain area pointed out that the vast majority of suppliers were local companies, employing local citizens, and if the ownership structure changed to the point that the mine's operation were jeopardized, these companies and their employees would lose out. As a consequence in less than 24 hours they had an open letter to the government signed by more than 60 percent of their key local suppliers stating that the original agreement should be honored and that what the government was doing threatened the jobs of citizens who elected them to create jobs.

Someone not local from government affairs recognized that several countries would be concerned by the local government's threat of not honoring a signed agreement and contract. That person arranged for letters and visits from the ambassadors of three large and powerful countries with high economic investment in the country, which happened within 12 hours.

Someone from finance gathered data when the international markets opened and news reached them to show the financial impact not just on the one company in particular but on all companies with a major presence in the country in question to show how international capital markets would react. This individual then solicited the help of others in the financial department not located in the country to get input from international bankers on what the implications for loan rates would be for the country and for companies doing business in the country and how that would impact the government's own budget if its international borrowing rates increased.

Someone local from the marketing department pointed out that there were many local employees the company had trained who, through that training, had qualified for and moved into significantly higher paying jobs. In collaboration with some consultants they came up with an advertising campaign within 24 hours featuring specific employees and put their short but powerful story on billboards and signs that government officials could easily see as they went to work in the morning.

While the team solved the country-specific problem and the government reversed its course and returned to abiding by the original agreement, the powerful lessons of being on this team could have been lost in the heat of battle. Instead, the company did a formal "after action review" and even documented the incident in a case study for internal use. Team members were interviewed to distill what they had learned that was unique to this situation and what lessons could be extracted and applied to other situations in the future. Clearly team experiences like this, if leveraged, can be powerful development vehicles for both the members as well as for individuals beyond the team.

However, our research suggests that merely throwing a diverse set of people together and then adding some folks from far off places to the mix on average will not automatically deliver great results or learning and development opportunities. Therefore, it is wise to assess the readiness of the team leader and members to tackle the specific challenge and leverage the learning. The following provide some simple assessment questions:

1. How much experience have the team leader and team members had working with people

    *   of different cultural backgrounds?
    *   of different functional backgrounds and training?
    *   of different company backgrounds (company size, industry, life cycle)?

2. How much training and education have the team leader and team members
    had in relation to:

    - general team dynamics?
    - cross-cultural communication?
    - multicultural and cross-functional team effectiveness?

As these basic questions suggest, adequate experience, education, and training
among the team members are critical factors in successful global teams. In our
experience and travels we have seen debris from numerous global teams that
crashed and burned because the members were thrown into the situation without
adequate experience or training. You wouldn't send a Piper Cub pilot to fly a
747. Both are airplanes flown by pilots, but there is a qualitative difference, just
as there is between domestic and global task forces and teams. So team leaders
and members should always be sure they understand how large a leap is expected
of them; and be certain they have adequate training for the global team challenges
they do take on.

Development strategy #4: travel

In our interviews, many executives talked about the power of extensive foreign
travel in developing various global leadership characteristics. In particular,
many mentioned the power of travel in developing global business savvy and
emotional connection. As one manager explained, "There's nothing like being in
India to help you understand the opportunities and challenges. Nothing compares
to sitting down to dinner with someone from Bombay to help you really relate
to them."

Most companies use foreign travel as an important and effective developmental
tool. In our study, 55 percent of Japanese firms reported that they use extensive
foreign travel as a key to developing global leaders, while only 40 percent of
European firms and 27 percent of U.S. firms use extensive foreign travel for this
purpose. We want to be clear that while Japanese, American, and European
executives traveled about the same amount, development expectations of that
travel differed significantly across countries.

A manager at a consumer products firm spoke to the issue of how much foreign
travel many executives experience:

> Last Monday, I ran into a colleague who had been waltzing around the
> world for 44 days—a personal best. His dog didn't even know him when
> he came home. That's the tradeoff. You're on the road to learn the details of
> the business.

As this quote suggests, getting a firsthand feel for the world can require logging a
lot of miles. The world is a pretty big place. However, logging the miles does not
necessarily lead to landing key insights. The key to becoming a global leader is

not just the *quantity* of foreign travel, but the *quality*. To be effective, travel must put potential global leaders in the middle of the country—its culture, economy, political system, market, and so on—without the "executive comfort cocoon" of a Western-style luxury hotel, car and driver, and choreographed itinerary.

For example, an interview with an executive of a large retail store revealed that he had traveled to Japan more than 20 times in the last three years. Each trip was approximately one week long, which translates into a cumulative five months in Japan. In that amount of time, this individual could have acquired substantial insights and knowledge about a wide variety of Japanese cultural, economic, and political issues. However, as the conversation progressed, it became clear that the executive did not really understand the country at all. Further probing into his past visits revealed that the executive was always met at the airport, always stayed at the same luxury hotel, always had a car and driver to take him to appointments, always had a bilingual employee with him, and always had his entire itinerary set up by the local office before his arrival. In short, this executive had experienced the same week 20 times. In spite of the opportunity the frequent trips to Japan provided, this self-created cocoon guaranteed that little learning would take place.

As we mentioned in Chapter 4, John Pepper, past CEO at Procter & Gamble, set a completely different example for his employees. Rather than insulating himself behind the typical perks of limousines and dutiful staffers, John Pepper set a goal to visit five families in each country. He wanted to talk with the families and learn how they use household products. His actions communicated the message that international travel should be used as an opportunity to learn more about the various countries, cultures, and consumers that make up P&G's global marketplace. His travels in France helped him rearrange his mental map concerning the French preference for front-load washers and their resistance to top-load washers. This in turn helped him embrace the duality of managing a new cold-water detergent brand on a global basis, while at the same time finding a way to meet the local needs of getting the detergent to distribute evenly throughout the wash when used in front-load washers. Eventually, this led to an innovative solution. The company developed a new system based on a plastic ball, designed to be filled with detergent and placed in a front-load washer along with the dirty clothes. During the wash cycle, the detergent is distributed evenly through small holes in the ball.

International travel can be made more effective in developing global leaders in two specific ways: taking detours and getting wet.

Since contrasts are often the things that help us stretch and rearrange our mental maps, it is important to get off the beaten path and take detours. The following quote from a senior executive in a British oil company reflects how effective global leaders approach travel as a developmental opportunity:

> When I travel, I try to experiment as much as possible. When I am in Beijing, I like finding someone who can take me down the dirty back allies. I like going to grungy local restaurants and back alley bars. I don't want to take the tourist route. Recently, when I was in Turkmenistan, I asked our guy

to take me to the local market and then to a local bar. I loved it. I ask people unconstrained questions: Why do you do that? How do you do that? Sometimes they are offended, but often they are extremely pleased that you asked.

Getting wet really amounts to diving deep into the waters of the society in terms of what shopping, education, homes, and so on are really like for the people who live there. This is in effect what John Pepper accomplished by visiting the homes of real people rather than having local office staffers provide reams of market research data on living styles. If you want to get wet, look for opportunities to engage all your senses—sight, hearing, smell, taste, and touch. Engaging all your senses makes the difference between merely observing and actually experiencing a new place when you travel to it.

At 3M, Margaret Alldredge described how managers are encouraged to dive deep into the society and learn as much as possible from their travels so they can share their insights with others. 3M has formalized a process for disseminating the lessons gained from international travel. After an international trip, the traveler organizes a "brown bag lunch" to present what he or she has learned about the country visited. Knowing that one must make a presentation enhances the motivation to extract lessons worthy of presenting to peers back home and, as a consequence, enhances the level of learning during international trips. In addition, the presentations facilitate vicarious learning within the firm and enable others to build from a higher base of knowledge when going abroad.

As you think over the international trips you've taken and future trips you may anticipate, consider the following questions:

1. What "detours" have you taken or plan to take in relation to

    - eating (shops, open markets, stores)?
    - lodging (hotels, inns, apartments)?
    - recreation (sports, camping, hiking)?
    - entertainment (theater, dance, music)?
    - shopping (markets, stores, centers)?

2. How deeply have you plunged into the country in terms of

    - people's homes?
    - transportation?
    - religion?
    - education?
    - cultural activities?
    - government and politics?

In summary, foreign travel must be somewhat frequent if it is to be used as a global leadership development tool; however, whether your company has a formal program such as 3M's or not, you need to take steps to enhance the *quality* of what you learn from your travels. Take detours. Be willing to venture off the beaten path. The fact that a path is beaten means it's unlikely you'll learn something on it that competitors don't already know. Remember, if you do what you've always done, you'll learn what you already know.

Recommendations

So how can the 4Ts make an impact on your development as a global leader throughout your career? We examine this question in more detail in the next chapter. Still, we should emphasize several points here.

First, even though we place the burden of responsibility for development on the individual's shoulders, we believe that senior executives have a responsibility to make sure that the company has both the quantity and quality of leaders it needs in order to ensure prosperity for years to come. Jack Welch, past CEO of GE expressed this same sentiment this way: "Headquarters at GE doesn't run companies. It runs a school that teaches how to run companies, and does it so well that GE maintains a huge trade surplus in talent. That's my job. We spend all our time on people. The day we screw up the people thing, this company is over."[3]

Second, there seems to be little substitute for an international assignment in terms of developing the mindset needed for global leadership responsibilities. Because many organizations do not think about international assignments from a systematic or strategic development perspective, you must make sure that you do. Two excellent books covering these issues in detail are *So You're Going Overseas: A Handbook for Personal and Professional Success* and *So You're Coming Home*.[4] Not all international assignments are of equal strategic value for the organization or your personal development. In general, look for assignments that will give you the opportunity to link the local operation to regional and corporate headquarters. Technology transfers are especially likely to provide opportunities to integrate and coordinate activities between the local unit and regional or worldwide units. Think carefully about accepting an assignment that will put you out in the "wilderness" with little reason to coordinate with others. While this type of assignment and autonomy can be very enjoyable and personally rewarding, it is a better route for someone who wants to become a country specialist than for those who want to develop broader, global perspectives.

Third, take advantage of formal training and education opportunities that focus on international aspects of business. Especially seek out programs that draw participants from a variety of functional and geographic backgrounds. To the extent possible, also seek out programs that give you an opportunity to interact with individuals from other companies and industries.

Fourth, although it may not always be possible, seek cross-cultural and cross-functional team membership experiences before you seek out or accept cross-cultural and cross-functional leadership opportunities. If you do have the opportunity to lead a cross-cultural and cross-functional team, be sure to assess members' knowledge and skills relative to global team dynamics. Do not assume that all the members are equipped to deal effectively with diverse team dynamics. To the extent that skills are lacking and the team's task is important and visible, you would do well to try to get some training for the team before it becomes fully involved in the project.

Finally, make sure that you seek out detours and learning opportunities during international travels. In one sense, none of us have the time for these detours; however, from another perspective, you cannot afford not to take them. If you want a competitive advantage over others, you need to see and experience things they don't. You've got to get off the beaten path.

With these recommendations in mind, let's now examine in more detail how these strategies for developing global leadership capabilities change over the course of your career and how you can continue to pursue them.

Notes

1 Stroh, L., Mendenhall, M. E., Black, J. Stewart, and Gregersen, Hal B. (2005). *International Assignments: An Integration of Research and Practice.* Hillsdale, NJ: Erlbaum.
2 Ibid.
3 Stewart, T. (1999). "The Contest for Welch's Throne Begins: Who Will Run GE?" *Fortune,* January 11, p. 27.
4 Black, J. Stewart and Gregersen, Hal B. (1998) *So You're Going Overseas: A Handbook for Personal and Professional Success.* San Diego, CA: Global Business Publishers; Black, J. Stewart and Gregersen, Hal B. (1999) *So You're Coming Home.* San Diego, CA: Global Business Publishers.

10 Intersecting your career stage and leadership development

While companies want and need more global leaders, in a recent survey we conducted, only 14.3 percent of the firms indicated that they had a comprehensive global leader development system. Recall from Chapter 1 that 82 percent of companies reported to us that they don't have enough global leaders to meet their needs. In combination this suggests that the global leader talent gap is not going to close quickly. This either represents a great challenge or opportunity, depending on your perspective.

For the individual leader, it suggests that you should not wait on or depend on the company for your global leadership development. If your company has a system, count yourself lucky and take full advantage. If you are responsible for developing future leaders and your company has a comprehensive system, then you can add the greatest value to the company by ensuring that you identify and connect to the system individuals with the greatest interest in and aptitude for global leadership. But if your firm is like the vast majority and does not have a comprehensive system, the challenge or opportunity for developing yourself or others as the case may be is on your shoulders.

In the previous chapter we discussed at length the benefits and unique development power of the 4Ts (Transfers, Training, Teams, and Travel). All of that is also relevant in this chapter as well. However, in our extensive interviews and research, it became quite clear that the exact role and use of the 4Ts vary by career stage. Therefore, in this chapter, we want to highlight the extent and way the 4Ts should be used, depending on whether you or the people you are responsible for are early, mid, or later in their career. The summary of the differences of the objectives of each of the 4Ts by career stage is presented in Table 10.1. The rest of the chapter examines each of the 4Ts in more detail by career stage. That way, if you want, and depending on your situation, you can skip straight to the career section that is most relevant for you personally and/or for the people you have the opportunity to develop.

Early career development

Individuals do not become global leaders instantly or easily. As we have mentioned, experience constitutes 70 to 80 percent of the needed development.

Table 10.1 Development objectives and career stages

Developmental activity	Early career stage	Mid-career stage	Late career stage
Global transfers	No P&L Awareness Shorter-term Testing	P&L responsibility Cross-functional Long-term Testing	P&L responsibility Global or regional Long-term Final polishing
Global training	Perspective Awareness Functional skills	Perspective General mgr. skills Action learning Networking	Senior executive skills Networking Action learning
Global teams	Team Member Single function/ cross-cultural Cross-functional	Team Leader Single function/global Cross-functional	Global team leader Mentor to junior team leaders
Global travel	Awareness Testing	Learn Share	Connections and relationships Building others

Training and formal feedback constitute the rest. The reality is that it simply takes time to accumulate the needed experience and training. What executives have said from their own experience and from developing others is that it takes at least 10 years to accumulate the requisite development if it could be all perfectly planned and sequenced. The reality is that it is almost never perfectly planned or sequenced and sometimes it is just accidental. As a consequence, if you are yourself early in your career, you should start your global development now. If you are responsible for others who are early in their careers, the message is the same but with added emphasis, because the impact that you can have is much bigger when you do the math. To get a grasp of your potential impact, simply multiply the number of young leaders whose development you influence by the number of years of their careers that remain. But whether you are yourself early in your career or are responsible for the development of others who are early in their careers, the bottom line message is the same: start the development today. This message should be amplified if you are in a company in which the global leader development system is less than ideal.

If you yourself are in the early stages of your career and are in a company with a less than ideal global leader development system, then the situation represents both a challenge and an opportunity. It is a challenge primarily because, with few systematic development mechanisms in place, you may find it difficult to "sell" your development needs to individuals who have the authority to give you the development opportunities you need. However, the lack of established development programs is also a great opportunity. For example, we know of one young manager who raised the need for cross-cultural training for young managers with several executives. This young woman had a double challenge, because she was in a fairly invisible job and department, and the company had done virtually nothing in the way of formal cross-cultural or international training for young managers. Not all the executives who heard this young woman's arguments were persuaded, but two key executives were. As a consequence, the executives authorized the young woman to organize a seminar for younger managers. Not only was she one of the first participants in the program, but she became much more visible to other executives, who in the end had to sign off on their subordinates who attended the seminar.

If you are responsible for the development of young leaders and if your firm lacks a fully constructed and integrated development system, you too have both a challenge and opportunity. In this situation, however, we typically hear much more about the challenges than the opportunities. In fact, when we talk to the most senior leaders, we hear not just about what challenges not having a full system create but hear even more about why the company doesn't have an integrated system. The most common explanations we hear from senior executives about why their company does not have a fully constructed and integrated global leader development system fall into three buckets: too expensive, too vague, too risky.

Too Expensive. Many executives explain their lack of a system by arguing that a whole—"soup to nuts"—system is just too expensive. Identifying who has interest in and potential for global leadership and figuring out what are the right transfers, training, teams, and travel for the development of leaders over 10 years or more for a given leader costs too much. They comment further that the high cost is not just in the direct expenses but in the time and energy required to design, develop, and deliver such a system. Having looked at companies with such systems, we cannot argue. A fully constructed and integrated system is not cheap; that's for certain. However, there are costs and consequences of not having a system as well. In that sense it is no different from constructing or not constructing a factory. If you build a factory, you have all the direct and non-direct costs. These you can calculate. But if you don't build the factory, you also have potential costs and consequences. If demand for the product the factory would produce exceeds supply (as it does for 82 percent of companies in the case of global leader demand and supply), then if you don't build the factory, you either miss out on all the revenue that would come from what the factory would produce or you have to purchase the supply to sell from someone else. This is why, after articulating this analogy, we often ask the following questions:

- What is the cost of not having the right number and quality of leaders you need?
- Have you ever had to pass on a global expansion, merger and acquisition (M&A), or joint venture (JV), or other opportunities because you did not have enough leaders with the requisite capabilities?
- Have you ever had senior leaders make tactical or strategic blunders because they were not given adequate development? What have been the costs of those mistakes?
- Have you ever had leaders who didn't have the right global development injure relationships with customers, suppliers, regulators, government

officials, communities, NGOs, or other stakeholders? What have been the costs of those mistakes?

It doesn't take much more than this to make the point. In fact, not long ago in a consumer products company we were having this basic conversation. The executive admitted that recently they had a failed product launch, not because of fundamental problems with the product, but because the leader had little experience understanding the nuances of regulations that governed the product around the world. The botched launch cost more than $30 million. That was ten times the global leader development budget at the time.

Too Vague. In addition to explanations that global leader development is too expensive, senior executives also tended to explain to us the lack of development because of the target being too vague. For example, recently at a Japanese firm the senior leader said that global leader development was too vague and then asked a series of questions: What is a global leader? What capabilities should be developed? How best should these be developed? Who should be developed? As you can see, these questions are actually pretty focused and, therefore, the problem was not that the target of global leadership development was too vague, but that the answers to these questions from his staff were not compelling. This incident is typical of what we have encountered with regard to the explanation that global leadership development is too vague. Hopefully, the research we've conducted helps provide some concrete answers to many if not most of these questions, and therefore helps reduce this objection.

Too Risky. The third most common explanation for why companies don't have integrated development systems is because it is too risky to develop talent, especially young talent. When we asked executives to explain, virtually all of them had a variation on the following:

> This new generation is different. They don't think about job stability or company loyalty the way my generation does. For example, we put together a fairly intensive and well-designed multi-module program a couple of years back. It was great development. Participants had interactions with senior executives; they met with suppliers, customers, and the like; they worked on projects; they presented to the board; the whole thing. Then we lost several of the members to competitors. My HR guys told me that with direct and indirect costs (including the participants' time) thrown in, the cost was over $100,000 per participant. I could have just written a check to my competitors instead of financing the development of their future employees.

No argument from us that losing employees after investing so much is frustrating. However, in focusing on who left, executives lose sight of two other critical issues. The first is who stayed with the company and what impact on their ability to contribute did the development have. One may exist, but we have yet to come upon a case where the company lost all employees who participated to competitors or other employers. The second issue they lose sight of is what would have happened to those young leaders if the company had done nothing. To assume that those leaders would have stayed with the company without any investment in their development as global leaders is, in our experience, folly.

Bottom line, if you are responsible for the development of young leaders, whether you are a line manager or in HR, to say (or allow more senior executives to maintain) that a fully constructed and integrated global leader development system is too expensive, too vague, or too risky is, on the basis of our research, not very defendable. You have to ask what are the costs and consequences of not investing, of not clarifying, and not risking. The answer is probably somewhat different for different companies, but we have no evidence that the costs and consequences are anything close to zero.

Transfers

The expense of international transfers causes most firms to restrict them to more senior managers. There are, however, some exceptions to this rule. For example, American Express has a program in which it selects five young, high-potential U.S. managers and five non-U.S. managers and sends them on 18-month international assignments, half the usual length. ColgatePalmolive has a similar program.

Even if your firm does not have this type of program, you might consider what Kelly Barton did as a young manager in a software company. Kelly graduated with a degree in Japanese Studies. She had lived in Japan for a semester as an undergraduate student and was reasonably fluent in the language. Although Japan was a strategically important country and the base of her firm's Asia operations, it was so expensive to send people there that the firm had basically stopped sending expatriate managers. Kelly recognized that Japan represented an important consumer and competitor base in the video and computer game software industry. She also knew that if she could get even a short assignment there (6 to 18 months), she could gain exposure to other important Asian countries. Given the potential growth of the overall Asian market in video games, Kelly was convinced that exposure to the region would be of lasting value.

Leveraging her knowledge of how to live cheaply in Tokyo, Kelly proposed to go to Japan on a short assignment without a full expatriate package. If the company would pay the large deposits usually required when renting an apartment in Japan, Kelly offered to go there without any extraordinary allowances, like housing or general cost-of-living increases. Through internal networking, she had already discovered two projects in the company's Japan office that were a perfect fit with her capabilities. Both projects were expected to take less than 18 months to complete.

Kelly's request was reviewed and in the end granted. Interestingly, despite her background in Japan, Kelly found that working there provided a whole new set of insights about the country. Her exposure to other Asian countries, especially China, also turned out to be a bit different from her expectations. The differences, however, helped broaden her perspective in a way that never could have happened without living and working overseas.

Kelly's experience helps illustrate the key elements of an international assignment early in your career. First, the assignment needs to focus on a single country. Unless young leaders' personal and family backgrounds are such that they have lived in a variety of countries, it is wise to test early if they will do well effectively adjusting to and performing in a single foreign setting. While adjusting to one country is no guarantee that they will have the mentality to deal with the world, it is a better predictor and certainly a better development mechanism than staying at home without the international assignment.

Although the term of the assignment does not necessarily need to be short, given that the main purpose is to broaden awareness, especially of oneself, longer-term assignments may not be necessary or advisable. Early career international assignments provide unique development opportunities to create a heightened self-awareness about young leaders' specific global leadership strengths and weaknesses. These experiences can also enhance their inquisitiveness about the international business domain in general. With this development purpose in mind, it makes little sense to attach profit-and-loss (P&L) or other significant responsibilities to early-career international assignments. Still, even without intense job responsibilities, these assignments are a great way for the company to get an early idea about the candidate's long-term global leadership potential.

Training

Unfortunately, few of the companies we surveyed or interviewed provide formal global leadership training for young managers. Many, however, do provide training in functional skills. This is quite logical. Early in one's career, mastering specific functional or technical capabilities is simply required. However, it does not take much to add some international dimensions to these programs. For example, without breaking the bank, participants can be drawn from a region rather than just one country. This early exposure to colleagues outside one's home country can not only elevate perspective at the time but can provide networks that can be leveraged over time.

If you add global leadership or business elements to a program for young leaders, it is important to keep in mind and help them appreciate that the main objective is to heighten awareness and broaden perspective on global business and leadership issues. As a consequence, participants may not have immediate opportunities to apply all the great global content of the program. A participant's ability to get this issue of immediate and delayed application alone can tell you something more about their future global potential. Patience and proper application at the right time in the right situation are one of the keys to successful global leadership, where the situation from one country to another or from one region to another varies. Exercising good judgment about what to do—or not do—with what they learn can be just as important as the program content itself. In training programs we have been involved with, we have seen cases in which young managers were so excited by the content that they lost sight of their position in the company and exercised poor judgment in determining the line between effectively pushing the organization and stepping too far outside acceptable limits. Even here this is a forgivable mistake of young exuberance, assuming the individual learns from it.

Teams

While global task forces and teams may be all the rage, they can be difficult animals to ride. As one executive from Texas observed: "It's plain dumb to try and ride big, Brahma bulls right out of the chute as a young tike. You need to break in riding bucking calves first." Early in a career, it is wise to have young high-potential talent serve as team members on a single functional team that has members from various countries throughout a given region. Keeping the functional discipline constant—as with a marketing task force, for instance—will give the young talent more time and mental energy to focus on the cultural issues that the diverse members of the team bring.

One executive recalled her early experience on a global advertising team. The team, charged with developing a global advertising strategy for a new product, was composed of members from all major regions in the world. Even though the team members shared similar technical and functional knowledge, the differences in advertising strategy in the various countries led initially to near chaos. Although everyone spoke English, it soon became clear that each member was speaking a different language. That is, the underlying assumptions about advertising effectiveness, media plans, etc. were significantly different. It wasn't until group members learned how to communicate their underlying assumptions and draw out those of others that team members could finally see and understand each other.

Once a young talent has experience as a member on a single function but multicultural team within a region, the next logical step would be membership on a cross-functional team within the same region. At that point the talent can leverage past understanding about the various countries and cultures of team members and begin the process of understanding how different functional perspectives can filter and affect how people see and approach various problems. By then they should be well positioned to examine the nuances that different cultural backgrounds can have on these functional perspectives.

Later, you should look for opportunities to put the young leaders who did best on these earlier teams on multicultural *and* cross-functional teams. In this type of team, not only do members learn how to bridge national or regional culture gaps, but they learn how to bridge functional culture gaps as well. As one manager reported, "Sometimes the gap in perspective and values between finance and marketing can be as great as that between Taiwan and England."

Travel

Most young talent does not have lots of opportunities to travel to various countries. In our research and consulting experience, one of young managers' most frequent complaints concerned inadequate opportunity for international travel. This is normal and natural and probably not perfectly resolvable. However, an effective backdoor method is to involve young talent in situations, such as negotiations, in which foreigners visit you. These types of situations often involve reciprocal visits to their homeland and office. If the young leader is a valuable member of the team, it may be worthwhile to invite them along on the next trip.

Keep in mind that travel early in one's career is a great way to increase overall awareness—awareness of different markets, governments, consumers, competitors, business customs and practices, etc. Published country briefings, such as those offered by firms like Craighead International,[1] can be a valuable way to get young and inexperienced talent up to speed before they travel to the country. This way they can ask better questions and gain sharper insights about the country.

Early in a career young leaders should be careful about taking "detours." As young talent, they should be advised that they do not have the same credibility as a more senior manager in justifying detours or side trips. Therefore, they are not as likely to be given the benefit of the doubt when someone is trying to decide whether their half-day tour of the *Tsukiji* fish market in Tokyo was a great learning experience about the country's distribution system or not. This is not to say that they should not take detours off the beaten business path, just that they should take them wisely.

Young talent should also be coached that those with whom they travel are watching them. Sometimes they may even deliberately be testing them. For example, John Huntsman, Jr., former vice chairman of Huntsman Corporation, traveled with young managers to see specifically how they respond to being "out of their element."

> I'd take people on negotiating sessions overseas for technology transfers or in dealing with foreign groups who come here. You can pretty much separate out those people who can mix well with foreign groups, as against those who just clash. The personalities that seem to flourish . . . are those who are open. I mean, they're typically open-minded. They sit back before they speak, and they think about the implications a little bit more than the typical American knee-jerk reaction. And I think you see that through experience, by basically sharing the negotiating table with them, or seeing them in action with foreign delegations.

In short, traveling can be an excellent way early in one's career to enhance awareness and gain some visibility with senior managers. As a more senior manager, like John Huntsman, you can use travel as a way to get an early read on young managers. However, it's important not to read too much into the results of early travel experiences. Making a mistake or experiencing a bit of culture shock at age 23 is not foolproof evidence that the person does not have what it takes to be a great global leader.

Cautions

Regardless of what specific development opportunities young talent are provided with, two cautions are in order. First, both the company and the specific individuals should take care not to overinterpret the results of these opportunities. People change and weaknesses can be overcome. Second, once awareness has been raised in individuals of their potential weaknesses, it is critical to provide coaching, mentoring, or general guidance about how to turn these into strengths. Without this guidance, young talent may set off in unproductive corrective directions.

Mid-career development

In our experience, midcareer is the most challenging stage in terms of global leadership development. This time period mixes rigorous development and serious testing. Unlike early career opportunities that are primarily developmental in nature, mid-career opportunities are quite often intended to provide significant development and a test to determine whether individuals have the potential to become a senior officer in the global corporation.

Transfers

Despite the expense of international transfers, in our recent survey of over 100 medium and large firms, 70 percent of the firms plan to increase the number of managers sent on international assignments over the next five years, while 18 percent plan to keep the number the same, and 12 percent expect to reduce the total number. However, of those planning to increase the total, the mix is different from the past. In the past, the vast majority of mid-career expatriates were sent from the company's "home" country out into the world. Now, it is as likely that it might be "inpatriation" (i.e., sending a "foreigner" into the home country) or "transpatriation" (i.e., sending someone not from the home country somewhere other than their native country). Consequently, it is wise both to signal to employees the importance of international mobility and to systematically gather data on employees' willingness to move internationally.

So what should an international assignment look like to maximize its unsurpassed global leader developmental potential? First and foremost, ideally it should have profit-and-loss responsibility. In our interviews with individuals identified by their companies as future global leaders, these people indicated that P&L responsibility made them wrap their minds around the overall business and how their business fits in with others across the corporation's worldwide network in a way that even large function jobs or projects simply could not. These individuals explained that it was the breadth of the responsibility that helped them gain "a truly global perspective." One manager at American Express indicated that while he was running marketing in Japan, he did not completely appreciate the global aspects of the business. It wasn't until he became president of the Japan operation that his perspective became truly global.

If P&L responsibility is not possible, try to give mid-career high-potential leaders an assignment with cross-functional dimensions. Keep in mind that most senior positions in a global company require a comprehensive perspective. That is, leaders will need to see not just across the borders of countries, but across the borders of divisions, products, and functions within the company. An international assignment that provides opportunities to do this has the greatest developmental potential. This, however, does not mean that companies should not offer international assignments that don't measure up to these ideals. Our research shows that any international assignment has the potential to help develop and prepare mid-career talent for global leadership positions in ways that staying at home just can't. Many of the executives we interviewed had never experienced an ideal assignment; yet they benefited significantly from the international assignment in their global leadership development. In fact, they would always take the assignment again if given the choice between a less than ideal international assignment and no overseas experience at all.

Finally, make sure that candidates' personal and family situation allows them to seek assignments at least three years long. Assuming a candidate hasn't lived in the foreign country before, it will take him or her eight to twelve months to adequately adjust to living and working there. It will also require six to nine months to prepare adequately for their return home. This leaves only a little over a year in a typical three-year assignment to focus fully on the job at hand, let alone use it to develop global leadership capabilities and create value for the firm.

While we stress the development potential of international assignments, the reality is that during the assignment candidates will be tested and evaluated in terms of their current abilities as well as their long-term potential. Thus, firms should do all they can to ensure that the international assignment succeeds. In addition to picking up a copy of *So You're Going Overseas*, which we recommended in the previous chapter, you may want to take a look at another book that offers a comprehensive discussion of foreign assignments: *Globalizing People through International Assignments*.[2]

Training

We've learned from our experience and research that mid-career managers are the primary beneficiaries of formal global leadership training. A majority of companies we interviewed and surveyed don't currently have programs for high-potential mid-career managers, but they plan to add such programs in the near future. Excellent programs can enhance awareness and perspective concerning global business and leadership issues. On any existing or in-planning program, we can recommend emphasizing the following three characteristics.

First, ensure that the program focuses on general management skills. Although in-depth functional programs with international dimensions can be of some value, by mid-career the greater development value comes from programs that focus on integrating various disciplines (e.g., finance, marketing, human resources, strategy). For example, one of the authors of this book was heavily involved in the design and launch of a new program at IMD in collaboration with the Amos Tuck School of Business at Dartmouth College called Transition to Business Leadership that was focused specifically on this objective.

Second, look for programs that have action-learning components. Unlike early career managers, at mid-career leaders want and need opportunities to apply program content. One of the best ways is to have some business challenge built right into the program. As we mentioned earlier, Carrefour's global leadership program had a significant project built into the program design. Participants actually spend over a third of the total program working on real company issues assigned by the president. A professional facilitator was assigned to each team to help with nightly debriefings, team dynamics, and project content in order to avoid disasters and raise the probability of the team's success. Sunkyong, Samsung, 3M, Takeda, NYSE, Christie's, Mars, Nestlé, Rio Tinto, Lexmark, GE, and many, many more companies all have executive development programs with substantial global action-learning components.

Third, ensure that the program portfolio provides within- and across-company networking opportunities. One of the great benefits of Exxon's Workshop on Global Leadership is that it includes high-potential mid-career managers from throughout Exxon's worldwide operations. The same with Shell's Group Business Leadership Program (GBLP). The programs allow individuals to get to know each other personally and to leverage those relationships in facilitating the company's increasing efforts to coordinate activities on a global basis long after the program is over. The participation of IBM, Goldman Sachs, Brunswick, and others in a consortium program allowed its high-potential managers to leverage relationships with individuals outside their industry as well as benchmark themselves against non-competitors. Sending mid-career leaders to high-profile open enrollment programs at the top-ranked schools can also enhance networking. For example, the *Financial Times* ranks the top schools in terms of open and custom programs every year and this list can give companies a quick indication to which schools they might want to consider sending their leaders.

Teams

Most mid-career leaders told us in interviews that being members of "global teams" no longer has the glamor and allure it did when they were in their early twenties. Experience has taught them that global teams are indeed difficult animals to ride. Ideally, mid-career leaders have already had the opportunity to be a member of at least a couple of multicultural and cross-functional teams, so at this point they need team leadership opportunities.

As with team membership, it is wise to first confer leadership of a single functional team with members from various countries throughout a given region. Keeping the functional discipline constant can be very valuable early in the development of a mid-career leader. Unlike when they were younger, mid-career leaders no longer have the luxury of sitting back and simply observing how differently Germans and Chinese view challenges, such as establishing a global brand identity. As the team leader, they have to get people with these very different views to work effectively together. Complicating this with different functional backgrounds too early in the learning curve can be a recipe for mid-career disaster.

Executives also pointed out important risks and pitfalls that need to be managed for global teams to function as an effective developmental strategy. The first caution was the risk of asking someone to lead a cross-functional, multicultural global team with lots of virtual components too early in their career or without enough experience in these types of team settings. One executive related the following:

> I knew one young woman who had lots of potential, but she got put in charge of a task force with people from four different countries and three different functional backgrounds. The team had a total meltdown, and she had no chance. She was inadvertently set up for failure and didn't even know it until it was too late.

In addition, executives pointed out the pitfall of giving leaders global teams without adequate training in the dynamics and effective process skills relative to diverse teams. Several executives indicated that the pressure of having to deliver something without adequate "diverse team process" training consistently led to less than optimal results. A common problem was the domination of the group by one individual or a coalition. The takeover and the associated suppression of diverse ideas and perspectives were typically justified by the offenders by the "need to get something done." However, this approach rarely resulted in superior deliverables. Therefore, be sure that team leaders, and even members, have the requisite knowledge of and skills for diverse team dynamics. If the leader or team members don't, do all that you can to get them some training or coaching before the team gets too far into the process. It's trite but true: "An ounce of prevention is better than a pound of cure."

In contrast, effective global team leaders figured out what was going wrong with their group dynamics and subsequently created norms for the team concerning issues such as conflict resolution or decision making. While this usually resulted in a reasonable deliverable from the team, valuable time was lost while the group dynamics were being fixed. Furthermore, the deliverable was often less than it could have been if team members had been adequately trained in the first place.

Travel

Unlike young managers early in their careers, most mid-career managers whom we interviewed or surveyed were on the road plenty. As a consequence, they likely don't need more. The issue for mid-career leaders is not the quantity of the travel but the quality and the development objectives. Just as the number of international trips changes between early and mid-career, so too do the purposes.

International travel at the mid-career stage has two main global leadership development objectives.

The first purpose of travel for mid-career leaders is *to learn*. This is not to say that they can or should ignore the business purpose of the trip. There is always a business purpose to the trip—someone to see, documents to review, negotiations to conduct, etc. The business purpose of an international trip is a given. Our experience is that if the assigned individuals weren't capable of accomplishing whatever the business purpose is, they wouldn't be getting on the airplane in the first place. But if that's all they accomplish, then they will have missed out on the full global leadership development potential of international travel. As we have said, the best way to learn new things is to take "detours," to get off the beaten business path. The advantage of being midway through one's career is that these individuals are likely to have some latitude in taking these detours because of the credibility they've built up over the years.

They can enhance this credibility relative to the detours by *sharing what they learn*, which is the second basic developmental purpose of travel during mid-career. As we mentioned earlier, 3M has formalized a series of brown-bag lunches in which learnings from various international travels are shared and discussed. Even in the absence of a formal program like the one at 3M, nothing is likely to prevent individuals from organizing such a lunch and sharing insights with subordinates or peers.

Consider, for example, Dale Smith of 3M. During every trip he takes to Latin America, about once a quarter, Dale makes sure to take some sort of detour. Often he'll ask a local national what cultural value is core in the country and what place, event, or activity best captures that value. To the extent possible, he will then try to visit the historical site, watch the event, or participate in the activity. Upon return to his base in Florida, Dale always makes it a point to invite one of more of his staff out to lunch. In addition to reviewing the business results, Dale describes the detour he took and what he learned from it. In talking with one of Dale's subordinates, it's clear that not only does he convey the business results and the cultural knowledge he picked up, but he also sets an example for his staff as a leader who tries constantly to learn from new experiences. In the long run, this may have a bigger impact than any of the specific lessons Dale learns or shares.

Caution

The fact that mid-career global leadership development opportunities have both development and testing purposes creates one key caution. If the company overemphasizes the "testing" aspects of these experiences, it will likely cause individuals to hyperfocus on delivering "results." This is not bad per se, and you certainly cannot ignore delivering results. However, an overemphasis on results can lead to risk-averse behavior. This is unfortunate, because in most cases the "ability to take risks and act outside the box" is a key global leader skill. Thus, becoming obsessed with "hitting the numbers" may well cause individuals to miss out on the development opportunities they need to reach greater leadership responsibilities. True, missing the numbers will probably lower their chances of advancing to the next level as well. However, one executive we interviewed put it this way: "Too many managers think that doing well where they are now is sufficient to move them along in their careers. I want to see them do well now and *also* demonstrate that they can learn and grow enough to be ready for the next level." It is trite but true: "What got them here will not get them there." As a consequence, the company has to be somewhat mindful of encouraging the learning aspects of transfers, training, teams, and travel without causing people to mistakenly believe that results don't matter. As the same time, companies must take care not to underemphasize learning and overemphasize results to the point that people mistakenly think that results are the only things that matter.

Late career development

Late career development is the weakest link in most companies' global leadership development efforts. Many companies falsely assume that either individuals have it or don't by that point in their career. The issue is not whether individuals have it or not; the key issue is, how refined is what they have? Given the broader scope of senior management positions and the more strategic impact of decisions at that level, small refinements in global leadership capabilities can produce significant payoffs to both the individuals and the company. As a consequence, companies should view global leadership development at this stage as a period of specific refinement and polishing. It will also likely be a time of final testing.

Transfers

As we mentioned, most companies plan to increase the number of managers sent on international assignments. They also plan to broaden the "traffic patterns" of these transfers. Instead of most expatriates coming from the home country and being sent out to various foreign units, in a hub-and-spoke pattern, firms increasingly are transferring the best person (regardless of nationality) to the position. They are trying to be "passport-blind" in making these assignments.

An international assignment in someone's later career stage represents an opportunity to polish specific capabilities and become personally familiar with strategic geographies. For example, all managers headed for senior positions within Komatsu serve at least one assignment in the United States. This is because U.S.-based Caterpillar is Komatsu's toughest competitor the world over. The president of General Motor's operations in Asia confided that GM expects most of its growth over the next 10 years to come in Asia. As a consequence, an assignment in Asia represents a strategic opportunity to learn firsthand about what may well be the most important consumer region in the world for GM long into the next century.

In addition to the strategic importance of the locale, we mentioned before that our interviews with exemplar global leaders found that P&L responsibility was an important dimension in maximizing the developmental potential of an international assignment. This was especially true for individuals in the later career stage.

Training

From our experience and research, late-career executives receive very few opportunities for formal global leadership training. However, a number of the companies we interviewed and surveyed believe this is a shortcoming and plan to add programs in the near future. Programs that add value for senior executives are not easy to design or implement, but in general programs for these executives should emphasize three characteristics.

First, the programs should have a strategic and external focus. For example, programs should have a heavy dose of content that examines global strategy and structure, competitive intelligence, strategic alliances, and joint ventures. These programs should include case studies and discussions that focus on the dynamics of integrating business activities across divisions, products, functions, and geographies and on determining which business activities are best localized. Many if not most business schools do not have programs pitched at this level. Generally the largest schools such as IMD, Harvard, INSEAD, and Wharton have open enrollment programs for senior executives. While these programs are not cheap, they attract senior executives from across the globe and typically involve the school's best faculty.

Second, programs for senior executives should have action-learning components. In order to be of value, however, these components need to have the potential to push participants, to help them identify areas in need of polish and refinement. They do not have to be just projects. For example, as part of a program we put participants in teams in which they have to manage a crisis that includes actors hired as protesters, media interviewers, government officials, and the like. We videotape the team's responses and then analyze the video with participants and provide executive coaches for further insights and development actions.

Or, as another example, imagine that you just returned from a two-week action-learning project in Vietnam. The objective of your team project was to assess the political risk and market potential of the country. The deliverable was to be a report and presentation to the executive committee of the company about whether or not to enter Vietnam, and, if so, how best to proceed. As you step off the plane, weary from a 20-hour flight, you are confronted by a reporter and TV crew. They hound you with questions about your trip:

- Is it true that you have been investigating the potential of opening operations in Vietnam?
- Can you confirm the rumors that you signed a memorandum of understanding while you were there?
- Is it true that you will be closing your factory in Kentucky and moving it to Vietnam?

- Has the U.S. government put any pressure on you one way or the other concerning your firm's activities in the country?

How would you react to the situation? At some point your senior executives will likely confront such a scene. How good are their public relations skills? What if this mock confrontation took place when they landed in Vietnam? How well would they do? The point is, you want to look for or design programs to stretch your senior leaders who are on the cusp of becoming your global leaders. You don't want them confronting some of these issues in real life in real time for the first time. This is why pilots get extensive training in simulators. You don't want a senior captain to announce, "We've just had one engine go out and this is my first time experiencing this, so together we will see how it goes. Keep your fingers crossed for me."

Clearly some things can't be anticipated such as when Captain "Sully" Sullenberger of US Airways flight 1549 lost both engines after taking off from LaGuardia Airport in New York because of a bird strike and had to land in the Hudson River in 2009. However, that was not the first time he had piloted an Airbus A320 with virtually no engine thrust. In his book, Captain Sully talks about how on a crystal-clear and calm night on approach to San Francisco he throttled back the engines to near idle to glide the plane in.[3] Without that sort of refinement and practice before the crisis, it is debatable whether he could have done what he did and landed the plane in water with all passengers surviving.

Training for executives is about refinement not the basics. But this last bit of polish is likely all they need to be a truly effective global leader. Keep in mind, however, that having come this far, and having received lots of positive reinforcement about their capabilities over the years, they will probably need a program that shocks the system, a program that stretches them, to make visible their areas that need refinement.

Third, senior executives need programs that provide within- and across-industry networking opportunities. One of the great benefits of GE's Global Leadership Program is that it brings senior managers together from throughout GE's worldwide operations. The four-week program allows individuals to get to know each other at a level that can truly facilitate a company's efforts to coordinate activities globally.

One of the great things about open enrollment programs such as IMD's Breakthrough Program for Business Leaders, or INSEAD's Advanced Management Program, or Harvard's Advanced Management Program is that they bring participants across the world and from across many different industries. They are also long enough that participants are almost forced to look outside themselves, outside their culture, outside their company, outside their industry.

Teams

Senior executives in a variety of companies said they felt a keen responsibility to select and develop future top executives. However, several expressed frustration at the difficulty of "picking stars that will really shine." Part of this frustration grew out of not having had the opportunity to personally lead a global team. Often this was because their companies had moved so quickly into global arenas that they were responsible for several global teams without having been the leader of a single global team themselves. This lack of experience caused some executives to make mistakes in choosing other executives to lead global teams. As one senior executive said to us, "I never had the opportunity to lead a truly global team. I didn't fully understand what it took. It took a couple of mistakes in selecting [global team leaders] before I really understood what it was all about."

Leading a global team can easily represent a microcosm of the dynamics of running a global organization. As a consequence, team leaders can gain insights into their strengths and weaknesses, while they still have a chance to take care of any necessary refinements. While leading a global team before guiding a global division seems to be the ideal, at least one European executive managed to do both at the same time. He leveraged lessons learned while leading a global team to help better structure and run a global product division. If you are in charge of a global unit and have not had the opportunity to lead a truly global team, you should identify a salient business issue and put together and lead a global team. You can then leverage the lessons learned from leading the global team and apply them in your overall unit.

Finally, as we mentioned before (and it's worth repeating), be sure that the team leader and the team members have the requisite knowledge and skills for diverse team dynamics. And yes, once again: "An ounce of prevention is better than a pound of cure."

Travel

Most executives in the later stage of their careers pointed out that they had more travel demands, let alone opportunities, than they could possibly meet. As one executive at Kimberly-Clark lamented, "If I took every trip for which there was a business reason or justification, I would never be home." Senior leaders travel when business reasons make it compelling to do so. However, in addition to the normal business reasons for the trip, in the later stage of their careers, leaders should focus on choosing international travel opportunities that provide the chance to do two things.

First, they should take advantages of trips that help form and solidify relationships. Jon Huntsman, Jr. stressed the need to travel in order to connect with business partners on a personal basis.

> We won't do business with people who we don't enjoy being with. You become friends first. Then you begin talking about business. But, we're not just going to do business blindly. We like to pick and choose. We go into a country, like in Australia, and there's the Packer family. And our families are very close, and his son James, who's now running the business, is one of my very good friends, and that comes first. It's the relationship before the

business. The business will go up and down, but we try to keep the personal relationship always intact and unharmed.

Second, senior leaders should take advantage of trips that help them build others as leaders. There exists no way yet to "digitize" relationships and the nuances that go along with them. If senior leaders are trying to develop and build leaders in a foreign locale, it's hard to do that simply through email, fax, or even the phone. It often has to be face to face for the richness of the exchange and communication to take place. Or senior leaders might consider taking someone along on the trip who could benefit from the mentoring they could provide. As we mentioned earlier, for younger high-potential talent early in their careers, simply listening to the descriptions of distant negotiations, governmental protocol, market situation, or competitors just doesn't have the same impact as being there in person. Senior leaders should seriously consider opportunities where they could take younger talent along to help develop them.

Cautions

Our work also uncovered an important weakness relative to late-career global leadership development: firms constantly underutilize their "foreign" talent base. This observation applies to most multinational companies regardless of country of origin: Japan-based firms underutilize their non-Japanese talent; U.S.-based firms underutilize their non-U.S. talent; Germany-based firms underutilize their non-German talent; and so on. Global firms cannot afford to continue to believe that the best global leaders are primarily those of the parent company's nationality. Top management at SCG in Thailand have embraced this vision. They estimate that they will need 30 percent of their global leaders by 2016 to be non-Thai. Today it is less than 10 percent. Thus, they have to invest in identifying and developing their non-Thai talent. Their international assignment traffic patterns are changing. As they move toward Stage 5 in their global development, they recognize that they have to give up the old hub-and-spoke mentality, with headquarters as the source of all global leadership talent.

Our work also uncovered a surprising lack of linkage among global leader development, turnover, and overall succession planning. Specifically, the "bench strength" in most firms is quite weak, and the development plan is either not in place or is inadequate, given the turnover levels among upper-middle- and senior-level executives. While less than 15 percent of the firms have a comprehensive global leader development system, those that did had better financial performance than those that did not.

Conclusion

Our study of companies as they move forward into the uncharted territories of the global frontier produced several conclusions. Clearly, effective global strategies and structures cannot be formulated without capable global leaders. Even with good global strategies and structures, effective execution is what ultimately separates the winners from the losers. Successful execution of global strategies and structures is impossible without adequate numbers of high-quality global leaders. Executives in the companies we interviewed consistently complained that they have neither sufficient numbers nor the desired level of global leadership talent. Global leaders, like athletes or musicians, need some natural talent.

However, this talent must also be developed. Because you cannot become a global leader overnight, companies must take a systematic and multifaceted approach to the process. For the best results, the development approach should vary depending on career stage. Despite the need for companies to take a more proactive and systematic approach to the development of global leaders, *none of the outstanding global leaders we interviewed simply waited for their companies to map out the territory and trade routes to global leadership development.* Without exception, these individuals ultimately shoulder development responsibility themselves. They not only push the global business frontiers, but the frontiers of their own careers and development as well. They use any development opportunities the company offers, request ones not offered, and create something out of nothing to ensure that they, like you, become the next generation of global leaders.

Notes

1 Craighead International (www.craighead.com, 1-203-655-1007) (accessed 23 September 1998).
2 Black, J. Stewart and Gregersen, Hal B. (1998) *So You're Going Overseas: A Handbook for Personal and Professional Success.* San Diego, CA: Global Business Publishers; Black, J. Stewart, Gregersen, Hal B., Mendenhall, Mark E., and Stroh, Linda (1998) *Globalizing People through International Assignments.* Reading, MA: Addison-Wesley.
3 Sullenberger, C. (2009). *Highest Duty* (with Jeffery Zaslow), New York: HarperCollins.

11 Mapping your future as a global leader

Our immediate neighborhood we know rather intimately. But with increasing distance our knowledge fades . . . until at the last dim horizon we search among ghostly errors of observations for landmarks that are scarcely more substantial. The search will continue. The urge is older than history. It is not satisfied and it will not be suppressed.

(Edwin Hubble, reflections in his last scientific paper)

We live in an age of constant discovery. Explorers in a variety of fields continue to expand the scope of human knowledge: With the Hubble telescope, we can peer deeper into space, seeing stars and galaxies that we have never before beheld. On earth, we now travel deep into the oceans, discovering sea life that was previously unknown. Yet with all this exploration, we are reminded that in spite of all that we can now see and understand, there is still so much more to learn.

Similarly, in the constantly changing global marketplace, personal and organizational frontiers stretch beyond the horizon as the vast oceans did for the explorers of old and as endless space does for astronomers today. Firms pushing into this new frontier are in desperate need of global leaders to help them forge ahead. They need global leaders who can help make sense of the changing psychology of the employment contract, sift through the opportunities and pitfalls in developing markets, and create cohesive and effective teams of individuals from different countries, cultures, and functional disciplines. While the challenge of global leadership is significant, the good news for you is that they are in short supply. There is a large global leadership gap waiting for you to fill.

Mapping your personal career frontier

Filling this leadership gap is easier said than done. The turbulence of the global market not only creates competitive challenges for companies but career challenges for individuals. For example, the globalization tsunami has already smashed the employment contract of the past into a thousand splinters. No longer do organizations promise secure and predictable careers in return for loyalty and solid performance. The turbulence of today's global environment shreds the reliable career maps upon which you once could chart your course. Career ambiguity has replaced the predictability of the past. The notion of long-term loyalty to a single company has been washed away and replaced with relatively uncharted career frontiers.

In the predictable business world of the past, the image of captain and ship was often used to describe the corporation and its leader. The image was not complete without the brave captain sailing the company out to sea. In this scenario, the thought of jumping ship was not an inviting one. Sharks lurked below, waiting to devour anyone foolish enough to leave the safety of the vessel.

Times have changed. The symbolism of this old image has shifted. Today, the ship does not represent the company; it is your own career, and you have to be the captain. The winds of opportunity blow from many directions and the waves constantly change. In conquering these challenges, your career path will not follow a nice straight line. Instead you will have to tack right and left; you will have to keep moving, growing, and developing. These tacking maneuvers may be within the same company or they may be across different companies. Unlike what was true in the past, there is no way to reliably predict whether your career path should be navigated within one firm or across many.

By evoking this transformed image of ship and captain, we do not want to create the impression that firms do not care about retaining high-potential individuals, or that they are doing nothing to generate global leader development systems. In fact, our experience with senior executives in most firms suggests just the opposite. At companies like 3M, Colgate-Palmolive, and Shell, executives spend considerable time, energy, and money on developing cadres of future global leaders. As we pointed out earlier, though, our surveys of the terrain found that most firms have, at best, stitched together some ad hoc programs. Fewer than 10 percent have comprehensive global leader development plans.

This fact leads to two key insights. First, while the vast majority of companies are without comprehensive development systems, they still face a rapidly expanding need for global leaders. As a result, you may not have the luxury of waiting for your firm to develop a comprehensive plan before moving full speed ahead with your own global leadership development. Second, if most firms today do not have comprehensive development systems, then they surely didn't have them in the past. Yet, as we have tried to demonstrate, there are effective global leaders *today.* If their companies did not have comprehensive development plans, how did they become the capable leaders they are today? When we put this question to these exemplar leaders, to a person, the answer was the same: They did not wait for their companies to lay out a global leader career map. While they took advantage of every opportunity the company offered, they assumed full responsibility for charting their own career course. The path they charted anticipated the need for global leadership capabilities by several years and at times, decades. For example, Michael C. Hawley, former CEO of Gillette, began his international career in 1966 by running Gillette's import–export operation in Hong Kong. Over the next 20 years, he lived and worked on five different continents. Long before most executives understood the need for a global outlook, he was already in China back in 1979 helping Gillette begin operations in that country. With executives like Michael Hawley, companies like Gillette will catch and ride the gigantic wave of globalization rather than get wiped out by it.

Today's effective global leaders have all come to the same basic conclusion: to be successful you must become your own career cartographer, your own ship's captain. If you wait for your company to figure out and implement a comprehensive global leader development plan, it just might be too late. It may be too late because many of the global leadership opportunities will have passed you by and been taken by others who were more prepared. It may be too late because if you wait, you will still be standing at the starting line as hundreds and perhaps thousands of other high-potential managers join the race.

To become your own career cartographer, keep in mind that becoming a global leader is not an overnight process. As a consequence, first movers today produce competitive advantages tomorrow. The responsibility for these early (as well as for mid- and late) career moves resides with you. One exemplar manager put it this way:

> If the global future for companies is uncharted, why should a person's global career be any different? And if winning companies cannot afford to simply wait and copy their competitors' moves, why should individuals be any different? I didn't know exactly where I needed to head in order to enhance my value the most, but I knew I couldn't wait for someone to map it out for me. I knew I had to take that responsibility myself.

While Chapters 9 and 10 described in general terms the ways in which successful global leaders develop themselves, the precise sequencing and content of transfers, training, teams, and travel are in your hands. Accurate personal assessment is the key to being able to create an effective career map.

For example, if an international assignment is the single most powerful means of developing global leader characteristics and you haven't had one yet, are you prepared to take one on? Not every international assignment is right for you (nor are you necessarily right for every assignment) and now may not be the right time, but have you done a careful assessment of yourself and your family situation to know what assignments and timing would be appropriate? While books such as *So You're Going Overseas* are important to read once you've been presented with an opportunity, they are probably of most value long before the opportunity appears. Only through advance assessment of yourself, your industry, firm, and family can you have enough time to make the necessary preparations and changes. And only in making them early will you be in a position to both maximize the business results and the development potential of an international assignment.

Without exception, every exemplar global leader we interviewed was a self-employed cartographer, busily mapping out his or her career. Consider the path that Steve Burke charted. As we mentioned in Chapter 3, Steve embarked early on a self-designed path that ultimately led to a senior executive position. He initially worked at General Mills, learning the ropes of marketing by pushing Yoplait yogurt. This experience gave Steve valuable lessons in marketing that prepared him for a career move to Disney, heading up part of its consumer products division. From the beginning, Steve tapped into employee creativity and went on to build the Disney retail store concept from the ground up. Starting with zero revenues, Steve built the Disney stores into a $500 million-a-year operation in five short years. Not willing to rest on success or familiar territory, Steve actively sought out his next position in an entirely different part of the company: theme parks.

Steve made this significant tack in his career course and ended up in France helping turn around the EuroDisney theme park in the 1990s. During this experience, he had to acquire a whole range of new skills related to park operations and European business that he had never needed when running Disney's retail stores. Working with the Paris-based EuroDisney team as well as with executives at Burbank headquarters, Steve helped put the theme park back in the black.

Steve then took his time and searched for a return assignment that would leverage his growing skill base and still provide development opportunities. He found just such an assignment back in America. Steve's first job back was identifying and building strategic synergies between Disney and Cap Cities/ABC after their recent merger. Not having worked in the television and film business before, Steve was again faced with a challenge from which he acquired new capabilities. Before long he made another move and took a senior executive position in charge of ABC's television and radio stations, which required that he master the tricky world of programming.

Most recently, Steve has taken another significant career tack. He was made the CEO of NBC Universal, a new addition to Comcast, where he was chief operating officer before this move.

Steve—just like Tony Wang or Gary Griffiths—never waited for someone else to take control of his career. He put himself at the helm. Of course he sought advice from colleagues and bosses to guide his choices, but he never left his ultimate career fate in someone else's hands. Further, Steve, recognizing—like all exemplar global leaders—the necessity of tacking left and right, has followed a fairly convoluted path that has crisscrossed countries, industries, companies, and functions. This kind of flexibility prepared Steve, and will prepare you, for all the unforeseen frontiers encountered in today's global business world.

Global leadership: a personal journey of discovery

While some companies do more than others to develop global leaders, in the final analysis the road to global success is a personal journey of discovery. As you sail off into the waters of the new global marketplace, you will learn volumes about markets, technology, competitors, customers, suppliers, and the like. As we have described, such learning and the inquisitiveness that produces it are at the core of effective global leadership. However, more important even than learning about markets, technology, competitors, customers, or suppliers, you must prepare for and look forward to learning about yourself.

As you sail forward, will you be like the drill rig operator in Asia who maintained his ethical standards by refusing to pay bribes of a few thousand dollars to a corrupt government official even though the opportunity costs of an idle rig are tens of thousands per day? Will you be like Jon Huntsman, Jr., and look beyond the nationality and language of people and emotionally connect with them as individuals? Will you be like Tony Wang and relish the opportunity to bring together diverse organizational resources outside your line of authority to pull off a critical global deal? In essence, are you excited about this personal journey of discovery to know where you stand as a global leader?

As you embark on your leadership journey, keep in mind Henry David Thoreau's advice to become

> the Lewis and Clark . . . of your own streams and oceans; explore your own higher latitudes . . . be a Columbus to whole new continents and worlds within you, opening new channels, not of trade, but of thought . . . it is easier to sail many thousand miles through cold and storm and cannibals . . . than it is to explore the private sea, the Atlantic and Pacific Ocean of one's being.

This journey may well prove the most important one to take as we continue into the twenty-first century. It will also prove the most difficult, since the real journey is one of personal discovery—discovery not so much of distant markets but of yourself.

Consider Gary Griffiths's experience at the Warsaw Marriott. Gary took that international assignment with limited overseas business experience. He worked for years as an accountant in a public accounting firm before taking an accountant's job at a smoothly running western U.S. Marriott hotel property. When Gary left that world of stability and flew to Poland, he had no idea what kinds of surprises he would face. At first, he clung to the certainty of his past—when he came across familiar Mars candy bars for the first time in Poland, he grabbed five. Not because he was starving, but because he wanted to hold on to what was soothing and familiar. Yet the sweet taste of the candy bars wore off fast as Gary faced a mountain of uncertainty in Warsaw. Nearly every day, Gary faced challenges for which he had no ready answer. What do you do when:

- over 100 phones are stolen from the hotel during its first week of operations?
- a guest commits suicide in the hotel lobby by jumping from the second-floor balcony?
- you need cash to start up the hotel, but can't get a business bank account?
- one night's lodging costs a customer four million zlotys (the local currency) and when they attempt to pay for a night's stay, there are more digits in the price than the computer can calculate?
- you have to get truckloads of cash to the bank in a cash-starved economy?

- you have to account for purchasing $4,000 worth of food for the restaurant each day that must be picked up by a truck driver in an open market and paid for in cash?
- you can't get a phone line or refrigerator in your home for months?

For Gary, questions like these went on and on. Faced with constant uncertainty, Gary confronted more than one defining moment that forced him completely out of his comfort zone. These were the times when he was ready to give up and go home because he just wasn't sure he could rise to the challenge. But he stuck it out. He came to realize through these tough experiences that "the reality of the situation is just that, the reality." What he had been comfortable with in the past just wouldn't work in the present. As a result, he looked deep into the mirror and discovered a flicker of flexibility that he fanned into a flame—a flame that any global leader must have in order to succeed. Over time, Gary discovered that he thrived on the uncertainty and challenges of the environment he faced. He confronted the new reality of doing business in Poland by first confronting himself. If he had known in advance the exact level of craziness he was to face, and if you had asked him if he was up to it, he honestly might have said, "NO." In retrospect, he knows the experience was invaluable: "In the most important ways, I improved myself."

Experience is the forge through which ordinary people become extraordinary global leaders. It is said that the swords of the Japanese samurai are among the best in the world. Each blade is shaped in the hottest fires. The metal is folded over and over a thousand times. It is pounded repeatedly into itself until it fuses at the molecular level. Finally, it is sharpened with the greatest precision. In much the same way, we discover the real nature of our personal leadership "metal" by seeking out and confronting the greatest international challenges that lie before us. Just like a samurai sword, we become the very best when our character is forged in the hottest fires, pounded on by the most difficult experiences, and sharpened with continuous learning. There are few paths in life that offer greater opportunity and challenge than the one to global leadership. For that reason, there are few paths in life more rewarding. And for now, it is still the road less traveled. In this very personal journey of discovery, we wish you all the best.

Appendix
Global Leadership Inventory™

Global Leadership Inventory™ is a proprietary assessment instrument of an individual's global leadership potential that we developed on the basis of our extensive study and research. It is designed to give feedback to the individual about his or her strengths and weaknesses. It also outlines specific actions that can be taken to improve one's overall global leadership profile. The questions below are a sample of those in the official instrument. They are designed to give you a rough idea of your strengths and weaknesses. The official version of the instrument is available only through the Global Leadership Institute at Globalleadershipinstitute.net.

Assessing your competencies as a global leader

To assess your current global leadership competencies, please answer the following questions:

1. I have a good understanding of my company's business model (how it makes money).

   Strongly Disagree   *Strongly Agree*
   1   2   3   4   5   6   7

2. I have a clear sense of other companies' strategies in our industry.

   Strongly Disagree   *Strongly Agree*
   1   2   3   4   5   6   7

3. I personally know the key decision makers in my business unit/division.

   Strongly Disagree   *Strongly Agree*
   1   2   3   4   5   6   7

4. I generally know who to contact to get things done in my business unit/division.

   Strongly Disagree   *Strongly Agree*
   1   2   3   4   5   6   7

5. I genuinely care about and understand people whose cultural backgrounds are different from mine.

   Strongly Disagree   *Strongly Agree*
   1   2   3   4   5   6   7

6. I like to spend as much time as possible with my employees.

   Strongly Disagree   *Strongly Agree*
   1   2   3   4   5   6   7

7. I consistently display high ethical standards when I represent my company to outsiders.

   Strongly Disagree   *Strongly Agree*
   1   2   3   4   5   6   7

8. In conversations with other employees, I support my company's strategy and its leadership.

   Strongly Disagree   *Strongly Agree*
   1   2   3   4   5   6   7

9. I thrive in an uncertain environment.

   Strongly Disagree   *Strongly Agree*
   1   2   3   4   5   6   7

10. I don't like my job to have too much structure.

    Strongly Disagree   *Strongly Agree*
    1   2   3   4   5   6   7

11. I am very good at differentiating between those of my company's products and services that should be globally standardized and those that should be locally tailored.

    Strongly Disagree   *Strongly Agree*
    1   2   3   4   5   6   7

12. I recognize that a lot of what my company does needs to be modified as it enters new international markets.

    Strongly Disagree   *Strongly Agree*
    1   2   3   4   5   6   7

13. People say that I am constantly examining experiences and extracting the lessons that can be learned.

    Strongly Disagree   *Strongly Agree*
    1   2   3   4   5   6   7

14. Whenever I need energizing, I pursue new experience learning.

    Strongly Disagree   *Strongly Agree*
    1   2   3   4   5   6   7

15. I actively seek out unfamiliar territory and opportunities for learning.

    Strongly Disagree   *Strongly Agree*
    1   2   3   4   5   6   7

Scoring

Scoring this sample instrument is relatively easy. Simply add your circled numbers together for each of the following clusters of questions.

Total score for questions 1–4:

25–28	You have excellent organizational and business savvy.
21–24	You have good organizational and business savvy.
17–20	You have average organizational and business savvy.
16 and below	You have a major deficiency in organizational and business savvy.

Total score for questions 5–8:

25–28	You have unbending integrity and an excellent ability to connect emotionally with others.
21–24	You have strong integrity and a good ability to connect emotionally with others.
17–20	You have average integrity and a fair ability to connect emotionally with others.
16 and below	You have a major deficiency in integrity and a poor ability to connect emotionally with others.

Total score for questions 9–12:

25–28	You have excellent ability to embrace uncertainty and balance tensions.
21–24	You have good ability to embrace uncertainty and balance tensions.
17–20	You have average ability to embrace uncertainty and balance tensions.
16 and below	You have a major deficiency in your ability to embrace uncertainty and balance tensions.

Total score for questions 13–15:

25–28	You have excellent inquisitiveness
21–24	You have good inquisitiveness.
17–20	You have average inquisitiveness.
16 and below	You have a major deficiency in inquisitiveness.

Index